Transatlantic Finance in the Age of Revolutions

Mark Edward Hay

Transatlantic Finance in the Age of Revolutions

Hope, Baring, and the Financing of the Sale and Purchase of Louisiana

palgrave
macmillan

Mark Edward Hay
Erasmus University Rotterdam
Rotterdam, Zuid-Holland
The Netherlands

ISBN 978-3-031-65231-8 ISBN 978-3-031-65232-5 (eBook)
https://doi.org/10.1007/978-3-031-65232-5

This Palgrave Macmillan imprint is published by the registered company Springer Nature Switzerland AG
The registered company address is: Gewerbestrasse 11, 6330 Cham, Switzerland

Voor mama,
to dad.

Preface

This book has been long in the making. The first steps were taken during my doctoral studies at King's College London, culminating in 2016. Since then, the research has progressed in leaps and bounds until being picked up again in earnest in early 2022. The postponement of publication is due to two reasons. The first relates to my career development. After two years of laborious, tenuous employment in academia, which one can only escape through Herculean effort and luck, I was fortunate to find an appointment at the Erasmus University Rotterdam, which turned permanent with promotion in early 2021. However, with promotion comes increased responsibility and workload. It is found that research often is the first to suffer. Supposedly, the workload becomes more manageable with experience, but I am yet to reach that point. The second relates to a fluctuating health, culminating in a lengthy period off work. I thank the *Holland Protonen Therapie Centrum* in Delft for pushing boundaries, that is both the boundaries of science and my boundaries. Unconsciously, perhaps another reason has contributed to the postponement of this research, which is a sense that too much is published. For example, more publications relevant to the Louisiana cession have appeared than can be read in a lifetime. Much good is produced, but along with the good comes the mediocre (mine not excluded). This insight has fed a reluctance to publish for the sake of publishing, though perhaps that is also an easy excuse for a person who finds more joy in archival research and discussion than publication. In any case, I would thank my editor, Ellie Duncan, for her seemingly infinite patience and positivity.

My health scare forced me to rethink the character of this publication. Initially, this book was entitled: "Financing the Sale and Purchase of Louisiana: Hope, Baring and the Migration of International Finance". The subtitle was ill-phrased, and would need to have been amended, but the thrust of the book was to use the financing of the cession of Louisiana as a case study to reflect on how international finance navigated the tumultuous Age of Revolutions, with a particular focus on the changes to the Amsterdam market for international government lending, Amsterdam credit networks, and shift of the epicentre of international finance from Amsterdam to London. The desire to publish some findings speedily drove me to drop the analysis on the changes to international finance in favour of focussing on the case study, except for a few observations in the conclusion. The decision was difficult, but it is felt to have worked out well. The publication now sticks close to the primary sources, and there is no attempt to frame the research findings. It is thus accessible to the academic community and the broader public alike.

To me, research is a solistic experience. Yet, I have incurred many debts along the way. At King's College London, my supervisor, Dr Michael Rowe, has been a great influence on my early years. There is not a publication or new line of research that passes him by. The Economic History Society has had a profound impact on my academic development and career. The appointment to Power Junior Research Fellow allowed me to explore the Dutch archives in depth, and it offered the opportunity to step back from the bustle of academia to reflect and develop longer lines of inquiry. Still, it is at Erasmus University that I have come into my own as an academic. The Erasmus History Department is unconventional both for being embedded in the broader framework of Social Sciences and for consisting largely of early career academics. I have yet to encounter a department that matches the energy, dynamism, egalitarianism, and openness of our department. In true spirit, I would like to thank the collective department for welcoming me into their midst.

My research has brought me to many archives. I have been warmly received by all, though one archive towers above all, and this is the Baring Archive. True to its history, Baring is a pioneer, nowadays in opening up the archives of this important house in the history of commerce and banking. Not only has the Baring Archive digitised large parts of its collection, but they have also set up academic collaborations to study the archives, and they convene workshops for researchers of the collections. The Baring Archive workshop of 9 February 2024 offered me the opportunity to present my research. The feedback has allowed me to sharpen and qualify my findings. I would like to thank Clara Harrow, the archivist at the Baring Archive, on whose intimate knowledge of the collection I have oft relied.

As for any research, funding is key to success. As the first steps in this research were taken during my doctoral studies, I would like to acknowledge the assistance offered through the Arts & Humanities Research Council, the Fundatie van de Vrijvrouwe van Renswoude, the Dr. Hendrik Muller's Vaderlandsch Fonds, the Prins Bernhard Cultuurfonds, King's College London's Graduate School, and the Royal Historical Society.

I conclude with two personal notes. This publication was in part intended as the next chapter in a career-long debate with my colleague Dr Aaron Graham (1984–2023), on the intersection of Dutch and British early modern trade and finance. This debate will have to wait, but only for now. Finally, I would like to acknowledge the influential role of Hilda Wijnhoud, Francis "Fransje" Hay, and Millicent Hay, without whom this book would probably have been published sooner, but the journey would have been all the more boring.

Tunbridge Wells
February 2024

Mark Edward Hay

The original version of the book has been revised. A corrections to this book can be found at https://doi.org/10.1007/978-3-031-65232-5_6

Contents

List of Tables

CHAPTER 1

Introduction

Abstract The introduction positions the research through a discussion of the historiography of the financing of the cession of Louisiana, the history of Hope, and the history of Baring. Furthermore, the introduction discusses the primary source material that has been employed for this study, as well as its use and limitations.

Keywords Hope & Co. archive · Baring archive · Historiography of the financing of the Louisiana Cession

The history of Louisiana can tell many stories. It can tell the story of the origins and the expansion of the international rise of the United States, it can tell the story of the collapse of the French colonial empire in the Americas, it can tell the story of European imperialism or how European rivalry globalised from the mid-eighteenth century, it can tell the story of the dispossession and marginalisation of native populations, or it can be used to reflect on the Atlantic slavery and the importance of the labour of enslaved populations in European and American state and order building. This study is limited in aims and scope. It aims to tell the story of the financial mediation that facilitated the execution of the treaty and conventions on cession of Louisiana from France to the United States.

M. E. Hay, *Transatlantic Finance in the Age of Revolutions*, https://doi.org/10.1007/978-3-031-65232-5_1

Much has been written on the Louisiana cession, primarily in the two countries directly involved in the transaction, the United States and France. In the United States, the Louisiana cession is referred to as the Louisiana purchase. The key words "Louisiana + Purchase" yield 22,085 secondary sources in the catalogue of the Library of Congress. This only regards sources with the words "Louisiana Purchase" in the title. Many more works without the key words in the title explore the topic. In France, the Louisiana cession is referred to as the sale of Louisiana. The Biliothèque Nationale de France's Gallica website yields 10,432 secondary sources with the key words "Louisiane + Vente". This book is not concerned with the American acquisition of Louisiana, the French disposal of the territory, or the Franco-American diplomatic agreement that allowed for the transfer. This book is focussed on the financial operation that underlay the diplomatic agreement and allowed for the Louisiana territory to be transferred to mutual satisfaction. To keep this tome without reasonable bounds, the historiographical discussion is narrowly focussed too. It does not discuss American and French domestic politics before, during, and after the cession, nor the international context of the cession. The historiography is focussed on those works that examine the financial aspects of the Louisiana cession, and that deal with the principal actors involved in the financial operation, that is the merchant-banking houses Hope of Amsterdam and Baring of London. Besides, at the time of writing, the author was informed that Professor Dr Alexander Mikaberidze is working on a new history of the Louisiana cession. This updated history would be the starting point for insight into the domestic and international politics of the cession.

Historiography

Before exploring the financial operation to facilitate the cession of Louisiana from France to the United States, we must define what the Louisiana operation is. The historiography is clear that the United States purchased the Louisiana Territory from France for $15 million.[1] Because

[1] R.W. Hidy, *The House of Baring in American Trade and Finance. English Merchant Bankers at Work 1763-1861* (Cambridge, MA: Harvard University Press, 1949), 33; P. Ziegler, *The Sixth Great Power. A History of One of the Greatest of All Banking Families, the House of Barings, 1762-1929* (New York: Alfred A. Knopf, 1988), 70; P.E. Austin, *Baring Brothers and the Birth of Modern Finance* (London: Pickering & Chatto, 2007),

the United States did not possess the means to purchase Louisiana outright and because France hoped to receive payment sooner rather than later, a financial operation needed to be developed. For two reasons, it is difficult to define this financial operation.

First, the contracting parties had different conceptions of the Louisiana operation resulting from different answers to the question of what was transacted. For France, the Louisiana operation meant a financial operation that accelerated payments for the sale of Louisiana. For the United States, the Louisiana operation was an operation to acquire the funds to purchase the Louisiana Territory. These two operations are not the same. A quarter of the purchase price, \$3.75 million, was settled through the United States assuming French debt to private American citizens. This was a post-facto settling of accounts that benefitted France, but it was not part of the financial operation. For France the Louisiana operation thus entailed a scheme for accelerated payment to the sum of \$11.25 million. Because the United States assumed this debt to American citizens, from an American perspective, this sum is part of the Louisiana operation. Moreover, because this sum of \$3.75 million lacked any foundation, the American payments to American citizens exceeded this amount.[2] Another point to consider is that the United States purchased from France only the political authority over Louisiana. In the decades after 1803, the United States entered into multiple treaties with Native American tribes to buy the soil rights, of the so-called Indian title. These treaties spawned a

206, n42; M.D. Peterson, *Thomas Jefferson and the New Nation: a Biography* (Oxford: Oxford University Press, 1975), 760; P. Branda, *Le prix de la gloire. Napoléon et l'argent* (Paris: Fayard, 2007), 256; S. Pagé, *L'Amérique du Nord et Napoléon* (Paris: Nouveau Monde/Fondation Napoléon, 2003), 77; R.G. Kennedy, *Mr. Jefferson's Lost Cause. Land, Farmers, Slavery, and the Louisiana Purchase* (Oxford: Oxford University Press, 2003), 183; E.W. Lyon, *The Man Who Sold Louisiana. The Career of François Barbé-Marbois* (Norman, OK: Oklahoma University Press, 1942), 121; T.K. McGraw, *The Founders and Finance. How Hamilton, Gallatin, and Other Immigrants Forged a New Economy* (Cambridge, MA: Belknap Press of Harvard University Press, 2012), 241–242; J. Orbell, *Baring Brothers & Co., Limited. A History to 1939* (London: Baring Brothers & Co., Limited, 1985), 15; D. Tearle, *Barings Bank, William Bingham and the Rise of the American Nation. A Transatlantic Relationship from the Revolutionary War through the Louisiana Purchase* (London and Jefferson, NC: McFarland & Co., 2010), 160.

[2] J.E. Winston and R.W. Colomb, "How the Louisiana Purchase Was Financed", *The Louisiana Historical Quarterly* 12/2 (Apr., 1929), 203; T. Donaldson, *The Public Domain. Its History, with Statistics* [...] (Washington DC: Government Printing Office, 1880), 105.

plethora of financial operations and transactions that Robert Lee approximates at about $2.6 billion, or, adjusted for inflation, more than $8.5 billion in 2012.[3] From an American perspective, all these transactions are included in the Louisiana operation. As this study aims to shed a light on the financial mediation, the Louisiana operation is defined as the sum that required financing to facilitate the execution of the diplomatic treaty on the Louisiana cession, $11.25 million.

The second point to consider is the gradation of the operation. Financial operations tend to draw out and to bifurcate due to the changing international, political, and economic circumstances. Usually this occurs when one of the contracting parties encounters an obstacle to completion of their part in the operation, after which the affected part would be redeveloped, leading to a new, second-order operation. In complex or drawn-out operations this could occur several times. Moreover, second-order operations could be merged together or with different operations entirely, or (parts of) it could require further redevelopment, leading to a complex web or interrelated operations that expanded beyond its original spatial and temporal bounds. The Louisiana operation that the financial mediaries developed spawned several second and third-order operations that extended the original operation into the Baltic trade, the reconstruction of the French navy, the American secondary market for bonds, and American credit operations in Europe. Whilst interesting, these derivative operations require in-depth archival research in a variety of locations and broader contextualisation that would take this tome beyond its intended deadline and length. Therefore, this study is focussed on the primary operation on Louisiana.

There has not been much scholarly interest in the primary Louisiana operation as developed by financial mediaries. Two scholars to have studied the operation are E.J. Winston and R.W. Colomb, who wrote an article entitled "How the Louisiana Purchase Was Financed".[4] Employing a recent publication of American primary source material relevant to the Louisiana Purchase, Winston and Colomb retraced the financial transaction to quantify the sum paid by the United States, the sum received by France, and the sums earned by financial mediaries. Based on an

[3] R. Lee, "Accounting for Conquest: The Price of the Louisiana Purchase of Indian Country", *The Journal of American History* 103/4 (March, 2017), 921–942.

[4] Winston and Colomb, "How the Louisiana Purchase Was Financed", 189–201.

overview of the American redemption that was requested from the Treasury Department, Winston and Colomb calculated the purchase price at $23,527,873, and they assessed that France received Fr.60 million in American bonds. However, France discounted the bonds for Fr.8 million, so she received only Fr.52 million. The discount fee of Fr.8 million went to financial mediaries, who Winston and Colomb identified as Baring and Hope. The authors also mention interest payments, discounts, and commissions for brokers, but they do not specify who these are.

Winston and Colomb's sum for the United States has become a mainstay in the historiography.[5] Possibly, the sum was based on a report prepared for Congress by Thomas Donaldson.[6] However, the calculations of American interest payments do not match up with the interest rate and the redemption schedule that Winston and Colomb presented. Either the calculations are off, or some information has not been disclosed. The former is difficult to assess because the calculations are not explicated. The latter is difficult to assess because no reference is provided. A second issue regards the treatment of the financial mediaries, Baring and Hope. Winston and Colomb discuss the financial mediation as being done by the two houses in tandem. In fact, political intervention by the British government caused a rift between the two houses, which affected the nature of the Louisiana operation.

Another scholar to examine the financing of cession of Louisiana is P.J. van Winter. He published three pieces: an article entitled "De verkoop van Louisiana" [The sale of Louisiana], the chapter "Louisiana 6%" in his two-volume study on the role of Amsterdam trade and finance in the economy of the early United States, and an article entitled "Louisiana gekocht en betaald" [Louisiana, bought and sold].[7] All publications are based on the research that Van Winter conducted for his two-volume study, for which he consulted the Hope archives and select American

[5] R.D. Bush, *The Louisiana Purchase. A Global Context* (New York and London: Routledge, 2014), 67-68; J. Kukla, *A Wilderness So Immense: The Louisiana Purchase and the Destiny of America* (New York: Anchor Books, 2004), 320.

[6] Donaldson, *The Public Domain. Its History, with Statistics*, 105.

[7] P.J. van Winter, "De Verkoop van Louisiana", *Tijdschrift voor Geschiedenis* 47 (1932), 41-61; P.J. van Winter, Het aandeel van den Amsterdamschen handel aan den opbouw van het Amerikaansche Gemeenebest, 2 vols (The Hague: Martinus Nijhof, 1927-1933), II: 368-391; P.J. van Winter, "Louisiana gekocht en betaald", in *Bijdragen en Mededelingen van het Historische Genootschap* 75 (1961), 37*-56*.

archives. The first and last publications are popular articles based on readings he gave. The chapter contains the annotated research findings. Van Winter's research focusses mostly on the politics of the Louisiana cession. Only a small part is dedicated to the financial operation that was developed by the financial mediaries. And then Van Winter principally explores the Louisiana operation in the context of his broader research interest, Dutch-American economic relations in the eighteenth and early nineteenth century. His aim is to answer the question of why Baring, and in their tow Hope, were awarded the Louisiana business by the United States, rather than the Amsterdam houses that had traditionally serviced American debt. Van Winter concluded the awarding of the business to Baring of London was indicative of the migration of the centre of international finance from Amsterdam to London, though he did acknowledge that Amsterdam houses were awarded a minor role at a later point. However, Van Winter also failed to pick up on the changes to the consortium that mediated the cession of Louisiana, which saw Baring replaced to an extent by Amsterdam houses, probably because Van Winter did not consult the Baring archives. Quantifying the transaction is of secondary interest to Van Winter. He correctly established the price that the United States paid, though he did not quantify the interest payments. He estimated the sum received by France to be Fr.50,325,000. This is lower than Winston and Colomb because Van Winter picked up on one renegotiation of the terms of payment, for which France paid a fee. However, he missed out on other, minor fees paid by France. Van Winter did not quantify the profits made by the financial mediaries, perhaps because he does not pick up on the changes to the consortium.

A more recent study on the financing of the Louisiana cession is forthcoming by Professor Dr. Larry Neal. However, the publication is due after the deadline for this manuscript. That said, going by previous work, one can only state that Dr Neal's forthcoming study is much looked forward to and should be consulted alongside and contrasted with this study.

Several studies have appeared on the house of Baring. The best known is probably Ziegler's *The Sixth Great Power* of 1988.[8] The book explores the history of Baring, 1762–1929. The first four chapters deal with the period relevant to this study. Ziegler was encouraged to write the monograph by the partners of Barings Bank, and he had unrestricted access to

[8] Ziegler, *The Sixth Great Power.*

the archives. The book is well researched, and it should be consulted by any researcher of Baring. However, one does feel that Ziegler has come to identify too intimately with his subject of study, in particular with Francis Baring. One reads statements like: "[Francis was] one of the most remarkable men of his generation", "[Francis] possessed that precious knack of establishing what lay inside [books] without actually reading he contents", and "from a very early age he [Francis] commanded respect and people listened to what he had to say confident that it would be worth hearing".[9] Such a rose-tinted view does not do justice to the uphill battle that Francis fought to establish his house. Worse still, the view distorts Ziegler's perspective on the history of Baring. For example, whilst Ziegler identifies the connection with Hope as crucial to the rise of Baring, he views the relationship very much from the perspective of Francis' aims and ambitions, and he frames the history of Baring and Hope around this perspective.[10] In fact, alongside Francis' aims and ambitions were Hope's aims and ambitions, which had a role in shaping the collective history too, arguably even more so than Francis'. Furthermore, Ziegler stays rather superficial in the examination of the business operations of Baring. For example, the financing of the transfer of Louisiana is only briefly discussed.[11] The outline of the operation is clear, but the twists and turns of the operation, which are often revealing of the limits of ambition and how to overcome obstacles to success, remain obscured.

In addition, there are three studies that examine the history of Baring in the context of American economics and politics. The first is Hidy's *The House of Baring in American Trade and Finance*.[12] This is a great work that is well researched, including the business operations. The book has but one flaw, which is that the analysis is based on a small body of primary sources. The research was conducted prior to and during World War Two. Hidy had only limited opportunity to visit the archives in London, and when he did in 1939, much of the archive had been moved out of London to keep it safe from bombing. Hidy's study is thus based principally on

[9] Ziegler, *The Sixth Great Power*, 17–18.

[10] Ziegler, *The Sixth Great Power*, 54–55.

[11] Ziegler, *The Sixth Great Power*, 70–72.

[12] Hidy, *The House of Baring*.

the Baring Papers, which are located in Canada. These are mostly relevant for the period from 1836.[13] Only two out of the sixteen chapters discuss the history of Baring up to 1815. Considering the limited access to primary sources, Hidy sticks to a factual account of these years. Hidy discusses the Louisiana operation only fleetingly, but because he did not have access to all sources, he was not able to piece together a complete picture.[14] The second is Austin's *Baring Brothers and the Birth of Modern Finance*. The study is mostly relevant to the later nineteenth-century history of Baring. Very few pages are dedicated to the years up until 1815. Those reflections on these years seem mostly based on secondary sources, which are not always cited correctly. In particular, Austin seems to follow the work of Orbell closely.[15] Because Austin has not consulted primary sources for the early history, too many inaccuracies have crept in. To give just one example, Austin speaks of "Messrs Baring and Hope" travelling to Paris to negotiate a loan in 1817.[16] Henry Hope had passed away in 1811 already, and the last Hope had withdrawn from the partnership in 1813. Austin briefly touches on the financing of the cession of Louisiana, but his observations are factually incorrect: he incorrectly states that Alexander Baring and the American minister of the Treasury Albert Gallatin worked together in the negotiations in Paris, he is incorrect in the allocation of Louisiana stock to Baring and Hope, and he is incorrect in the size and site of French payments.[17] Inaccuracies like this make Austin's work unreliable. A third book to discuss the history of Baring in the context of American economics and politics is Tearle's *Barings Bank, William Bingham and the Rise of the American Nation*.[18] The book examines the interesting Baring-Bingham connection, which shifts the focus onto the early history of Baring and onto Alexander Baring rather than Francis Baring. That said, the thrust of the research is on William Bingham and his role in building the United States. Baring is considered only as a facilitator to Bingham. Tearle discusses the financing of the cession of Louisiana, but his understanding of the financial operations is

[13] Hidy, *The House of Baring*, xxi–xxii.

[14] Hidy, *The House of Baring*, 33–34.

[15] Austin, *Baring Brothers*, 26; Orbell, *Baring Brothers*, 26.

[16] Austin, *Baring Brothers*, 12.

[17] Austin, *Baring Brothers*, 17–18.

[18] Tearle, *Barings Bank*.

incorrect. He picks up on some changes to how the Louisiana operation was originally envisaged, but not all, such as Baring's withdrawal and the consequences this had for the allocation of Louisiana stock, the resource mobilisation operations, and the payments to France.[19]

A final publication on the history of Baring is Orbell's *Baring Brothers & Co., Limited. A History to 1939*.[20] Orbell was the archivist at the Baring Archive, and this shows in the publication. Orbell has a meticulous knowledge of the Baring archives, which he translated into an excellent study of the house. Orbell stayed very close to the sources, and he resisted the temptation to extrapolate from the sources to comment on the exceptionality of Baring. Of all the publications on the history of Baring, this book has been the most useful. It should be read prior to and alongside the consultation of the archives. If there is one flaw in the publication, it is that it is not annotated, meaning that one must comb the archives to find the source that Orbell refers to, though this job has become increasingly easy with the ongoing digitisation.

In sum, Baring is relatively well-served in the historiography. The broad outlines of the history of Baring are well known, as are some of the twists and turns in their business operations that came to define the history of the house, mostly the operations in America. However, not all early operations are examined in depth. For a full understanding of the history of Baring, this void must be filled. Furthermore, with the exception of Orbell, the historiography is framed by two perspectives. First is the tendency to want to account for Baring's success and its rise to greatness. There is merit in this line of inquiry, but it overlooks or disregards failure. In fact, viewing Baring's history through the prism of failure holds important lessons for understanding the rise of Baring. It not only shows how the house addressed adversity, but it also reveals that Baring was quick to draw better lessons from failure than many of their peers, which the author has come to view as perhaps Baring's most important quality. Second, the history of Baring is viewed through the narrow prism of the house. Outside influences are minimised or understood only insofar as they support Baring. In fact, Baring operated in a network of associated houses, and the changing interaction with the component parts of this

[19] Tearle, *Barings Bank*, 159–161.

[20] Orbell, *Baring Brothers*.

network is much revealing of how Baring responded to the array of obstacles it faced in its rise to prominence. In particular, the house of Hope was an important influence on Baring, and the history and archives of Hope do need to be consulted alongside that of Baring. Within this narrow perspective on the house of Baring, the figure of Francis Baring looms large. Francis is presented as a man of exceptional qualities, who made all the right decisions all the time, leading to a merchant-banking house that towered above all others. The prominence of the house of Baring is undisputed, but it was not exceptional, particularly not in the years to 1815. And Francis Baring had good qualities. He was intellectually gifted, alert to new business opportunities, quick to assess all the moving parts and slot them together into a profitable operation, and he worked very hard, despite his lifelong ill health. But Francis had his flaws too. He was overly ambitious, stubborn, he had little patience for those with lesser abilities, but most of all he was quarrelsome. Francis had a strained relationship with his older brother John, whilst his relationship with his younger brother was outright bad. Francis was distant from his eldest son Thomas, disappointed in his second son Alexander, disillusioned with his third son Henry, and depressed by his fifth son George. He had high hopes for his fourth son, William, but he was sickly and passed away before the relationship could flourish. Francis got along well enough with his son-in-law Charles Wall, but only because he was compliant. Francis only occasionally got along with his more independent-minded son-in-law, Pierre César Labouchere. Francis kept good relations with persons on whom he relied, such as Robert Voûte and Henry Hope in business, or the Earl of Shelburne in politics, but he failed to build networks of patronage, or of friendship, for himself. The history of Baring could benefit from a less idealised consideration of Francis and a greater focus on the contribution of other family members to the history of the house of Baring. For the late eighteenth and early nineteenth century, this person is Alexander Baring.

The house of Hope is less well served in the historiography. There is but one monograph on the house, Buist's *At Spes Non Fracta. Hope & Co. 1770–1815.*[21] The work was commissioned by Hope & Co. in 1953. Buist was granted unfettered access to the Hope archives for a period of 20 years. He intended to write a comprehensive history of the house

[21] M.G. Buist, *At Spes Non Fracta. Hope & Co. 1770–1815. Merchant Bankers and Diplomats at Work* (The Hague: Bank Mees & Hope NV, 1974).

from its origin to the present, similar to what Ziegler has done for Baring. However, Buist was quick to limit the study to the years up until 1815.[22] This was a good decision, because it has allowed for an in-depth discussion of Hope's early business operations. The publication has fourteen chapters, each of which deals with one business undertaking. Not only the outlines and outcomes of the business operations are presented, but the twists and turns in the operation are discussed at length, so that one gets a sense of how Hope dealt with setbacks, improvised, learnt, and adapted. Alas, Buist has not discussed the operation to finance the cession of Louisiana. It is unclear why not. As a student of Van Winter, he was well aware of the topic. Perhaps Buist was unable to collect sufficient primary source material. Part of the archival sources relevant to the Louisiana operation are located in the Baring Archive, which Buist did not consult. There is also a chapter on the history of the family and the firm. Buist presents a realistic picture, highlighting the flaws along with the strengths. He does not idealise the family. One comment is that Buist has not fully grasped the changes to the partnership from 1802 onwards, and the associated rise to prominence of Pierre César Labouchere. The reason for this may lie in the fact that Buist did not locate the private archives of Pierre César Labouchere, which ended up in the Baring Archive.

In sum, if there is any criticism of the work of Buist, it is directed at what has not been studied: the Louisiana operation and the history of the family and the firm, 1802–1815. Both omissions relate to Buist not having accessed the archives of the house so intimately connected to Hope, the house of Baring. This study aims to address both topics.

Primary Sources

Chapter 3 is based on the study of 610 primary sources, though a great deal more have been read. The transcriptions run for 175,000 words, or 250 pages. 526 sources (79%) are drawn from the Hope archives. 72 sources (11%) are from the Baring archives. 48 sources (7%) are from various American collections. 17 sources (3%) have been found in the French national archives. The numbers add up to more than 610 sources, because there are duplicates. Based on a reading of the archives, it is felt

[22] Buist, *At Spes Non Fracta*, IX-X.

that this body of sources represents about 75–80% of the original material. About 10% of the archival material was purposefully destroyed by Hope and Baring because they did not want to leave a paper trail. About 5–10% of relevant archival material would be contained in the collections of associates, such as De Smeth of Amsterdam, Willings & Francis of Philadelphia, or the papers of William Bingham. Not all relevant collections have been located—some may be lost. Those collections that have been located would contain only information indirectly relevant to the Louisiana operation. Therefore, they have not been prioritised. Up to 5% of the archival material relevant to this study has not been consulted because either the source has been mis-indexed and therefore not found, the source is inaccessible, or the source has been overlooked because it is only a small excerpt of an otherwise irrelevant communication. That said, it is felt that any new information will not fundamentally revise financial operations as presented in this study.

The archives of Hope & Co. have been very important to this study.[23] There are three reasons for this. First, Hope had a central role in the Louisiana operation, and so most communications started and ended with Hope. Two, at the time of the Louisiana operation, Hope had two offices, one in Amsterdam and one in London. And so, in addition to incoming and outgoing communications to relevant parties, one finds internal Hope communication on the Louisiana operation. Three, Hope was obsessed with archiving. Often, not only the principal copy of a communication is found, but second and third copies, as well as drafts at various stages of completion. A drawback of the Hope archives is that the archive is indexed only at a supra level, meaning that one must comb through large parts of the collection. Fortunately, the *Stadsarchief Amsterdam* [Amsterdam City Archive] has started digitising its collections.

Baring had a different approach to archiving. Francis Baring worked mostly from memory. Many papers were destroyed, and only the most important pieces were retained. And so whilst Baring has only a modest share in the sources that have been employed for this study, they carry greater weight. The Baring archives are held by the ING Bank in London. The archives of the early history of Baring, including sources relevant to the Louisiana operation, have been collected into the Northbrook

[23] The Netherlands, Stadsarchief Amsterdam [NL-SA], 735 *Archief van de Firma Hope & Co. met verwante archiefvormers*.

Papers.[24] Some additional collections have been added to the Baring Archive. These include the private papers of Pierre César Labouchere, which have been important to this study.[25] A large part of the Baring archives have been digitised.

For Hope and Baring's interactions with Washington, the American archives in the Library of Congress and the National Archives have been consulted.[26] In hindsight, this was not necessary. Most, if not all, of the sources relevant to the financing of the Louisiana cession have been published in print. The printed sources are listed in the footnotes. The archives of the foreign relations of the French executive power, 1799–1815, have been consulted for insight into the French perspective.[27] Few French sources have been digitised.

Despite the relative abundance of primary sources, working with the material to reconstruct the Louisiana operation has been challenging. The Louisiana operation was politically and financially sensitive. The Louisiana cession had political ramifications for the United States, France, Spain, Britain, and the Netherlands, and the financing of the cession interested not only the United States, France, and Britain but also rival bankers. Hope and Baring recognised the sensitivity of the operation, and they took several precautions to ensure secrecy. In principle, as much as possible the discussions on how to set up and develop the Louisiana operation were done in person.[28] This was possible because Hope had an office in London, and because Alexander Baring and Pierre César Labouchere frequently travelled between Amsterdam, Paris, and London. Clerks and associates were only given a minimum amount of information, and they were bound to secrecy. And even when persons involved in the Louisiana operation met, not all persons had the right to broach

[24] United Kingdom, Baring Archive [UK-BA], *Northbrook Papers* [NP].

[25] UK-BA, *Deposits & Gifts* [DEP], 208 *Papers of the Labouchere Family, 1621–1822.*

[26] United States of America, Library of Congress [USA-LoC], *Louisiana Miscellany*; United States of America, National Archives [USA-NA], Record Group [RG] 46 *Records of the US Senate, 1803–1805*; USA NA, RG/56 *General Records of the Department of the Treasury, Documents relating to the Purchase of Louisiana.*

[27] France, Archives nationales [FR-AN], Archives du pouvoir exécutief, 1789–1815 [AF], IV *Secrétairerie d'état impériale et cabinet de Napoléon 1er.*

[28] "Francis Baring to Labouchère, 15 February 1803", UK-BA, NP1/A/4/4; "Francis Baring & Co. to Hope & Co., 15 October 1803", NL-SA, 735/300; "Alexander Baring to Labouchere, 24 March 1804", NL-SA, 735/303.

the topic. For example, when a representative of the house of De Smeth, who played an important role in the operation, travelled to Paris where Alexander Baring was negotiating with the French regime, he was not allowed to discuss the financial operation unless hinted at by Alexander.[29] When Hope and Baring did put pen to paper, they took further measures. To start, much correspondence was destroyed after it had served its purpose.[30] Hope and Baring also employed a cypher in their correspondence.[31] It appears that this was quickly dropped. However, this only meant that the houses reverted to their usual parlance, which contained many abbreviations and codes: all accounts were given a code, which could be reused when the account was closed, and individuals were usually referred to by their initials. The person is identified easily enough when it regards a principal actor, but for some of the clerks, this has not been possible. In cases when the sender has not been identified, the house is stated as the sender. The challenges to working with the primary source material have been overcome thanks to a disagreement that emerged between Francis Baring and the house of Hope over the division of profit on the Louisiana operation, which forced all principal actors to put their thoughts and actions to paper. This cache of papers has become the Rosetta stone that has been used to corroborate other sources.

Where possible, the paper trail has been retraced to the original source. Secondary literature has been referenced only when the original sources have not been found. That said, all the secondary sources referenced in this book, particularly those discussed in the historiography, have been important in contextualising the research. It is felt that this publication is but a small piece of the puzzle that can be slotted into the overall historiography. All primary sources are referenced at the end of the last sentence that draws from that source. In most cases, the reference comes after a few sentences, but for some primary sources, the reference comes at the end of the paragraph or section. The reference can thus be intersected by other references.

[29] "Labouchère to Francis Baring, 24 February 1803", UK-BA, NP1/A/4/5.

[30] "Alexander Baring to Labouchere, London, 23 July 1804", NL-SA, 735/304.

[31] "Cypher", UK-BA, NP1/A/4/10; "Cypher", NL-SA, 735/299.

References

PRIMARY SOURCES

Archival Sources

The Netherlands, Stadsarchief Amsterdam [NL-SA]:
735 Archief van de Firma Hope & Co. met verwante archiefvormers
Amsterdam Office:
Correspondence with Baring:
- 299: 1803–1805.
- 300: 1803–1805.
- 303: 1803–1811.
- 304: 1804.

United Kingdom, The Baring Archive [UK-BA]
Northbrook Papers [NP]/1/A:
4. Louisiana Purchase Papers.

SECONDARY SOURCES

Austin, P.E., *Baring Brothers and the Birth of Modern Finance* (London: Pickering & Chatto, 2007).

Branda, P., *Le prix de la gloire. Napoléon et l'argent* (Paris: Fayard, 2007).

Buist, M.G., *At Spes Non Fracta. Hope & Co. 1770–1815. Merchant Bankers and Diplomats at Work* (The Hague: Bank Mees & Hope NV, 1974).

Bush, R.D., *The Louisiana Purchase. A Global Context* (New York and London: Routledge, 2014).

Donaldson, T., *The Public Domain. Its History, with Statistics* [...] (Washington DC: Government Printing Office, 1880).

Hidy, R.W., *The House of Baring in American Trade and Finance. English Merchant Bankers at Work 1763–1861* (Cambridge, MA: Harvard University Press, 1949).

Kennedy, R.G., *Mr. Jefferson's Lost Cause. Land, Farmers, Slavery, and the Louisiana Purchase* (Oxford: Oxford University Press, 2003).

Kukla, J., *A Wilderness So Immense: The Louisiana Purchase and the Destiny of America* (New York: Anchor Books, 2004).

Lee, R., "Accounting for Conquest: The Price of the Louisiana Purchase of Indian Country", *The Journal of American History* 103/4 (March, 2017), 921–942.

Lyon, E.W., *The Man Who Sold Louisiana. The Career of François Barbé-Marbois* (Norman, OK: Oklahoma University Press, 1942).

McGraw, T.K., *The Founders and Finance. How Hamilton, Gallatin, and Other Immigrants Forged a New Economy* (Cambridge, MA: Belknap Press of Harvard University Press, 2012).
Orbell, J., *Baring Brothers & Co., Limited. A History to 1939* (London: Baring Brothers & Co., Limited, 1985).
Pagé, S., *L'Amérique du Nord et Napoléon* (Paris: Nouveau Monde/Fondation Napoléon, 2003).
Peterson, M.D., *Thomas Jefferson and the New Nation: a Biography* (Oxford: Oxford University Press, 1975).
Tearle, D., *Barings Bank, William Bingham and the Rise of the American Nation. A Transatlantic Relationship from the Revolutionary War through the Louisiana Purchase* (London and Jefferson, NC: McFarland & Co., 2010).
Winston, J.E., and Colomb R.W., "How the Louisiana Purchase Was Financed", *The Louisiana Historical Quarterly* 12/2 (Apr., 1929), 189–201.
Winter, P. J. van, "De Verkoop van Louisiana", *Tijdschrift Voor Geschiedenis* 47 (1932), 41–61.
Winter, P.J. van, "Louisiana gekocht en betaald", in *Bijdragen en Mededelingen van het Historische Genootschap* 75 (1961), 37*-56*.
Winter, P.J. van, *Het aandeel van den Amsterdamschen handel aan den opbouw van het Amerikaansche Gemeenebest* (The Hague: Martinus Nijhof, 1927–1933).
Ziegler, P., *The Sixth Great Power. A History of One of the Greatest of All Banking Families, the House of Barings, 1762–1929* (New York: Alfred A. Knopf, 1988).

CHAPTER 2

Louisiana in Politics and Diplomacy

Abstract This chapter sets the backdrop for the financial operations that followed from the Franco-American agreement on the transfer of Louisiana. First, it briefly explores the importance of Louisiana to those actors that had a direct interest in the transfer of the territory, that is France, the United States, Spain, and Britain. Second, the chapter briefly retraces the history of the negotiations on the transfer of Louisiana, concluding in the signing of the diplomatic treaty and conventions.

Keywords Spanish Louisiana · French Louisiana · Pinckney's treaty · Trans-Appalachian West · Jay's treaty · Retrocession of Louisiana · Cession of Louisiana · European Disengagement from America

This chapter sets the backdrop for the financial operations that followed the Franco-American agreement on the transfer of Louisiana.[1] First, it briefly explores the importance of Louisiana to those actors that had a direct interest in the transfer of the territory, that is United States, France, Spain, and Britain. Second, the chapter briefly retraces the history of the

[1] Adapted from: A.P. Whitaker, *The Mississippi Question 1795–1803. A Study in Trade, Politics, and Diplomacy* (New York and London: D. Appleton-Century Co., 1934).

M. E. Hay, *Transatlantic Finance in the Age of Revolutions*,
https://doi.org/10.1007/978-3-031-65232-5_2

negotiations on the transfer of Louisiana, concluding with the signing of the diplomatic treaty and conventions.

Bourbon Louisiana

The territory that the United States purchased from France, commonly referred to as the Louisiana Territory, was vast, stretching across the North American continent from Canada to the Gulf of Mexico. It was generally accepted that the lands drained by the Mississippi River and its tributaries defined the limits of Louisiana, but the exact boundaries were unclear. They were not established until 1812, when the state of Louisiana was admitted to the United States of America. As recognised today, the territory that was purchased in 1803 covers approximately 2.20–2.29 million square kilometres of land (see Map 2.1). This is slightly under a quarter of the size of the United States of America in 2024. In 1803, however, the Louisiana Territory equalled the size of the newly independent American republic.[2]

The Spanish were the first Europeans to venture into the region that became known as Louisiana. In 1541, the Spanish conquistador Hernando de Soto explored the south-eastern part of North America, including Louisiana. Ever since, Europeans—Spanish, French, Dutch, Swedish, and English—were known to trade and live with the Native American tribes, but few remained definitively. The history of French Louisiana starts in 1669, when an expedition under René-Robert Cavelier, Sieur de La Salle crossed the Great Lakes to Ohio and Illinois. The expedition did not venture onto the Mississippi, but it did establish that the river emptied into the Gulf of Mexico. La Salle returned to Canada to prepare a larger expedition, but it was not until 1681 that he set off. On 9 April 1682, the expedition reached the mouth of the Mississippi, where La Salle asserted the right of discovery of the Mississippi River, which gave claim to all the lands drained by that river and its tributaries. In the following decades, France reinforced her claim by constructing settlements and military outposts across the territory, with New Orleans,

[2] M. Klein, "Louisiana: European Explorations and the Louisiana Purchase. A Special Presentation from the Geography and Map Division of the Library of Congress", unpublished essay (Library of Congress, Geography and Map Division, undated, accessed via: https://www.loc.gov/collections/louisiana-european-explorations-and-the-louisiana-purchase/about-this-collection/ (21 September 2023), 1–10.

Map 2.1 The Territory of Louisiana, 1803–1813. "Map of the Louisiana Purchase Territory", USA-NA, RG/49 *Records of the Bureau of Land Management*

strategically located at the mouth of the Mississippi, soon becoming the primary settlement. France may have succeeded in claiming and securing the vast territory, but French Louisiana remained sparsely populated, ill-managed, and economically underdeveloped. The territory never became self-sufficient, and it relied on financial injections from France for its development and defence.[3]

When France lost her Canadian possessions in the Seven Years' War, defending Louisiana became too difficult and expensive. Rather than allow the territory to fall to Britain, on 3 November 1762, by the Treaty of Fontainebleau, the French King Louis XV ceded Louisiana to his Spanish cousin Carlos III. The Treaty of Paris of 10 February 1763, which brought peace between France, Spain, and Britain, confirmed the cession of Louisiana to Spain, though the boundary between Spanish North America and British North America was revised in favour of Britain by ceding to Britain all former French Louisiana east of the Mississippi River. This territory, referred to by the British as the Western Territories, was not organised into new colonies, or attached to existing colonies, but proclaimed crown lands. Spain also ceded Florida to Britain to round off the Spanish and British empires in the Americas.[4]

[3] A good starting point for any study of French Louisiana is: G.R. Conrad (ed.), *The Louisiana Purchase Bicentennial Series in Louisiana History. Volume I: The French Experience in Louisiana* (Lafayette: The Center for Louisiana Studies, 1995). See also: W.R. Smith, *Brief History of the Louisiana Territory* (St. Louis: The St. Louis News Company, 1904), 3–28; J.F. Bannon, "The Spaniards in the Mississippi Valley. An Introduction", in J.F. McDermott (ed.), *The Spanish in the Mississippi Valley 1762–1804* (Urbana: University of Illinois Press, 1974), 1–5; D.R. Farrell, "Reluctant Imperialism: Pontchartrain, Vauban and the Expansion of New France, 1699–1702", *Proceedings of the Meeting of the French Colonial Historical Society* 12 (1988), 35–45; S.G. Lemann, "The Problems of Founding a Viable Colony: The Military in Early French Louisiana", *Proceedings of the Meeting of the French Colonial Historical Society* 6/7 (1982), 27–35; J. Pritchard, "Population in French America, 1670–1730: The Demographic Context of Colonial Louisiana", in *French Colonial Louisiana and the Atlantic World,* ed. B.G. Bond (Baton Rouge: Louisiana State University Press, 2005), 175–203; G.C. Din, "Empires Too Far: The Demographic Limitations of Three Imperial Powers in the Eighteenth-Century Mississippi Valley", *Louisiana History: The Journal of the Louisiana Historical Association* 50/3 (Summer, 2009), 261–268; C.A. Brasseaux, "The Image of Louisiana and the Failure of Voluntary French Emigration, 1683–1731", *Proceedings of the Meeting of the French Colonial Historical Society* 4 (1979), 47–56.

[4] A.S. Aiton, "The Diplomacy of the Louisiana Cession", in *Louisiana Purchase Bicentennial Series Volume II. The Spanish Presence in Louisiana 1763–1803*, ed. G.C. Din (Lafayette: The Center for Louisiana Studies, 1996), 11–27; Smith, *Brief History of the Louisiana Territory*, 29.

The transfer of Louisiana to Spain was anything but smooth. The inhabitants of Louisiana were unenthusiastic about Spanish rule. Initially, their fears were allayed by the last French Director-General of Louisiana, Jean-Jacques Blaise d'Abbadie, who claimed that little would change in practice. However, shortly after the Treaty of Paris, Carlos III of Spain embarked on a comprehensive reorganisation of his empire, which focussed on integrating the diverse territories into a more coherent polity. Two steps were taken. First, through the stricter regulation of commerce and a crackdown on illicit trade, commercial activity would be limited to trade with the metropole and with select colonial ports. For most of Spanish America, this in fact meant a loosening of the overly strict existing commercial regulations. For Louisiana, it meant a reorientation from the French empire, in which trade flowed from Canada in the north through Louisiana to the Caribbean Islands in the south and vice versa, to the Spanish empire, in which Louisiana, located at the fringes of Spanish America, had to elbow its way into established commercial networks. The inhabitants of Louisiana found this reorientation too disruptive. Furthermore, Louisianans found that private trade, including the lucrative slave trade, was now classed as illicit trade, and thus forbidden. This threatened many livelihoods. Second, the boundaries of the empire were to be strengthened. Louisiana, located at the north-eastern border of Spanish America, was to become a *barrera*, or barrier, protecting the empire against the neighbouring British. This was to be done through the construction of fortifications and the resettlement of populations to occupy strategic sites. The fortification of Louisiana was not so much a problem, though disagreement did arise over who would foot the bill, Spain or the inhabitants of Louisiana. The resettlement of populations was more controversial because it uprooted communities and upset the social relations that the patchwork of diverse communities had with each other and Native American tribes. Such issues were difficult to manage in times of competent government, but in the case of the transfer of Louisiana to Spain, these issues became impossible to manage due to a political vacuum that had emerged. After the decision to cede Louisiana to Spain had been taken, the French authorities were keen to transfer the territory as soon as possible, if only to be relieved of the financial burden of government. However, when the new Spanish governor, Antonio de Ulloa, arrived to take possession in 1766, he brought with him only 90 soldiers. He felt this was too few to maintain Spanish authority, and so he refused to accept the transfer of Louisiana. This unhappy state of affairs lasted until 1768, when the inhabitants of Louisiana took matters into their own hands and revolted. The revolt was put down with force, but no compromises were made, and so the dissatisfaction lingered. Due to the divisive politics, and because Louisiana contributed little to the treasury as compared to Spain's Southern American and Caribbean colonies, Spanish interest in developing the northern frontier of the empire was limited.[5]

Louisiana would have remained a backwater of the Spanish empire had not the American War of Independence changed the geopolitics of the region. The American Revolutionaries, with French, Spanish, and to a lesser extent Dutch assistance, defeated Britain and secured their independence at Paris on 3 September 1783. The war was no less of a success for Spain. Two days after Paris, Britain signed a peace with the Bourbon monarchies at Versailles, ceding East Florida and West Florida to Spain, which effectively turned the Gulf of Mexico into a Spanish lake. The cession altered Louisiana's position in the Spanish empire. Louisiana remained part of the northern boundary of Spanish America,

[5] A good starting point for any study of Spanish Louisiana is: G.C. Din (ed.), *Louisiana Purchase Bicentennial Series Volume II. The Spanish Presence in Louisiana 1763–1803* (Lafayette: The Center for Louisiana Studies, 1996). See also: Bush, *The Louisiana Purchase*, 14–35; J. Adelman, *Sovereignty and Revolution in the Iberian Atlantic* (Princeton: Princeton University Press, 2006), 22–33; A.J. Kuethe and K.J. Andrien, *The Spanish Atlantic World in the Eighteenth Century. War, and the Bourbon Reforms, 1713–1796* (Cambridge: Cambridge University Press, 2014), 231–345; Smith, *Brief History of the Louisiana Territory*, 30–39; P.J. Kastor, *The Nation's Crucible. The Louisiana Purchase and the Creation of America* (New Haven, CT: Yale University Press, 2004), 26–29; F. Kolb, "The New Orleans Revolt of 1768", *Louisiana History: The Journal of the Louisiana Historical Association* 59/1 (Winter, 2018), 5–39; G.C. Din, "Protecting the 'Barrera': Spain's Defenses in Louisiana, 1763–1779", *Louisiana History: The Journal of the Louisiana Historical Association* 19/2 (Spring, 1978), 183–211; C.A. Brasseaux, "Confusion, Conflict, and Currency: An Introduction to the Rebellion of 1768", *Louisiana History: The Journal of the Louisiana Historical Association* 18/2 (Spring, 1977), 161–169; J.P. Moore, "Antonio de Ulloa: A Profile of the First Spanish Governor of Louisiana", *Louisiana History: The Journal of the Louisiana Historical Association* 8/3 (Summer, 1967), 189–218; P.H. Boulle, "French Reactions to the Louisiana Revolution of 1768", in *The French in the Mississippi Valley*, ed. J.F. McDermott (Urbana: University of Illinois Press, 1965), 143–157; R.L. Woodward Jr., "Spanish Commercial Policy in Louisiana, 1763–1803", *Louisiana History: The Journal of the Louisiana Historical Association* 44/2 (Spring, 2003), 133–147.

but it was more interconnected from east to west, thus potentially alleviating the difficulties of commercial integration.[6] However, it was not long before Louisiana became a site of tension and conflict between the North American powers.

Louisiana in American Politics

The tension revolved around three interconnected issues: imperial boundaries, the problem of neighbourhood, and access to the Gulf of Mexico. Whilst de jure Britain had ceded her American possessions to the United States, de facto Britain contested the boundaries of the cession and she continued to expand her presence in North American southwards from Canada to Ohio and the Great Lakes area. Spain contested the cession of the Western Territories, which France had transferred to Britain in 1763, and which Britain, in turn, had transferred to the United States in 1783. The United States adhered to a strict interpretation of the treaties of 1763 and 1783, which extended the boundaries of the American republic to the shores of the Great Lakes in the north and the Mississippi in the west. The overlapping claims turned a large part of North America, running from the Great Lakes in the north to the Floridas in the south, and with the Mississippi as its western boundary and the original thirteen states of the United States as its eastern boundary, into a contested geopolitical space. In American historiography, this territory is referred to as the trans-Appalachian West. Both Britain and Spain embraced the emergence of a contested trans-Appalachian West, as it served their interest to have a buffer zone separating the geopolitical rivals of North America. For the United States, this state of affairs caused a second problem, the so-called problem of neighbourhood. The founders of the United States considered the possibility of the emergence of an independent American state outside the union the greatest threat to the American Republic, because a North America composed of multiple independent states would necessarily give rise to a continental order similar to Europe, in which the sovereign states

[6] A.W. Haarmann, "The Spanish Conquest of British West Florida, 1779–1781", *The Florida Historical Quarterly* 39/2 (Oct., 1960), 107–134.

competed for influence and frequently engaged in warfare. The geopolitical rivalry over the trans-Appalachian West brought this concern into focus.[7]

Settlers had drifted into the trans-Appalachian West since France's claim to the Mississippi watershed, but overall migration was relatively low. When the territory between the Mississippi and the Appalachian Mountains was ceded to Britain after the Seven Year's War, westward migration from the Thirteen Colonies increased. However, the British authorities did not want the area settled, because they wished to remain in friendly relations with the native tribes on their western borders, and so they forbade settlement in the area and ordered illegal settlers to remove themselves. This policy was difficult to enforce, but it became even more so during the American War of Independence, when the disruptions of war led people to seek safety beyond the zones of conflict. By the end of the war, the population of the trans-Appalachian West numbered in the tens of thousands. With American independence, the restrictions on westward migration were removed, and the expanding population of the United States poured over the Appalachian Mountains in search of a better future. These settlers of the trans-Appalachian West became an important voice in American politics when they clamoured for political and economic rights.[8]

The demands posed a challenge to the American government because it focussed American politics on important matters that the young

[7] A. Taylor, *American Revolutions. A Continental History, 1750–1804* (New York: W.W. Norton & Company, 2016), 333–404; C.P. Kakel III, *A Post-Exceptionalist Perspective on Early American History. American Wests, Global Wests, and Indian Wars* (Cham: Palgrave Pivot, 2019), 29–35; J.H. Clapham, "From the Peace of Versailles to the Second Peace of Paris, 1783–1815", in *The Cambridge History of British Foreign Policy, 1783–1919*, eds A.W. Ward and G.P. Gooch, 3 vols (Cambridge: Cambridge University Press, 1939), I: 149–156; A.P. Whitaker, *The Spanish-American Frontier: 1783–1795. The Westward Movement and the Spanish Retreat in the Mississippi Valley* (Gloucester, MA: Peter Smith, 1962), 9–46; S.F. Bemis, *Pinkney's Treaty. America's Advantage from Europe's Distress, 1783–1800* (New Haven: Yale University Press, 1960), 1–217; F. Furstenberg, "The Significance of the Trans-Appalachian Frontier in Atlantic History", *The American Historical Review* 113/3 (June, 2008), 655–659; R.R. Stenberg, "The Boundaries of the Louisiana Purchase", *The Hispanic American Historical Review* 14/1 (Feb., 1934), 32–64; P. Onuf and N. Onuf, *Federal Union, Modern World. The Law of Nations in an Age of Revolutions, 1776–1816* (Madison, WI: Madison House, 1993), 123–134.

[8] Kakel III, *A Post-Exceptionalist Perspective*, 35–45; Whitaker, *The Spanish-American Frontier*, 47–62; Furstenberg, "The Significance of the Trans-Appalachian Frontier", 652–654.

republic had not yet reflected on, such as whether to allow outward migration from the original thirteen states, and if so how to control it, and whether the United States was to expand, and if so how to integrate new territory into the union. As American politicians became bogged down in debate, the restless western settlers sought ways to forge an independent future, entertaining the wildest ideas from invading and overthrowing the Spanish authorities in Louisiana, to requesting incorporation into Spanish Louisiana, and declaring independence. Not yet having reached a political consensus on how to deal with the trans-Appalachian West, the United States hoped to quell any thought of independent political action by securing, if not yet political rights, then at least commercial opportunities for the western settlers. The best way to do so was thought to be through gaining access to the Gulf of Mexico via the Mississippi River, from where commerce could flow into the Atlantic.[9] The drive for commercial access to the Gulf of Mexico brought the United States into negotiations with Spain.

The Spanish authorities were ambivalent towards the American overtures. On the one hand, Spain still hoped for her claims to the Western Territories to be accepted. Were this the case, it made good sense to economically develop the region and to woo the western settlers with commercial concessions. On the other hand, were Spain's territorial claims rejected, it made better sense to refuse American demands in the hope of attracting migrants to Spanish Louisiana to counterbalance the lingering anti-Spanish sentiment and to strengthen the border with the United States, at least if the anti-American sentiment of the settlers could be enflamed. Furthermore, economic concessions to the United States would undermine Carlos III's drive to forge a more coherent empire. Ultimately, Spanish imperial reform took precedence over potential territorial expansion, and Spain restricted navigation of the Mississippi to Spanish vessels. Occasionally, Spain would temporarily or conditionally open navigation of the Mississippi to western settlers as her interests in the

[9] J.E. Lewis Jr., *The American Union and the Problem of Neighborhood. The United States and the Collapse of the Spanish Empire, 1783–1829* (Chapel Hill: University of North Carolina Press, 1998), 1–24; E. Hinderaker, *Elusive Empires. Constructing Colonialism in the Ohio Valley, 1673–1800* (Cambridge: Cambridge Univertsity Press, 1997), 226–244; Furstenberg, "The Significance of the Trans-Appalachian Frontier", 652–654, 663–668; Whitaker, *The Mississippi Question*, 3–26, 101–115; W.E. Hemphill, "The Jeffersonian Background of the Louisiana Purchase", *The Mississippi Valley Historical Review* 22/2 (Sept., 1935), 177–190.

region evolved, but the United States never gained unconditional access, no matter how hard she pushed.[10]

European Disengagement

It was war in Europe that brought the contestation over the trans-Appalachian West to a resolution. When the French Revolution turned into a continental European war in 1792, the United States proclaimed neutrality. However, lacking the means to defend American neutrality, the newly elected George Washington Administration found American shipping preyed on by both Britain and France. The economic war became unsustainable for the United States, forcing Washington to choose accommodation with one of the two powers. Despite a strong pro-French faction in American politics, the United States opted for accommodation with Britain, culminating in the Treaty of Amity, Commerce, and Navigation of 19 November 1794, or Jay's Treaty as it is referred to in American historiography. The treaty offered Britain commercial concessions, and it secured America's continued neutrality in the European war. For the United States, in addition to resolution of some minor issues, the treaty secured the withdrawal of British troops from the trans-Appalachian West and a commitment to resolve an outstanding border dispute between the United States and Canada.[11]

The Revolutionary Wars also changed the Spanish rationale regarding the navigation of the Mississippi. After her defeat by Revolutionary France, Spain concluded a peace with France at Basel on 22 July 1795. At San Ildefonso, on 19 August 1796, Spain went one step further and signed a treaty of alliance with France that obliged her to join the war against Britain. Spain's rapprochement with France, alongside the Anglo-American rapprochement, raised fears for the security of Spain's American empire. To prevent any challenge, Spain concluded a treaty with the United States that offered several concessions, including free American navigation of the Mississippi, the right of deposit for American goods at

[10] Whitaker, *The Spanish-American Frontier*, 63–170; B. Tyler, "The Mississippi River Trade, 1784–1788", *Louisiana History: The Journal of the Louisiana Historical Association* 12/ 3 (Summer, 1971), 255–267; Woodward Jr., "Spanish Commercial Policy", 148–160; Din, "Empires Too Far", 278–283.

[11] Taylor, *American Revolutions*, 407; Clapham, "From the Peace of Versailles", I: 156–157.

New Orleans, as well as some rectifications to the common frontier.[12] For the United States, commercially the treaty—the Treaty of San Lorenzo, or Pinckney's Treaty—was not a great success. It appeased the restless inhabitants of the trans-Appalachian West, and thus the possible emergence of multiple independent American states in North America was avoided, but the territorial rectifications did not extend the American frontier to the Gulf coast, which meant that American trade still had to pass through Spanish territory at the goodwill of the Spanish authorities. The treaty was a mixed blessing for Spain too. It opened Spanish Louisiana to American commerce and immigration, which revived the local economy, but Washington's successful championing of the interests of the western settlers did raise questions over the extent to which they could be employed for Spanish ends.[13]

By 1800, Spain came to view Louisiana as a liability, both due to the renewal of European hostilities in 1798, which exposed her American colonies to attack, and due to the deterioration of relations between her ally France, and the United States, which culminated into the Quasi-War, into which Spain could be drawn. Simultaneously, regime change in France led to a change in French colonial policy. On 9–10 November 1799, a coup d'état overthrew the Directory in France, to replace it with a new Consular regime, with Napoleon Bonaparte soon establishing himself as the principal of three consuls. The figure of Napoleon Bonaparte looms large in history. He would go on to draw much of Europe into an empire, which was ushered into the nineteenth century through professionalisation, rationalisation, codification, and standardisation, forcing the parts of Europe beyond the empire to adopt similar reforms. However, in 1799, Bonaparte was but one in a long line of French politicians seeking to tame the Revolution. At this point, perhaps Bonaparte's greatest achievement lay in the fact that he managed to consolidate his coup d'état.[14]

[12] M. Kerautret, *Documents diplomatiques du Consulat et de l'Empire*, 3 vols (Paris: Nouveau Monde/Fondation Napoléon, 2002–2004), I: 51–58; Bush, *The Louisiana Purchase*, 111–121.

[13] Whitaker, *The Spanish-American Frontier*, 185–222; F.P. Renaut, *La question de la Louisiane, 1796–1806* (Paris: E. Champion, 1918), 12–48; A. Fugier, *Napoléon et l'Espagne, 1799–1808*, 2 vols (Paris: Félix Alcan, 1930), I: 2–30; Bemis, *Pinkney's Treaty*, 218–293; Whitaker, *The Mississippi Question*, 51–67, 85–97.

[14] M. Crook, *Napoleon Comes to Power: Democracy and Dictatorship in Revolutionary France, 1795–1804* (Cardiff: University of Wales Press, 1998), 71–95. For recent studies on Napoleon: M. Broers, *Napoleon. Soldier of Destiny* (London: Pegasus Books, 2014);

Consular France was eager to reconstruct a French colonial empire in the Americas. In part, the motivation for reconstructing a colonial empire was commercial. Bonaparte believed that if the French presence in the Americas was sufficiently large, a local economy could be constructed that could make the French colonial empire in the Americas self-sufficient and reduce the overall cost of inter-colonial commerce as well as trade with metropolitan France. All French colonies in the Americas could thus become more profitable, which benefitted not only the French treasury, but also French merchants, who had suffered much since the French Revolution. The vast Louisiana Territory would play an important role in this colonial economy because it had the potential to provide much-needed raw materials and agricultural produce. Furthermore, Louisiana offered entry to the American market for French produce and manufacture. For another part, the desire to reconstruct a French colonial empire must be seen in the context of France's rivalry with Britain. A sizeable and profitable French colonial empire could successfully challenge the seemingly ever-increasing British maritime and commercial dominance. In this light, Louisiana was indispensable because was ideally located to garrison the French forces necessary to defend the French colonies.[15]

The Retrocession of Louisiana

On 1 October 1800, Spain and France concluded the (Third) Treaty of San Ildefonso that retroceded the Louisiana Territory to France in exchange for a French promise to secure a territory in northern Italy for the Spanish Prince Luis of Bourbon-Parma. However, the Spanish First Secretary of State, Don Manuel de Godoy, was disinclined to give

M. Broers, *Napoleon. The Spirit of the Age: 1805–1810* (London: Pegasus Books, 2018); M. Broers, *Napoleon. The Decline and Fall of an Empire: 1811–1821* (London: Pegasus Books, 2022); P. Dwyer, *Napoleon. The Path to Power, 1769–1799* (London: Bloomsbury, 2007); P. Dwyer, *Citizen Emperor. Napoleon in Power* (London: Bloomsbury, 2013); P. Dwyer, *Napoleon. Passion, Death and Resurrection, 1815–1840* (London: Bloomsbury, 2018).

[15] A. DeConde, *The Quasi-War. The Politics of the Undeclared War with France, 1797–1801* (New York: Charles Scribner's Sons, 1966), 3–258; Pagé, *L'Amérique du Nord*, 66–68; P.R. Girard, "Rêves d'Empire: French Revolutionary Doctrine and Military Interventions in the Southern United States and the Caribbean, 1789–1809", *Louisiana History: The Journal of the Louisiana Historical Association* 48/4 Fall, 2007), 403–408; Whitaker, *The Mississippi Question*, 115–129.

up Louisiana only for the promise of territorial compensation, and so he actively worked to delay the retrocession of Louisiana to France. It was thus not until Bonaparte concluded the Treaty of Lunéville on 9 February 1801 with the Habsburgs, by which France gained the Grand Duchy of Tuscany in northern Italy, that Godoy felt assured of satisfactory compensation for the retrocession of Louisiana. At Aranjuez, on 21 March 1801, Godoy and Lucien Bonaparte signed a treaty that, amongst others, exchanged Louisiana for the Grand Duchy of Tuscany. On 11 April 1801, Carlos IV of Spain gave his royal consent to the exchange, with which the transfer came into effect legally.[16]

After the transfer of Louisiana was agreed on paper, France needed to take possession of the territory. The success of which, and indeed the success of reconstructing a French colonial empire, depended on three factors. First, France needed to replace the Spanish colonial administration and armed forces with French officials and troops. This required sending an expedition from Europe to Louisiana. The Franco-Spanish treaty of 21 March stipulated only that Louisiana would be transferred, but not how and when. So, before France could dispatch the expedition, these details needed to be hammered out. France was quick to open negotiations, but for reasons that were not entirely clear, Spain refused to engage. Quite possibly Spain delayed because it felt that, by refusing to withdraw her armed forces from Tuscany, France acted contrary to the spirit of the Franco-Spanish treaty also. In any case, the standoff was not resolved until October 1802. Furthermore, France's ability to take possession of Louisiana depended on France's relations with two regional powers, Britain, and the United States. Britain viewed a French return to Louisiana as a threat to her possessions and influence in America.[17] This was problematic for France because the powerful Royal Navy could prevent a French expedition from reaching Louisiana. And even if a

[16] Renaut, *La question de la Louisiane*, 49–71; Fugier, *Napoléon et l'Espagne*, I: 105–138; A.P. Whitaker, "The Retrocession of Louisiana in Spanish Policy", in *The Louisiana Purchase Bicentennial Series in Louisiana History. Volume II. The Spanish Presence in Louisiana 1763–1803*, ed. G.C. Din (Lafayette: The Center for Louisiana Studies, 1996), 40–58; D. Hilt, *Troubled Trinity: Godoy and the Spanish Monarchs* (Tuscaloosa: University of Alabama Press, 1987), 112–114; Bush, *The Louisiana Purchase*, 33–35; Whitaker, *The Mississippi Question*, 176–186. For the treaties, see: Kerautret, *Documents diplomatiques*, I: 159–162, 176–178.

[17] B. Perkins, "England and the Louisiana Question", *Huntington Library Quarterly* 81/3 (May, 1955), 282–284.

French expedition reached Louisiana, the territory remained vulnerable to a British attack. When France and Spain agreed on the retrocession of Louisiana, France was at war with Britain, but fortunately, by the summer of 1802, France and Britain were at peace, and so Britain was no longer an obstacle to taking possession of Louisiana. More serious was the attitude of the United States. The United States and Spain certainly had their disputes, but Spain had shown herself willing to consider American interests. The United States feared that a France that aimed to reconstruct an American empire around Louisiana would be less responsive to American interests. For instance, it remained to be seen if France would continue to grant the United States access to the Mississippi, which was such a divisive issue in American politics. Moreover, the American government was acutely aware that a return of France to North America could bring war to the continent in the case of a renewal of hostilities between Britain and France. Since the days of the Quasi-War, Franco-American relations had improved, but not to the point that American fears over a French return to Louisiana were removed. France did little to appease the United States. Instead, when the American government became aware of the impeding retrocession of Louisiana in early 1802 and confronted the French government on the issue, France simply denied any territorial exchange with Spain, though to be fair by early 1802 France and Spain had not yet reached an agreement over how and when to transfer the territory, so perhaps a confirmation of the transfer was premature.[18]

With the international obstacles to the transfer of Louisiana removed, or ignored, France was free to dispatch the expedition to take possession of Louisiana. Whilst negotiating with Spain for the date and conditions of the actual transfer, a French expedition was prepared at Dunkirk. When the definitive agreement for taking possession became known in Paris, the date for the departure of the expedition was set for 1 November 1802. But then the departure was delayed due to the difficulties in gathering the required ships, troops, and finances. Furthermore, at the last moment Bonaparte shifted the port of embarkation from Dunkirk to Hellevoetsluis, near Rotterdam in the Batavian Commonwealth (The Netherlands). In hindsight, this was an unfortunate decision. By the time the troops

[18] DeConde, *The Quasi-War*, 294–326; Bush, *The Louisiana Purchase*, 35–41; R.D. Smith, "Napoleon and Louisiana: Failure of the Proposed Expedition to Occupy and Defend Louisiana, 1801–1803", *Louisiana History: The Journal of the Louisiana Historical Association* 12/1 (Winter, 1971), 21–29; Pagé, *L'Amérique du Nord*, 68.

and material were transferred to Hellevoetsluis, winter had set in, which prevented the expedition from sailing out until March 1803. By this time, the international conditions for taking possession of Louisiana had deteriorated markedly. On 16 October 1802, the Spanish governor of Louisiana withdrew the American commercial privilege of the right of deposit in New Orleans.[19] It is doubtful whether the Spanish government had sanctioned this action and most certainly the action had nothing to do with France. Nevertheless, the United States interpreted it as a sign of what was to come, and France was suspected of having provoked the revocation. The cancellation of American commercial privileges reignited the fear of a North America composed of multiple independent states, which threatened the United States. Henceforth, the American government endeavoured to block the retrocession of Louisiana to France, or if that failed, to obtain a corridor to the Gulf of Mexico. Relations with Britain had deteriorated too. By March 1803, Britain and France were sliding towards war. Hostilities had not yet resumed, but the Royal Navy did station a squadron off the Dutch coast, which cast doubt on whether the French expedition would be allowed to sail out. In light of the reduced chances of successfully taking possession of Louisiana, Bonaparte abandoned the idea of reconstructing a French American empire.[20]

Franco-American Rapprochement

A political agreement on the sale of Louisiana by France to the United States of America was reached quickly. The negotiations were opened by the American Minister Plenipotentiary to France, Robert Livingston. Livingston was the scion of two prominent New York families, the Livingstons and the Beekmans. Robert initially followed his father in the legal profession when he was appointed the first chancellor of the

[19] "Proclamation of Juan Venture Morales, Intendant at New Orleans, New Orleans, 16 October 1802", [United States Department of State], *State papers and correspondence bearing upon the purchase of the territory of Louisiana* (Washington, DC: Government Printing Office, 1903), 54–55.

[20] Smith, "Napoleon and Louisiana", 29–40; E.L. Faber, "The Passion of the Prefect: Pierre Clément De Laussat, 1803 New Orleans, and the Bonapartist Louisiana That Never Was", *Louisiana History: The Journal of the Louisiana Historical Association* 54/3 (Summer 2013), 261–291; Lewis Jr., *The American Union and the Problem of Neighborhood*, 24–27; Whitaker, *The Mississippi Question*, 189–206; Bush, *The Louisiana Purchase*, 50–52.

New York Court of Chancery in 1777, but when the American War of Independence broke out, he became a prominent, if reluctant anti-colonial Whig politician. He was a member of the committee that drafted the Declaration of Independence, though historians generally agree that Robert was added to the committee only to have the name of a prominent New Yorker on the Declaration. In 1781, Livingston became the first American Secretary for Foreign Affairs, but he resigned in 1783, because he felt the position was not commensurate with his political abilities. The resignation is reflective of Livingston's need for recognition, fame, and power, which inevitably led to petty and self-defeating behaviour that impeded his ambition for high office. In 1789, Livingston joined the Republicans, which originated as a faction in Congress to oppose the centralising efforts and the pro-British orientation of the Federalist Party. In order not to confuse the Republicans with the current day Republican Party, they are often referred to as the Democratic-Republicans, or the Jeffersonian Republicans, after its founder Thomas Jefferson. When Jefferson secured his first presidency, Livingston was appointed minister to France.[21]

Since the retrocession of Louisiana to France had become known in Washington, Livingston worked to gain commercial access to the Gulf of Mexico. However, he made little headway with the French Minister of Foreign Affairs, Charles-Maurice de Talleyrand-Périgord.[22] Talleyrand started his career in the church, but he became a fervent anti-clericalist during the French Revolution, and he chose to place his talents at the service of the state. Setting out his views on France's foreign policy in a series of pamphlets and public speeches, Talleyrand caught the attention of the French government, ultimately leading to his appointment as Minister of Foreign Affairs in July 1797. Talleyrand was an early supporter

[21] C. Brandt, "Robert R. Livingston, Jr. The Reluctant Revolutionary", *The Hudson Valley Regional Review* 4/1 (Mar., 1987), 8–20; D.S. Alexander, "Robert R. Livingston. The Author of the Louisiana Purchase", *Proceedings of the New York State Historical Association* 6 (1906), 100–102; Taylor, *American Revolutions*, 408–414. For Livingston's craving for recognition and fame, see: F.W. Brecher, *Negotiating the Louisiana Purchase: Robert Livingston's Mission to France, 1801–1804* (Jefferson, NC: McFarland & Company, 2006).

[22] "Livingston to Madison, Paris, 1 September 1802", *State papers*, 51; "Livingston to Jefferson, Paris, 28 October 1802", *State papers*, 58–60; "Livingston to Madison, Paris, 11 November 1802", *State papers*, 61–62; "Livingston to Madison, Paris, 11 November 1802", *State papers*, 62–63.

of Bonaparte, and he was re-appointed Minister of Foreign Affairs by the First Consul after the coup of 1799.[23]

Because of Livingston's limited success in pursuing access to the Gulf of Mexico, in January 1803, Thomas Jefferson and James Madison decided to bolster the American delegation at Paris with James Monroe.[24] Jefferson, Madison, and Monroe were all Democratic-Republicans from Virginia, and they each consecutively served eight years as President of the United States. Jefferson held various public offices in local government until the outbreak of the American War of Independence, when he was delegated to Congress. Jefferson is best known as the primary author of the Declaration of Independence. After independence, Jefferson was appointed Minister Plenipotentiary for Negotiating Treaties of Amity and Commerce with Great Britain and other countries, a role which entailed establishing diplomatic relations with European powers. From 1785, Jefferson also served as Minister to France. He left Paris in 1789, hoping to return to Virginia, but an appointment to Secretary of State prevented this. Once in national politics, Jefferson soon became disenfranchised with the Washington Administration. He ran for president in 1796, but he came second to George Washington's successor John Adams, and was thus appointed Vice President. He took up the role, but the continuing disagreement over the direction of national affairs led to his founding of the aforementioned Democratic-Republicans. Jefferson won the 1800 elections, and he served as President of the United States from 1801 to 1809.[25] Jefferson selected James Madison as his Secretary of State. Madison's career was similar to Jefferson's. He served in Virginian politics before the War of Independence drew him into national politics. Madison is mostly known for his prominent role in drafting the

[23] E. de Waresquiel, *Talleyrand. Le prince immobile* (Paris: Fayard, 2003), 9–312; J. Orieux, *Talleyrand ou le sphinx incompris* (Paris: Flammarion, 1970), 67–385; M. Poniatowski, *Talleyrand et l'ancienne France, 1754–1789* (Paris: Librairie Académique Perrin, 1988); D. Cooper, *Talleyrand* (London: Bedford Historical Series, 1938), 11–125.

[24] "Jefferson to Monroe, Washington, 13 January 1803", Thomas Jefferson, *The Writings of Thomas Jefferson, Being his Autobiography, Correspondence, Reports, Messages, Addresses and Other Writings, Official and Private*, ed. H.A. Washington, 9 vols. (New York: Taylor & Maury, 1853–1854), IV: 453–456.

[25] Peterson, *Thomas Jefferson*; J.B. Boles, *Jefferson: Architect of American Liberty* (New York: Basic Books, 2017); J.J. Ellis, *American Sphinx. The Character of Thomas Jefferson* (New York: Vintage Books, 1998), 3–272.

Constitution of the United States. Madison succeeded Jefferson as President of the United States in 1809.[26] Jefferson and Madison considered Monroe the ideal candidate to pursue American interests more vigorously. Not only was Monroe closely aligned politically, but as a fellow Virginian, they felt he understood the importance of commercial access for the inhabitants of the trans-Appalachian West. Furthermore, Monroe had served as Minister Plenipotentiary to France in 1794–1796, so he was experienced in negotiating with the French.[27]

The American delegation at Paris was instructed to obtain all the territory east of the Mississippi. At the time it was believed that Spain had transferred the Floridas to France too, or was about to do so. Therefore they were instructed to acquire from France the territories of East Florida and West Florida, in addition to the port of New Orleans. However, if Spain had not transferred the Floridas to France, Monroe was to collaborate with the American Minister Plenipotentiary to Spain, Charles Pinckney, to obtain the Floridas from Spain either in a bilateral agreement, or through involving Spain in the agreement with France. The American government hoped to purchase the territory east of the Mississippi for Fr.30 million, but if necessary, the sum could be increased to Fr.50 million. In the case that France (or Spain) would only sell part of the territory east of the Mississippi, the American delegation could purchase the port of New Orleans for up to three-quarters of the sum, or the Floridas for one-quarter of the sum, whereby West Florida was valued twice as much as East Florida. If France refused to sell at all, the delegation was to insist on the right to construct an American port on the Mississippi. If France refused even this, Livingston and Monroe were to obtain expanded commercial privileges in New Orleans, including the right of deposit, the right to own real estate, and American consular representation in New Orleans.[28] In short, the instructions for the American

[26] G. Wills, *James Madison* (New York: Henry Hold and Company, 2002), 1–55; R.A. Goldwin, *From Parchment to Power. How James Madison Used the Bill of Rights to Save the Constitution* (Washington, DC: AEI Press, 1997), 15–54; L. Cheney, *James Madison. A Life Reconsidered* (New York: Penguin, 2015); I. Bryant, *James Madison. Secretary of State, 1800–1809* (Indianapolis: Bobbs-Merrill, 1953); A. Burnstein and N. Isenberg, *Madison and Jefferson* (New York: Random House, 2010).

[27] T. McGrath, *James Monroe. A Life* (New York: Dutton, 2020), 1–268; D.C. Gilman, *James Monroe* (Boston: Houghton Mifflin Company, 1911), 17–77.

[28] "Report of the committee to whom was referred a resolution providing for an additional appropriation of two millions of dollars for the purpose of intercourse with

delegation were flexible. For up to a sum of Fr.50 million, Monroe and Livingston were to acquire as much territory east of the Mississippi as possible, but if no territory could be acquired, the delegation could settle for commercial privileges.

Monroe's departure to France was delayed by his falling ill, but on 9 March 1803, he left New York for Le Havre.[29] Monroe's arrival on 10 April 1803 coincided with a conference in Paris between Bonaparte, Talleyrand, and François Barbé-Marbois, the Minister of the Public Treasury. At the meeting, Bonaparte informed his ministers that he had decided to sell Louisiana conditional on the price being no less than Fr.50 million.[30] It is generally accepted that the deteriorated international circumstances, the belief that a new war with Britain was inevitable, and the need for funds for the upcoming war were the primary reasons for Bonaparte to sell Louisiana.[31] The three factors were of course connected, but the fact that Bonaparte placed the negotiations for the sale of Louisiana in the hands of Barbé-Marbois, rather than in the hands of his Minister of Foreign Affairs, Talleyrand, may indicate that financial concerns were foremost on Bonaparte's mind.

Barbé-Marbois was the son of a prosperous merchant from Metz. He was destined to follow in his father's footsteps, but a fortunate connection with a rich protectress allowed François to study law in Paris. Initially, he had difficulty finding a job, but after changing his rather common name, Barbé, into the more genteel Barbé de Marbois, he found a position

foreign nations", *State papers*, 84–88; "Madison to Livingston, Washington, 18 January 1803", *State papers*, 69–71; "Madison to Pinckney, Washington, 18 January 1803", *State papers*, 80–81; "Madison to Pinckney and Monroe, Washington, 17 February 1803", *State papers*, 98–99; "Madison to Monroe, Washington, 2 March 1803", *State papers*, 114; "Madison to Livingston and Monroe, Washington, 2 March 1803", USA-LoC, *James Monroe Papers*, Series 1, Reel 2.

[29] "Monroe to Madison, New York, 22 February 1803", J. Monroe, *The Writings of James Monroe, including a collection of his public and private correspondence now for the first time printed*, ed. S.M. Hamilton, 7 vols (New York: G.P. Putnam's Sons, 1898–1903), IV: 2–3; "Monroe to Jefferson, New York, 7–9 March 1803", *The Writings of James Monroe*, IV: 4–8.

[30] F. Barbé-Marbois, *Histoire de la Louisiane et de la cession de cette colonie par la France aux États-Unis de l'Amérique Septentrionale; précédée d'un discours sur la constitution et le gouvernement des États-Unis* (Paris: Firmin Didot, 1829), 285–301.

[31] Y. Benot, *La démence coloniale sous Napoléon* (Paris: La Découverte, 2006), 102; Pagé, *L'Amérique du Nord*, 76–77; Kastor, *The Nation's Crucible*, 40–41; Bush, *The Louisiana Purchase*, 43.

in the French foreign service. Barbé-Marbois' intellectual faculties and talent ensured he rose through the ranks rapidly. After a spell as secretary to the French legation in Saxony, and chargé d'affaires in Bavaria, in 1779, Barbé-Marbois was posted to the Unites States, where he soon comfortably mingled with the elites of the rebellious Thirteen Colonies. In 1785, he was promoted to the prestigious position of Intendant of Saint-Domingue, where he remained until 1789, before returning to France. Under the various Revolutionary regimes, Barbé-Marbois' talents and experience were appreciated, but his loyalty to the Revolution was occasionally doubted, not least due to his aristocratic-sounding name. As a result, promotion was alternated with incarceration. Only through changing his name to less aristocratic Barbé Marbois did François avoid overzealous scrutiny, and he survived the Revolutionary turmoil with his reputation intact. When Bonaparte seized power in the coup of Brumaire, Barbé-Marbois lived in exile in Guyana, but a pardon allowed him to return to France. It was not long before Barbé-Marbois caught the eye of the First Consul. On 24 July 1800, Barbé-Marbois became a member of the Consular Council of State. And when, on 27 September 1801, Bonaparte curtailed the responsibilities of the Ministry of Finance by delegating the management of expenditure to a new Ministry of the Public Treasury, Barbé-Marbois became its head.[32]

The negotiations on the cession of Louisiana were opened on 11 April 1803, but the substantive discussions were postponed until the arrival in Paris of Monroe on 12 April. It took little difficulty to bring the two sides together. The first obstacle was the extent of the territory to be transferred. By now, it was clear that France had not obtained the two Floridas from Spain, so the American delegation entered the negotiations with the aim of securing New Orleans only. Much to their surprise, Barbé-Marbois offered the entire Louisiana Territory for sale. From the perspective of France, this offer makes sense. The port of New Orleans was the most valuable asset of the Louisiana Territory. Without it, the colony would only be a drain on the French Treasury. But even after the American delegation had accepted in principle to purchase the entire Louisiana Territory, it remained difficult to establish the exact boundaries of the territory. This difficulty was only overcome by deliberately leaving the delineation of the territory vague, which caused some problems for

[32] Lyon, *The Man Who Sold Louisiana*, 3–115.

the American government after taking possession of the territory. At the time, the potential difficulties were recognised by the American delegation and by Barbé-Mabois, but both parties gladly postponed the resolution in order to conclude the treaty.[33] A second issue was the price of the sale. As mentioned, Bonaparte insisted on at least Fr.50 million. The American delegation was authorised to pay a maximum of Fr.50 million, and so it would seem an agreement was within reach. However, considering that the entire Louisiana Territory was sold, rather than merely the port of New Orleans, Barbé-Marbois insisted on a price of Fr.80 million. Livingston was reluctant to depart from the instructions, but Monroe felt that the acquisition of the entire territory justified the extra cost, though conditional upon the sum including Fr.20 million of outstanding claims of American merchants on France. This sum of Fr.20 million was an estimate that lacked any foundation. Neither had the negotiators established a manner of repaying the American merchants. The claims of American citizens would cause some inconvenience for the American government, but in April 1803, both parties were too eager to finalise the sale to get bogged down in details.[34] On 2 May 1803, Livingston and Monroe, on behalf of the United States, and Barbé-Marbois, on behalf of France, signed one treaty and one convention, which were backdated to 30 April 1803: one treaty that transferred the Louisiana Territory to the United States and one convention that obliged the United States to pay France a sum of Fr.60 million.[35] A second convention obliged the United States to adopt French debts to American citizens to the sum of Fr.20 million. This was signed several days later and also backdated to 30 April.[36] To

[33] For the territorial complications arising from the Louisiana Purchase see: I.J. Cox, *The West Florida Controversy, 1798–1813. A Study in American Diplomacy* (Baltimore: Johns Hopkins Press, 1918); C.L. Egan, "The United States, France, and West Florida, 1803–1807", *The Florida Historical Quarterly* 47/3 (Jan., 1969), 227–252; R. Stenberg, "The Western Boundary of Louisiana, 1762–1803", *The Southwestern Historical Quarterly* 35/2 (Oct., 1931), 95–108.

[34] Barbé-Marbois, *Histoire de laLouisiane*, 301–330; "Livingston to Madison, Paris, 13 April 1803", *State papers*, 159–163; "Mr. Monroe's Journal or Memoranda, 27 April-2 May 1803", *State papers*, 165–172; "Livingston to Madison, Paris, 17 April 1803", *State papers*, 172–175; "Livingston and Monroe to Madison, Paris, 13 May 1803", *State papers*, 191–196.

[35] Barbé-Marbois, *Histoire de la Louisiane*, 332.

[36] "Traité Entre les Etats-Unis d'Amérique et la République Française, Paris, 30 April 1803", USA-NA, RG/11, TS/86/AO; "Première convention financière annexée, 30 April

come into effect, the treaty and conventions would need to be ratified by France and the United States, but the swiftness with which the agreement was made revealed that the political will was present on both sides of the pond.

Louisiana, Bought and Sold

Between April 1801 and March 1803, there was a small window of opportunity for Bonaparte to reconstruct a French colonial empire in America, centred on Louisiana. It was missed. It seems contradictory to Bonaparte's character to fail to seize the moment, and one may doubt the seriousness of Bonaparte's colonial ambitions. It might well be that the French expedition that was supposed to take possession of Louisiana, and which was endlessly delayed, was nothing more than a chip in European-turned-global rivalry. To Britain, a French Louisiana was a threat. To France, Louisiana was challenging to defend, and it required great investment and effort to become profitable. As long as the threat to Britain was greater than the cost to France, the possibility of a French return to North America could be used as leverage in international politics. However, once the threat of a French presence in North America became so great that Britain felt obliged to take countermeasures, such as the stationing of the squadron of ships off the Dutch coast, the leverage seized to be effective, and it made more sense to sell off the claim for funds that could be employed to increase French influence in continental Europe.

For the United States, the continued presence of European powers in the Americas carried risk. After independence, the young American republic was still finding its feet. Several big issues were yet unresolved, including what the borders of the United States were, how to deal with demographic pressures, whether to expand, whether to allow independent states outside the union to emerge, and what international relations best served American interests. These issues were difficult to resolve because

1803", NL-SA, 735/484; ibidem, FR-AN, AF/IV/1681/A, or: "Convention between the French government & the Minister Plenipotentiaries of America for the creation of 11,250,000 Dollars 6pct American Stock at the disposal of the former, 30 April 1803", NL-SA, 735/3754; ibidem, FR-AN, AF/IV/1681/A; "Seconde convention financière annexée, 30 April 1803", NL-SA, 735/484. Readily accessible through: Kerautret, *Documents diplomatiques*, I: 278–289. A payment schedule was concluded, but this was voided by later events: "Exécution de la convention conclue entre la République Française et les Etats-unis d'Amérique le 10 Floréal an XI [30 April 1803]", FR-AN, AF/IV/1681/A.

of the youthfulness of American politics and because European rivalry frequently spilled over into the Americas to alter the geopolitical environment, as such as was the case with the frequent cession of (parts of) Louisiana. What the United States most needed was a period of respite to address these unresolved political issues. The United States was fortunate for such a period to arrive in the late eighteenth and early nineteenth century, when European rivalry turned into a conflict to defeat Revolutionary and Napoleonic France, leading to European disengagement in the Americas.[37] The United States was quick to seize the moment. Treaties with Britain and Spain secured America's northern and southern borders and limited foreign exploitation of American vulnerabilities. The treaty with France doubled the size of the United States and secured her western border, but most importantly, it prevented the emergence of an independent state outside the union by opening the West to restless settlers.

The alignment of French and American interests ensured that the political negotiations on the transfer of Louisiana were concluded in less than three weeks. The financial operation, however, was yet to begin.

References

PRIMARY SOURCES

Archival Sources

The Netherlands, Stadsarchief Amsterdam [NL-SA]:
735 Archief van de Firma Hope & Co. met verwante archiefvormers
London Office:
Incoming Correspondence:
– 484: 1803–1805.
Deposited Archives:
Common Fund of Original Louisiana Stock:
– 3754: Register of correspondence, 1803–1812.
United States of America, Library of Congress [USA-LoC]:
James Monroe Papers:

[37] Taylor, *American Revolutions*, 407–408, 415–423; R. Blaufarb, "The French Revolutionary Wars and the Making of American Empire, 1783–1796", in *The French Revolution in Global Perspective*, eds S. Desan, L. Hunt, and W.M. Nelson (Ithaca & London: Cornell University Press, 2013), 148–162.

- Series 1: General Correspondence, Reel 2: 22 March 1796–8 October 1803.

United States of America, National Archives [USA-NA]:

- Record Group 11: *Perfected Treaties.*
- Record Group 49: *Records of the Bureau of Land Management.*

France, Archives nationales [FR-AN]

Archives du pouvoir exécutief, 1789–1815 [AF], IV Secrétairerie d'état impériale et cabinet de Napoléon 1er.

- 1681/A: Relations extérieures: États-Unis, An VIII-1813.

Printed Primary Sources

Barbé-Marbois, F., *Histoire de la Louisiane et de la cession de cette colonie par la France aux États-Unis de l'Amérique Septentrionale; précédée d'un discours sur la constitution et le gouvernement des États-Unis* (Paris: Firmin Didot, 1829)

Jefferson, T., *The Writings of Thomas Jefferson, Being his Autobiography, Correspondence, Reports, Messages, Addresses and Other Writings, Official and Private*, ed. H.A. Washington, 9 vols. (New York: Taylor & Maury, 1853–1854).

Monroe, J., *The Writings of James Monroe, including a collection of his public and private correspondence now for the first time printed*, ed. S.M. Hamilton, 7 vols (New York: G.P. Putnam's Sons, 1898–1903).

[United States Department of State], *State papers and correspondence bearing upon the purchase of the territory of Louisiana* (Washington, DC: Government Printing Office, 1903).

SECONDARY SOURCES

Adelman, J., *Sovereignty and Revolution in the Iberian Atlantic* (Princeton: Princeton University Press, 2006)

Aiton, A.S., "The Diplomacy of the Louisiana Cession", in *Louisiana Purchase Bicentennial Series Volume II. The Spanish Presence in Louisiana 1763–1803*, ed. G.C. Din (Lafayette: The Center for Louisiana Studies, 1996), 11–27.

Alexander, D.S., "Robert R. Livingston. The Author of the Louisiana Purchase", *Proceedings of the New York State Historical Association* 6 (1906), 100–114.

Bannon, J.F., "The Spaniards in the Mississippi Valley. An Introduction", in J.F. McDermott (ed.), *The Spanish in the Mississippi Valley 1762–1804* (Urbana: University of Illinois Press, 1974), 3-15.

Bemis, S.F., *Pinkney's Treaty. America's Advantage from Europe's Distress, 1783–1800* (New Haven: Yale University Press, 1960).

Benot, Y., *La démence coloniale sous Napoléon* (Paris: La Découverte, 2006).

Blaufarb, R.,"The French Revolutionary Wars and the Making of American Empire, 1783–1796", in *The French Revolution in Global Perspective*, eds S.

Desan, L. Hunt, and W.M. Nelson (Ithaca & London: Cornell University Press, 2013), 148–162.

Boles, J.B., *Jefferson: Architect of American Liberty* (New York: Basic Books, 2017).

Bond, B.G. (ed.), *French Colonial Louisiana and the Atlantic World* (Baton Rouge: Louisiana State University Press, 2005).

Boulle, P.H., "French Reactions to the Louisiana Revolution of 1768", in *The French in the Mississippi Valley*, ed. J.F. McDermott (Urbana: University of Illinois Press, 1965), 143-157.

Brandt, C., "Robert R. Livingston, Jr. The Reluctant Revolutionary", *The Hudson Valley Regional Review* 4/1 (Mar., 1987), 8–20.

Brasseaux, C.A., "Confusion, Conflict, and Currency: An Introduction to the Rebellion of 1768", *Louisiana History: The Journal of the Louisiana Historical Association* 18/2 (Spring, 1977), 161–169.

Brasseaux, C. A., "The Image of Louisiana and the Failure of Voluntary French Emigration, 1683–1731", *Proceedings of the Meeting of the French Colonial Historical Society* 4 (1979), 47–56.

Brecher, F.W., *Negotiating the Louisiana Purchase: Robert Livingston's Mission to France, 1801–1804* (Jefferson, NC: McFarland & Company, 2006).

Broers, M., *Napoleon. Soldier of Destiny* (London: Pegasus Books, 2014).

Broers, M., *Napoleon. The Decline and Fall of an Empire: 1811–1821* (London: Pegasus Books, 2022).

Broers, M., *Napoleon. The Spirit of the Age: 1805–1810* (London: Pegasus Books, 2018).

Bryant, I., *James Madison. Secretary of State, 1800–1809* (Indianapolis: Bobbs-Merrill, 1953).

Burnstein, A., and N. Isenberg, *Madison and Jefferson* (New York: Random House, 2010).

Bush, R.D., *The Louisiana Purchase. A Global Context* (New York and London: Routledge, 2014).

Cheney, L., *James Madison. A Life Reconsidered*(New York: Penguin, 2015).

Clapham, J.H., "From the Peace of Versailles to the Second Peace of Paris, 1783–1815", in *The Cambridge History of British Foreign Policy, 1783–1919*, eds A.W. Ward and G.P. Gooch, 3 vols (Cambridge: Cambridge University Press, 1939).

Conrad, G.R. (ed.), *The Louisiana Purchase Bicentennial Series in Louisiana History. Volume I: The French Experience in Louisiana* (Lafayette: The Center for Louisiana Studies, 1995).

Cooper, D., *Talleyrand* (London: Bedford Historical Series, 1938).

Cox, I.J., *The West Florida Controversy, 1798–1813. A Study in American Diplomacy* (Baltimore: Johns Hopkins Press, 1918).

Crook, M., *Napoleon Comes to Power: Democracy and Dictatorship in Revolutionary France, 1795-1804* (Cardiff: University of Wales Press, 1998).
DeConde, A., *The Quasi-War. The Politics of the Undeclared War with France, 1797–1801* (New York: Charles Scribner's Sons, 1966).
Desan, S., L. Hunt, and W.M. Nelson (eds), *The French Revolution in Global Perspective* (Ithaca & London: Cornell University Press, 2013).
Din, G.C. (ed.), *Louisiana Purchase Bicentennial Series Volume II. The Spanish Presence in Louisiana 1763–1803* (Lafayette: The Center for Louisiana Studies, 1996).
Din, G.C., "Empires Too Far: The Demographic Limitations of Three Imperial Powers in the Eighteenth-Century Mississippi Valley", *Louisiana History: The Journal of the Louisiana Historical Association* 50/3 (Summer, 2009), 261-292.
Din, G.C., "Protecting the 'Barrera': Spain's Defenses in Louisiana, 1763–1779", *Louisiana History: The Journal of the Louisiana Historical Association* 19/2 (Spring, 1978), 183–211.
Dwyer, P., *Citizen Emperor. Napoleon in Power* (London: Bloomsbury, 2013).
Dwyer, P., *Napoleon. Passion, Death and Resurrection, 1815–1840* (London: Bloomsbury, 2018).
Dwyer, P., *Napoleon. The Path to Power, 1769–1799* (London: Bloomsbury, 2007).
Egan, C.L., "The United States, France, and West Florida, 1803–1807", *The Florida Historical Quarterly* 47/3 (Jan., 1969), 227–252.
Ellis, J.J., *American Sphinx. The Character of Thomas Jefferson* (New York: Vintage Books, 1998).
Faber, E.L., "The Passion of the Prefect: Pierre Clément De Laussat, 1803 New Orleans, and the Bonapartist Louisiana That Never Was", *Louisiana History: The Journal of the Louisiana Historical Association* 54/3 (Summer 2013), 261–291.
Farrell, D.R., "Reluctant Imperialism: Pontchartrain, Vauban and the Expansion of New France, 1699-1702", *Proceedings of the Meeting of the French Colonial Historical Society* 12 (1988), 35-45.
Fugier, A., *Napoléon et l'Espagne, 1799-1808*, 2 vols (Paris: Félix Alcan, 1930).
Furstenberg, F., "The Significance of the Trans-Appalachian Frontier in Atlantic History", *The American Historical Review* 113/3 (June, 2008), 647–677.
Gilman, D.C., *James Monroe*(Boston: Houghton Mifflin Company, 1911).
Girard, P.R., "Rêves d'Empire: French Revolutionary Doctrine and Military Interventions in the Southern United States and the Caribbean, 1789–1809", *Louisiana History: The Journal of the Louisiana Historical Association* 48/4 Fall, 2007), 389–412.
Goldwin, R.A., *From Parchment to Power. How James Madison Used the Bill of Rights to Save the Constitution* (Washington, DC: AEI Press, 1997).

Haarmann, A.W., "The Spanish Conquest of British West Florida, 1779–1781", *The Florida Historical Quarterly* 39/2 (Oct., 1960), 107–134.

Hemphill, W.E., "The Jeffersonian Background of the Louisiana Purchase", *The Mississippi Valley Historical Review* 22/2 (Sep., 1935), 177–190.

Hilt, D., *Troubled Trinity: Godoy and the Spanish Monarchs* (Tuscaloosa: University of Alabama Press, 1987).

Hinderaker, E., *Elusive Empires. Constructing Colonialism in the Ohio Valley, 1673–1800* (Cambridge: Cambridge Univertsity Press, 1997).

Kakel III, C.P., *A Post-Exceptionalist Perspective on Early American History. American Wests, Global Wests, and Indian Wars* (Cham: Palgrave Pivot, 2019).

Kastor, P.J., *The Nation's Crucible. The Louisiana Purchase and the Creation of America* (New Haven, CT: Yale University Press, 2004).

Kerautret, M., *Documents diplomatiques du Consulat et de l'Empire*, 3 vols (Paris: Nouveau Monde/Fondation Napoléon, 2002–2004).

Kolb, F., "The New Orleans Revolt of 1768", *Louisiana History: The Journal of the Louisiana Historical Association* 59/1 (Winter, 2018), 5–39.

Kuethe, A.J., and K.J. Andrien, *The Spanish Atlantic World in the Eighteenth Century. War, and the Bourbon Reforms, 1713–1796* (Cambridge: Cambridge University Press, 2014).

Lemann, S. G., "The Problems of Founding a Viable Colony: The Military in Early French Louisiana", *Proceedings of the Meeting of the French Colonial Historical Society* 6/7 (1982), 27–35.

Lewis Jr., J.E., *The American Union and the Problem of Neighborhood. The United States and the Collapse of the Spanish Empire, 1783–1829* (Chapel Hill: University of North Carolina Press, 1998).

Lyon, E.W., *The Man Who Sold Louisiana. The Career of François Barbé-Marbois* (Norman, OK: Oklahoma University Press, 1942).

McDermott, J.F. (ed.), *The French in the Mississippi Valley* (Urbana: University of Illinois Press, 1965).

McDermott, J.F. (ed.), *The Spanish in the Mississippi Valley 1762-1804* (Urbana: University of Illinois Press, 1974).

McGrath, T., *James Monroe. A Life* (New York: Dutton, 2020).

Moore, J.P., "Antonio de Ulloa: A Profile of the First Spanish Governor of Louisiana", *Louisiana History: The Journal of the Louisiana Historical Association* 8/3 (Summer, 1967), 189–218.

Onuf, P., and N. Onuf, *Federal Union, Modern World. The Law of Nations in an Age of Revolutions, 1776–1816* (Madison, WI: Madison House, 1993).

Orieux, J., *Talleyrand ou le sphinx incompris* (Paris: Flammarion, 1970).

Pagé, S., *L'Amérique du Nord et Napoléon* (Paris: Nouveau Monde/Fondation Napoléon, 2003).

Perkins, B., "England and the Louisiana Question", *Huntington Library Quarterly* 81/3 (May, 1955), 279–295.
Peterson, M.D., *Thomas Jefferson and the New Nation: a Biography* (Oxford: Oxford University Press, 1975).
Poniatowski, M., *Talleyrand et l'ancienne France, 1754-1789* (Paris: Librairie Académique Perrin, 1988).
Pritchard, J., "Population in French America, 1670-1730: The Demographic Context of Colonial Louisiana", in *French Colonial Louisiana and the Atlantic World*,ed. B.G. Bond (Baton Rouge: Louisiana State University Press, 2005), 175-203.
Renaut, F.P., *La question de la Louisiane, 1796-1806* (Paris: E. Champion, 1918).
Smith, R.D., "Napoleon and Louisiana: Failure of the Proposed Expedition to Occupy and Defend Louisiana, 1801–1803", *Louisiana History: The Journal of the Louisiana Historical Association* 12/1 (Winter, 1971), 21–40.
Smith, W.R., *Brief History of the Louisiana Territory* (St. Louis: The St. Louis News Company, 1904).
Stenberg, R., "The Western Boundary of Louisiana, 1762–1803", *The Southwestern Historical Quarterly* 35/2 (Oct., 1931), 95–108.
Stenberg, R.R., "The Boundaries of the Louisiana Purchase", *The Hispanic American Historical Review* 14/1 (Feb., 1934), 32–64.
Taylor, A., *American Revolutions. A Continental History, 1750–1804* (New York: W.W. Norton & Company, 2016).
Tyler, B., "The Mississippi River Trade, 1784–1788", *Louisiana History: The Journal of the Louisiana Historical Association* 12/ 3 (Summer, 1971), 255–267.
Ward, A.W., and G.P. Gooch (eds), *The Cambridge History of British Foreign Policy, 1783-1919*, 3 vols (Cambridge: Cambridge University Press, 1939).
Waresquiel, E. de, *Talleyrand. Le prince immobile* (Paris: Fayard, 2003).
Whitaker, A.P., "The Retrocession of Louisiana in Spanish Policy", in *The Louisiana Purchase Bicentennial Series in Louisiana History. Volume II. The Spanish Presence in Louisiana 1763–1803*, ed. G.C. Din (Lafayette: The Center for Louisiana Studies, 1996), 40–58.
Whitaker, A.P., *The Mississippi Question 1795–1803. A Study in Trade, Politics, and Diplomacy* (New York and London: D. Appleton-Century Co., 1934).
Whitaker, A.P., *The Spanish-American Frontier: 1783–1795. The Westward Movement and the Spanish Retreat in the Mississippi Valley* (Gloucester, MA: Peter Smith, 1962).
Wills, G., *James Madison* (New York: Henry Hold and Company, 2002).
Woodward Jr., R.L., "Spanish Commercial Policy in Louisiana, 1763–1803", *Louisiana History: The Journal of the Louisiana Historical Association* 44/2 (Spring, 2003), 133–164.

Unpublished sources

Klein, M., "Louisiana: European Explorations and the Louisiana Purchase. A Special Presentation from the Geography and Map Division of the Library of Congress", unpublished essay (Library of Congress, Geography and Map Division, undated0, accessed via: https://www.loc.gov/collections/louisiana-european-explorations-and-the-louisiana-purchase/about-this-collection/

CHAPTER 3

The Hope-Baring Concern

Abstract This chapter discusses the history of the house of Hope and the history of the house of Baring from their origins to the early nineteenth century. It highlights the challenges that both firms faced in navigating the tumultuous Age of Revolutions, and how they grew closer to weather the storms. The chapter argues that from 1795 to 1823, Hope and Baring should be viewed as one consortium at the pinnacle of a network of associated houses that developed and executed operations collectively.

Keywords Hope & Co. · Francis Baring & Co. · Pierre César Labouchere · Alexander Baring

In the past years, the archives of Hope and the archives of Baring have been digitised and made available online. This has greatly facilitated research. It has also spawned a temptation to write a complete business history of the two firms. Taking solace from the fact that Marten Buist's twenty years of unfettered access to the Hope archives allowed him to write only a partial history of Hope until 1815, the author has concluded that a full history of Hope and Baring is not possible for a short publication like this. For this chapter it has been decided to focus only on those aspects of the histories of the two firms that relate to the financing of the sale and purchase of Louisiana, that is the difficulties they faced

M. E. Hay, *Transatlantic Finance in the Age of Revolutions*,
https://doi.org/10.1007/978-3-031-65232-5_3

in adapting to the new political, economic, and financial realities of the late eighteenth and early nineteenth century, the difficulties they encountered in ensuring the continuity of their firms, and the solutions they found. Both Hope and Baring engaged in numerous trades and financial operations at any one time, which often became intertwined. All trades and operations not directly relevant to financing the sale and purchase of Louisiana have been left aside. These can be learnt from the secondary literature, or the online archives. Neither are the finances of the firms discussed. The reason for this is, first that Hope's finances are better documented than Baring's finances, allowing for only an incomplete and skewed comparison. Second, the finances of Hope and Baring only make sense in comparison to other houses in their respective markets. Buist has adopted this approach. The author has not adopted it, because it would take the chapter beyond its stipulated word count.

House of Hope

The Hopes are of Scottish origin, though possibly with French roots, or at least with a strong family connection to France. The founding father of the Dutch Hopes is Henry Hope (also known as Hendrick Hope), with various spellings of the surname being recorded, including Hoop (Dutch) and Hop (French). He was born in Scotland around 1630. In the early 1660s, Henry moved to the Netherlands to settle in Rotterdam as a merchant trading on England. He was not successful in business. In the 1680s Henry relocated—some say fled—to London, only to be pursued by Dutch creditors. It is not known how Henry's debts were settled. Not long after returning to London, he passed away, leaving his debts to his wife Anna and their three children. It does seem that a settlement of sorts was agreed, because Henry and Anna's eldest son, Archibald Hope, returned to Rotterdam to resume his father's business under his own name. If Henry Hope is the founding father of the Dutch Hopes, Archibald Hope is the *pater familias* who rooted what was an unsuccessful immigrant family firmly in the Netherlands, both economically and socio-culturally. Under Archibald, the business prospered, allowing the house to diversify into trading on Ireland and the Americas. Archibald crowned his economic rise in the Netherlands with a marriage to Anna Claus, the daughter of a well-to-do Amsterdam button-maker and merchant. Archibald and Anna had eleven children. It was these children and their offspring who were to rise to the pinnacle of the Amsterdam capital market to establish the name of Hope as merchant-bankers of the first order.[1]

Of the nine of Archibald and Anna's children who survived into adulthood, most followed in their father's footsteps to become merchants. The third and fourth sons, John and James, set up independent trading businesses in Rotterdam, but they do not seem to have been more successful than the average Rotterdam merchant house. Not much is known of their persons or affairs.[2] Archibald and Anna's eldest son, Henry (1699–1737), joined his father's firm in 1723, changing the name of the firm to Archibald and Henry Hope. However, Henry was keen to make his own fortune. Not long after joining his father, he left to set up his own firm. He soon ran into difficulties and had to be bailed out by his parents to a sum greater than his share of the inheritance. This unfortunate episode coincided with a broader reorganisation of the Hope business. Whilst Henry had set up his own business, two other sons had joined their father's firm, Isaäc (1702–1766) and Zachary (1711–1770), the firm becoming known as Archibald, Isaäc, and Zachary Hope. The firm seized upon Henry's liquidation to expand trade with the Americas, and Henry was dispatched to Boston to become the firm's agent in the Americas. From 1735 onwards, the house would also enter into a new line of business, the shipping of colonists from Britain via Rotterdam to the Americas. The Hopes of Rotterdam were one of the first Dutch houses to engage in the large-scale transportation of English colonists to the Americas. Their entrepreneurialism was greatly rewarded, with both the Rotterdam House and Henry Hope in Boston prospering. In 1743, Archibald passed away and the firm was renamed Isaäc and Zachary Hope, but business continued to prosper.[3]

At this point, we can leave the Hopes of Rotterdam and turn towards Archibald, the younger (1698–1734), the second son of Archibald and Anna. Archibald was the first of the Hopes to move to Amsterdam, where he lived with his uncle Warner Lulofs, a successful stockbroker. After gaining much-needed experience, Archibald set up his own business, Archibald Hope. In 1724, he was joined by his younger brother,

[1] J.E. Elias, *De vroedschap van Amsterdam 1578–1795*, 2 vols (Amsterdam: N. Israel, 1963), II: 935–943; Buist, *At Spes Non Fracta*, 1–5.

[2] Elias, *De vroedschap*, II: 937.

[3] Elias, *De vroedschap*, II: 935, 937–942; Buist, *At Spes Non Fracta*, 11.

Thomas Hope (1704–1779), who became a full partner in 1726. The next year, 1727, Thomas married Margaretha Marcelis, the daughter of Jan Marcelis, a soap boiler and merchant of Amsterdam. This solidified his position amongst the mercantile elite of Amsterdam. The couple had one son, Jan (1737–1784), who was groomed to take a position in the firm. Margaretha died in 1758, but Thomas did not bother to remarry. One gets the impression that he was too fixated on growing the business.[4] Then, on 28 March 1733, Archibald passed away. He was buried in Rotterdam, which indicates he may have withdrawn from active participation in the business, as Buist argues. This corresponds with Thomas Hope's reputation of being the driving force of the house. Just before Archibald died, possibly when he withdrew from day to day management, the last of the brothers, Adrian (1709–1781) joined the firm. Adrian remained a lifelong bachelor and lived with his brother. One gets the impression with him too that he was merely interested in the firm.[5] After the death of Archibald, the Amsterdam house is renamed Thomas and Adrian Hope.[6] It was this firm that was to rise to world renown.

Under Archibald, the Amsterdam house was engaged in commodity trade on England and the Americas. After he passed away, Thomas and Adrian expanded the geographical focus of trade to encompass the whole of Europe and they followed in the footsteps of the Rotterdam House to engage in the profitable business of transporting colonists to the Americas.[7] A clear indication of the social integration and economic success of the Hope of Amsterdam was that in 1750 Thomas Hope was appointed by the Stadtholder to represent him as Director-General and Governor of the Dutch East India Company and the Dutch West India Company, with a remit to revitalise trade with these important markets.[8] This is not the place to dwell on Thomas' political career. Suffice it to highlight that the position drew Thomas and Adrian Hope's attention to the West Indian market. It was not long before Hope of Amsterdam became more heavily involved in trade in the West Indies. The West Indian market also

[4] Elias, *De vroedschap*, II: 938–939; Buist, *At Spes Non Fracta*, 13.

[5] Elias, *De vroedschap*, II: 939.

[6] Elias, *De vroedschap*, II: 937–939; Buist, *At Spes Non Fracta*, 5–8.

[7] Elias, *De vroedschap*, II: 1058–1059; Buist, *At Spes Non Fracta*, 11.

[8] Buist, *At Spes Non Fracta*, 8–9.

offered Thomas and Adrian the opportunity to branch out into banking by offering loans to planters, mostly in the Danish West Indies.[9]

When the Seven Years' War erupted in 1756, Thomas and Adrian Hope were well-positioned to benefit from the favourable market conditions for merchants based in neutral states. To start, they benefitted from Amsterdam's entrepot function to supply France and her allies with war materials. Furthermore, drawing on their recent experience in offering credit to planters, Hope of Amsterdam ventured into government lending by helping to place British government bonds on the Amsterdam capital market and remitting British subsidies to her continental allies.[10]

In 1762, it was decided to expand the business by recruiting two new partners.[11] The first partner was Jan Hope, Thomas and Margaretha's son. Despite his grooming, Jan was more interested in living the life of a country gentleman, who dabbled in politics, art, and science, than in banking. He continued to draw an income from the house until he passed away in 1784, but his involvement in the management of the firm was limited.[12] The second partner to join the firm was Henry Hope (1735–1811). Henry was the son of Henry, Archibald Sr.'s eldest son who had emigrated to Boston after his firm collapsed. He was the nephew of Archibald Jr., Thomas, and Adrian, and the cousin of Jan. At the age of 13, Henry was sent to England for an education. Upon completion of his studies in 1754, Henry took up an apprenticeship with Harman & Co., at that time known as Gurnell, Hoare, Harman & Co. Founded in 1740, Harman was a merchant-banking house based in the City of London. It is unknown how Hope and Harman became acquainted, but from Hope's archives, it is clear that the firms were closely associated, and their operations would become increasingly entangled over the next decades, in particular in trade and lending in Russia and Portugal. In 1760, Henry visited his uncles in Amsterdam, where he made such an impression that he was offered a partnership. Henry remained unmarried, preferring to dedicate his time to work. Though Jan would inherit his father's share in the company, it was Henry who succeeded Thomas as the driving force in

[9] J. van der Voort, *De Westindische plantages van 1720–1795. Financiën en handel* (Eindhoven: De Witte, 1973), 108, 292–293, 298–299.

[10] Buist, *At Spes Non Fracta*, 12.

[11] "Circular on the new partnership, Amsterdam, 1 January 1762", NL-SA, 735/520.

[12] Elias, *De vroedschap*, II: 933–934; Buist, *At Spes Non Fracta*, 17–18.

the firm.[13] Henceforth the Amsterdam firm would be known as Hope & Co..

The joining of the new partners coincided with a shift in the activity of the firm. The Hopes would continue to engage in trade, but increasingly they became involved in lending, in particular to foreign governments.[14] It is not sure what caused this greater focus on banking, but it may simply have been a case of mitigating risk and seizing new opportunities. The Seven Years' War was the start of a more contentious period of European history at a time when European conflict becoming increasingly global. On the one hand, this global European conflict increased the risk of trade. On the other hand, the increasing cost of global conflict revealed the European fiscal state to be inadequate for defending state interests, causing governments to seek capital on the markets.[15] Whilst the Hope archives are not conclusive on the matter, it has always been felt that it was Henry Hope who recognised the opportunities of the changing political climate.

Sweden was the first power that Hope managed to get hooked on Dutch credit. The tumultuous domestic politics of Sweden meant that King Adolf Frederick could not rely on his government to stabilise Sweden's public finances, which had deteriorated after her participation in the Seven Years' War. Therefore, the king turned to the Amsterdam bankers to finance Sweden's budget deficits. Initially, Sweden hoped to play off various Amsterdam banking houses to obtain the best conditions for her loans. Sweden had some success, but Hope's superior ability to place loans meant that they emerged as principal bankers to the Swedish court, though to maintain the king's custom the loan conditions were gradually amended in Sweden's favour. From 1767, Hope placed Holland current florins [guilders] (Hcf.)14.5 million in Swedish loans on the Amsterdam capital market. The relationship ended rather abruptly in 1787.[16] At this point, Hope preferred to focus on the more lucrative lending to Sweden's enemy, Russia. Initially, the Amsterdam house of Raymond and Theodoor de Smeth floated loans on the market on behalf

[13] Elias, *De vroedschap*, II: 935–936; Buist, *At Spes Non Fracta*, 16.

[14] Elias, *De vroedschap*, II: 1058–1059.

[15] J.C. Riley, *International Government Finance and the Amsterdam Capital Market 1740–1815* (Cambridge: Cambridge University Press, 1980).

[16] Buist, *At Spes Non Fracta*, 73–110; Riley, *International Government Finance*, 145–152.

of Russia, but from 1788, they were supplanted by Hope. Hope floated Russian loans to the sum of over Hcf.100 million. This sum does include Amsterdam loans to the Polish king and Polish magnates, which Tsarina Catherine the Great adopted after the partition of Poland, which transferred leveraged Polish estates and assets to Russian ownership. No other power was hooked on Dutch credit like Russia was, and the Russian loans were a great source of income and profit for Hope. That is not to imply Russia was exploited. Russian public finances were opaque and notoriously chaotic in the late eighteenth and early nineteenth century.[17] Not only was foreign capital needed, but it played an important role in establishing Russian credit, which was highly rated until the Revolution of 1917.[18] Hope also provided loans to other powers in these years, like Spain, Nassau-Saarbrück, and Bavaria, as well as to Polish magnates and the Polish king.[19] However, these states never became hooked on the Dutch capital.

Notwithstanding the success in business, the 1780s were a tumultuous period in the history of Hope. To start, the two experienced, senior partners died in quick succession. Thomas Hope passed away in 1779 and Adrian Hope passed away in 1781. To ensure the continuity of the firm, on 4 July 1782 a new partnership was signed admitting two new partners. The partnership was backdated to 1 January 1782 and was to run for a period of six years, until 31 December 1787. The first partner was Nicolas Baudouin, who had been an employee of Hope since 1765. Nicolas suffered from poor health and his contribution to the firm was limited. The second partner to join was John Williams. Under the contract, Henry Hope had a $^{35}/_{96}$ share, Jan Hope had a $^{49}/_{96}$ share and both new partners took a $^{6}/_{96}$ share.[20] John Williams was born in Cornwall in 1757,

[17] R. Bonney, "The Eighteenth Century. II. The Struggle for Great Power Status and the End of the Old Fiscal Regime", in *Economic Systems and State Finance*, ed. R. Bonney (Oxford: Clarendon Press, 1995), 368–371; R. Hellie, "Russia, 1200–1815", in *The Rise of the Fiscal State in Europe, c. 1200–1815*, ed. R. Bonney (Oxford: Oxford University Press, 1999), 481–506.

[18] Buist, *At Spes Non Fracta*, 93–274; Riley, *International Government Finance*, 153–165.

[19] Buist, *At Spes Non Fracta*, 20, 110–121, 280–281; Elias, *De vroedschap*, II: 1059–1061.

[20] "Contract Nicholas Baudouin, 3 April 1765", NL-SA, 735/538; "Contract Nicholas Baudouin, 1 February 1772", NL-SA, 735/538; "Partnership Henry Hope, Jan Hope, Nicolas Baudouin and John Williams Hope, Amsterdam, 4 July 1782", NL-SA, 735/521.

either in St Issey, St Ives, or St Ewe—the sources are inconclusive. Not much is known about the early life of John Williams. Buist's reading of the history of John Williams at Hope is that Henry Hope first encountered him when he was employed as a clerk in an Amsterdam merchant house. At the time John became seriously ill. Judging that he did not receive the medical care he needed to recover his health, Henry took John into the Hope household to allow him to recuperate, and he employed him in the firm thereafter. In April 1782, Henry arranged for John to marry Ann Goddard (1763–1820).[21] Ann was the daughter of John Goddard, a merchant of Rotterdam, and Henrietta Maria Hope, Henry Hope's sister.[22] Ann was the light in Henry's eyes and the marriage is understood to have aimed at binding John Williams more closely to the Hopes. As a token of gratitude to Henry, John adopted the Hope surname, thereafter being referred to as John Williams Hope. After Henry Hope passed away on 25 February 1811, in memory of Henry, John Williams dropped his middle name to become simply John Hope. John was a good deskman who served the Hopes loyally until he passed away on 12 or 18 February 1813. He grew from clerk to partner in 1782, and he became the senior partner by capital share of the partnership after the death of Henry in 1811.[23]

The author has always been puzzled by the recruitment and rise to prominence of John Williams. John was smart enough, but he was not overly burdened with intelligence or talent. He was risk-averse, irritable, and easily ruffled. He possessed little fighting spirit and, after Henry died, he revealed himself to be reluctant to honour previous agreements.[24] These are not good qualities for a deskman, let alone the senior partner of an internationally renowned merchant-banking house. It is nearly incomprehensible that Henry would have recruited John based on merit. The author has always felt that the recruitment and rise to prominence of John Williams was due to the relationship between Henry and John being more intimate than merely professional. The conduct of Henry

[21] "Prenuptial agreement between John Williams Hope and Ann Goddard, London, 8 March 1782", NL-SA, 735/2903; "Extracts of the wills of John Williams Hope and Ann Goddard", NL-SA, 735/2904.

[22] Elias, *De vroedschap*, II: 936–937.

[23] Buist, *At Spes Non Fracta*, 17, 375.

[24] Buist, *At Spes Non Fracta*, 243, 253–254, 426.

and John Williams gives rise to this assertion. Henry remained unmarried throughout his life, preferring the company of the Hope household instead. Of course, John Williams married Ann. In the historiography, it is assumed that the marriage was unhappy because Ann was "a woman of character" who had a public affair with a Dutch colonel, Jean François Baron de Dopff, which supposedly the timid John Williams dared not condemn.[25] It is undisputed that Ann had an affair, but this does not seem to have affected her relationship with John Williams. Ann, John Williams, their children, and De Dopff are frequently found forming one household.[26] Yet, at key moments in his life, John Williams revealed a clear preference for living with Henry. For example, in 1794, Hope fled the political turmoil in the Netherlands for the safety of London. In 1802, the Netherlands was deemed safe for business again and, amongst others, John Williams was sent to Amsterdam to re-open the Hope office. However, and despite his family having left for Amsterdam already, John Williams continued to linger in London, with Henry. Francis Baring, who was by now a close associate of Hope, grew increasingly frustrated with John Williams' reluctance to seize the business opportunities opening up on the continent.[27] But one does not find Henry berating John Williams for his procrastination. Similarly, in 1808, one finds John Williams deserting his post in Amsterdam to return to London to be by Henry's side in the last years of his life.[28] There is also the odd line in the correspondence between Henry and John Williams that supports the assertion. For example, in early 1805, Henry writes to John that, since John's departure from London, he laments the loss of intimacy and social comfort "of a bossom friend possessing all the virtues & amicable qualities necessary to perfect domestick comfort & happiness".[29] Of course, it may simply be that Henry and John felt the need to draw closer in times of adversity.

On 20 April 1784, Jan passed away, thereby freeing more than half of the share of the partnership. In 1763, Jan had married Philippina

[25] Elias, *De vroedschap*, II: 942; Buist, *At Spes Non Fracta*, 17.

[26] "Robert Voûte to Francis Baring, Middagten, 22 August 1804", UK-BA, NP1/A/3/16.

[27] Buist, *At Spes Non Fracta*, 402.

[28] Elias, *De vroedschap*, II: 936–937; Buist, *At Spes Non Fracta*, 56, 400–402.

[29] "Henry Hope to John Williams Hope, 1 January 1805", NL-SA, 735/464.

Barbara van der Hoeven, the daughter of a member of the *vroedschap* (city council) of Rotterdam. They had three children, Thomas (1769–1830), Adrian Elias (1772–1834), and Henry Philip (1774–1839).[30] The children inherited Jan's share, but their interests would be managed by Jan's wife until they reached maturity. Phillippina is mentioned explicitly in all contracts from the death of Jan until her sons came of age. It is clear she was consulted on affairs relating to the partnership, but she did not partake in the day-to-day management of the firm. Jan's management position thus remained vacant. Meanwhile, Baudouin's health had deteriorated to the point that he requested to withdraw from the firm. These two affairs encouraged Henry to reorganise the partnership. A new partner was found in Jan Casper Hartsinck, Cornelisz. (1755–1835). Although Hartsinck hailed from a prominent Amsterdam merchant family, he was a politician more than a banker. At the time of his recruitment, he was an alderman of Amsterdam.[31] A new partnership contract was drawn up on 12 May 1785, under which Henry Hope's stake increased to $^{37}/_{96}$ share, John Williams' stake increased to $^{14}/_{96}$ share, Jan's three children each took a $^{13}/_{96}$ share and Hartsinck was offered a $^{6}/_{96}$ share. The partnership was to commence on 1 January 1788 and run for a period of 14 years.[32] Baudouin was to remain in the firm until the new partnership commenced, but his poor health finally caught up with him. On 18 January 1787, he died of a stroke.[33] The vacancy was not filled, as the new partnership had anticipated his departure.

The new partnership was not stable. In late 1789, Hartsinck's position in the firm became untenable. It is not quite clear what occurred, but it seems that Hartsinck made some misstep in business that was of such magnitude that Henry demanded his immediate resignation. At first, Hartsinck seemed to acquiesce in his lot, but after Ms Hartsinck intervened to insist on a substantial pay out for her husband, the separation

[30] Elias, *De vroedschap*, II: 933–935; Buist, *At Spes Non Fracta*, 17–18.

[31] Elias, *De vroedschap*, II: 908–911, 1015.

[32] "Partnership Henry Hope, Nicolas Baudouin, John Williams Hope, Jan Casper Hartsinck and Wed. Jan Hope [Philippina Barbara van der Hoeven], Amsterdam, 12 May 1785", NL-SA, 735/521; "Contract Philippina Barbara van der Hoeven, Wed. J. Hope, Henry Hope and John Williams Hope, Amsterdam, 14 May 1785", NL-SA, 735/521.

[33] "Receipt of the payment of N. Baudouin's will, Amsterdam, 13 March 1787", NL-SA, 735/521.

turned acrimonious. A settlement was not reached until the intervention of a close associate of Hope with considerable diplomatic skill, Robert Voûte.[34] It was decided that Hartsinck would resign on 16 November 1789, ostensibly to take up a position in the Amsterdam city council. He received a hefty Hcf.500,000 in severance.[35] The sum would seem a reflection of a flawed partnership contract rather than Hartsinck having prevailed in the dispute. Hartsinck's share in the company was divided as follows. $^{1}/_{96}$ was allocated to John Williams Hope and Jan and Philippina's youngest two sons shared another $^{1}/_{96}$. Jan and Philippina's eldest son, Thomas, was made partner and received the remaining $^{4}/_{96}$ of Hartsinck, increasing his share to $^{17}/_{96}$. The new partnership would commence on 1 January 1790 and run until 31 December 1801, though with an automatic annual renewal if none of the partners withdrew within a one-year notice.[36]

Whilst Thomas' partnership ensured the continuity of the family as stakeholders in the firm, it did not resolve the challenges of managing the business. Thomas was not much engaged in the firm. He lived in London and was more interested in collecting art and antique furniture. He remained a silent partner. The two younger brothers did not become active in the firm either. Adrian lived in Amsterdam. He was known as a strange and unpredictable character. Opinions on his mental state range from mentally weak to insane. In October 1802, Henry Hope assumed power of attorney over Adrian, and excluded him from the firm, though Adrian continued to draw an income. After Henry died in 1811, Adrian's affairs were transferred to two Dutch associates of Hope, David Berck and Entrop Muller. When Adrian's mental faculties deteriorated even further, the family confined him to his estate of Bosbeek en Groenendaal, near Heemstede in the Netherlands, where he sat out his days until he passed

34 "John Williams Hope to Francis Baring, Amsterdam, 16 October 1789", UK-BA, NP1/A/1/1; "Robert Voûte to Francis Baring, Middagten, 22 August 1804", UK-BA, NP1/A/3/16.

35 "Act of resignation J.C. Hartsinck, Amsterdam, 16 November 1789", NL-SA, 735/521; "Receipt of payment to J.C. Hartsinck, Amsterdam, 24 November 1789", NL-SA, 735/521.

36 "Contract Henry Hope and John Williams Hope and Philippina Barbara van der Hoeven, Wed. J. Hope, Amsterdam, 16 November 1789", NL-SA, 735/521; "Partnership Thomas Hope, Amsterdam, 22 January 1790", NL-SA, 735/521.

away in 1834.[37] Henry Philip is known to have inspected Hope-Baring's investment in Maine lands together with Alexander Baring, but the correspondence of his hand is scarce, indicating that his role in the firm was limited. He remained a silent partner.[38]

So, more than a decade after the death of Thomas and Adrian, the house still had management vacancies to fill. It is at this point that Henry Hope recruited two able colleagues who were to play crucial roles in navigating Hope through the tumultuous years to come. The first was Robert Voûte (1747–1823), referred to as Bob or Swarte Bob. The Voûtes have their roots in La Chazottié in Languedoc. In the 1730s, several members of the family migrated to the Netherlands to avoid persecution for their protestant faith. Robert's father, Jean Jacques Voûte, settled in Amsterdam as a commodities broker specialising in coffee, tea, and dyestuffs. Jean Jacques was unfortunate in his private life. After the birth of two healthy children, his third child died before the age of one. Within a year, in 1739, his wife died giving birth to twins. The twins did not survive either. Jean Jacques' second marriage of 1741 was equally unfortunate. His second wife died giving birth to their son, who passed away shortly thereafter. Jean Jacques' marriage to his third wife, Susanne Icard was happier. The couple had ten children. Four sons, including Robert, entered their father's firm, which was renamed J.J. Voûte & Sons. It was these four sons and their offspring who made the firm into a respected house in the commodities trade.[39]

It is not known how Voûte and the Hopes became acquainted, but Robert worked for Hope since at least the 1780s. By 1792, the relationship was such that Robert withdrew from his father's firm to work exclusively for Hope. Voûte never became a partner in the firm, preferring to work for Hope on his own terms. Voûte played two important roles in the history of Hope. First, he was Hope's go-to man for advice on matters

[37] "Anthony Charles to Henry Hope, Amsterdam, 7 September 1802", NL-SA, 735/477; "Power of Attorney for Henry Hope, Amsterdam, 30 September 1802", NL-SA, 735/477; "Adrian Elias Hope to Henry Hope, Amsterdam, 8 September 1802", NL-SA, 735/477; "Henry Hope of Adrian Elias Hope, London, 12 October 1802", NL-SA, 735/462; "Adrian Elias Hope to Henry Hope, Amsterdam, 19 October 1802", NL-SA, 735/477; Elias, *De vroedschap*, II: 934–935; Buist, *At Spes Non Fracta*, 56, 243.

[38] Elias, *De vroedschap*, II: 935; "Henry Hope to John Williams Hope, 1 January 1805", NL-SA, 735/464.

[39] C.C. van Valkenburg et al., "Voûte", *Nederland's Patriciaat* 63 (The Hague: Centraal Bureau voor Genealogie, 1983), 421–436.

relating to the commodity trade. For example, Voûte played a crucial role in the attempt by Hope to corner the market for cochineal in 1787. The operation was unsuccessful. Hope failed to corner the market and the operation made a loss. The failure was in part the result of flawed information provided by Voûte.[40] Nevertheless, Hope shook off the failure and Voûte's continued prominence in the firm testifies to the regard in which Henry held him, as well as to the friendship they developed. The second role that Voûte played was even more important. If the Hopes can be described as merchant princes, then Voûte was their ambassador. Whenever tensions emerged between Hope and the governments, politicians, and rulers they dealt with, or even with partners like Hartsinck, Robert was dispatched to resolve the issues. For example, Hope's association with the House of Orange had strained its relations with the Dutch Revolutionary regime that came to power after the Batavian revolution of 1795. It was Voûte who was delegated to re-engage with the Batavian regime to ensure Hope could remain active on the Amsterdam capital market.[41] More important was his mission to the Russian court to ensure Russia's adherence to the terms of payment of the loans that Hope had provided.[42] Voûte also undertook missions to Vienna and London on behalf of Hope. From 1806 onwards, Robert became more involved in Dutch politics. He sat in the financial section of the Dutch Council of State during Louis Bonaparte's reign (1806–1810). After the Netherlands was annexed to the Napoleonic Empire, Voûte took several political positions. He served Napoleon well in the Netherlands and was made baron of the empire for his services. As a politician, he continued to use his influence on behalf of Hope. Robert Voûte does not feature in this study, but only because he was engaged in other matters of importance to the house.[43]

The second person to feature prominently in the history of Hope is Pierre César Labouchere (1771–1839). The family was originally known by the surname of Barrier. The Barriers came from Estremiac, in what was

[40] Buist, *At Spes Non Fracta*, 431–451.

[41] Buist, *At Spes Non Fracta*, 14–16, 44–45, 49, 183–184; J.C. Breen, "De feestelijke stemming na de restauratie van 1787", *Maandblad Amstelodamum* 5 (1918), 90.

[42] Buist, *At Spes Non Fracta*, 123–154.

[43] P.C. Molhuysen, P.J. Blok et al. (eds), *Nieuw Nederlandsch Biografisch Woordenboek*, 10 vols (Leiden: K.H. Kossmann, 1911–1937), II: 1508–1510; Buist, *At Spes Non Fracta*, 39, 433.

then the province of Gascony. They owned some estates and a vineyard entitled Labouheyre. The estate was expanded with a homestead, which was named De Labouchere. From the mid-seventeenth century, upward social mobility induced the Barriers to add the geographical qualification to their surname, thus becoming Barrier de Labouchere. Later they identified merely as Labouchere. Like the Voûtes, the family members were protestants. After the revocation of the Edict of Nantes in 1685, they departed their ancestral lands. They first settled in Orthez in the south of France, where they are known as cloth merchants, later relocating to Nantes in Brittany. By the 1720s, part of the family migrated to the Netherlands. Pierre was born in The Hague on 2 November 1771. At the age of 13, he was sent to apprentice with his uncle, a cloth merchant from Nantes.[44]

Western France was an important node in Hope's commercial and financial network. The Hopes developed an intimate and long relationship with many of the most prominent houses of the area, including Hottinguer and Le Couteulx, both of which would later gain renown as prominent Parisian banking houses.[45] The Laboucheres, though relative newcomers to Nantes, soon established themselves firmly amongst the mercantile elite of the region. It is then not surprising that when Hope sought a clerk for their French desk, they solicited suitable candidates from their network in Western France. Pierre, who had exhibited great intelligence and industry, was put forward. Pierre took up the position in 1790 and it was not long before talents were recognised.[46]

In 1795, Pierre was in London. It was here that he became enamoured with Dorothy Baring, the third daughter of Hope's business partner, Francis Baring. Pierre's pursuit of Dorothy's hand is infamous, and it is often quoted as revealing of the shrewdness and determination that

[44] "Extract of the Register of the Walloon Church in The Hague, 7 November 1772", UK-BA, DEP/208/19/7; "Short history of the Labouchere family, 17 January 1797", UK-BA, DEP/208/19/18; F. de Josselin de Jong, "Labouchère", *Nederland's Patriciaat* 49 (The Hague: Centraal Bureau voor Genealogie, 1963), 208–209; A. Labouchere Thorold, *The Life of Henry Labouchere* (London: Constable & Company, 1913), 1–2.

[45] M. Gérard, *Messieurs Hottinguer. Banquiers à Paris*, 2 vols (Paris: Banque Hottinguer, 1968–1972), I: 95–149; M. Zylberberg, *Capitalisme et catholicisme dans la France moderne. La dynastie Le Couteulx* (Paris: Éditions de la Sorbonne, 2001), 107–224.

[46] V. Nolte, *Fifty Years in Both Hemispheres, or Reminiscences of the Life of a Former Merchant* (New York: Redfield, 1854), 50–51.

served Pierre so well as a banker. Ostensibly, during one visit to Baring, Pierre had finally garnered the courage to ask Francis for his daughter's hand. However, Francis refused unhesitatingly. Pierre retorted by asking whether his partnership in Hope would make a difference to Francis' perception of his suitability, to which Francis admitted it would. Upon return to Hope, Pierre then asked Henry to be made partner in the firm, which Henry discouraged. Pierre replied by asking whether his marriage to Dorothy Baring would change Henry's opinion, to which Henry responded affirmatively. Having received his answer Pierre declared his engagement to Dorothy and he was made partner in Hope. That same day, he wrote to Francis Baring announcing his partnership and claiming the hand of Dorothy, which he promptly received. This anecdote can be traced back to the memoirs of his grandson, Henry Labouchere, and it has become a mainstay in the historiography ever since.[47] It pains the historian to question what has become a legendary anecdote, but unfortunately, there seems little merit to this reading of events. Pierre did not need a partnership to claim Dorothy's hand. He married Dorothy on 21 November 1796. Henry did require further convincing. Pierre was only made partner after the firm was reorganised in 1802.[48]

Pierre is sometimes described as cold, haughty, lacking in wit and refined education, and awkward in social settings. Such opinions seem based mostly on a description of him by Vincent Nolte (1779–1852).[49] Nolte was a gifted merchant-banker who gained notoriety as the managing partner of an American merchant-banking house. However, before he founded his firm, he was part of the Hope network, and Pierre recruited Nolte to become an agent for Hope. Despite the promotion, Vincent remained somewhat frustrated at what he considered the slow pace of his career progress, whilst simultaneously enviously eyeing Pierre's rapid rise through the ranks of Hope & Co..[50] Nolte's characterisation of Pierre does not chime with the correspondence he has left in the Hope and Baring archives. Pierre's writing gives the impression of an

[47] Labouchere Thorold, *The Life of Henry Labouchere*, 2; 'Un radical d'outre mer', *Le Temps*, 23 January 1912.

[48] "Sir Francis Baring's Notebook, 1763–1809", UK-BA, DEP/193/40; "Articles of Agreement, 5 October 1802", UK-BA, DEP/208/1.

[49] Nolte, *Fifty Years*, 51–52; Labouchere Thorold, *The Life of Henry Labouchere*, 3; Buist, *At Spes Non Fracta*, 64.

[50] Nolte, *Fifty Years*, 45–76; Buist, *At Spes Non Fracta*, 296.

exceptionally talented banker, who pursued profit with a singular determination. That said, whenever his pursuit pushed him onto a path that compromised his honour or the honour of Hope, Pierre would opt for the honourable route, even at the expense of profit.[51] An anecdote that reveals Labouchere's moral fibre and generosity of character is an incident of early 1813. At this point, John Williams Hope was obsessed with liquidating Hope's Amsterdam office and he was willing to cut loose all employees without consideration of backpay or pension. It was Pierre, who by this time had retired from the firm, who intervened to reallocate profits to pay Hope's employees.[52] As we shall see, it was Pierre who played a key role in the financing of the sale and purchase of Louisiana.

House of Baring

It is commonly believed that the Barings are of North German origin.[53] This is almost certainly wrong. The Barings had their roots in Groningen, in the north of the Netherlands, from where they gradually relocated eastward, eventually settling down in Bremen.[54] The Barings had a long tradition of civil service and service to God, but this changed with Johann Baring. Johann was the son of Franz Baring (1656–1697), a Professor of Theology, and Rebecca Vogds, the daughter of a prominent Bremen wool merchant. Franz died before the birth of Johann (1697–1648), and so the boy was raised by his mother's family. Johann was groomed for a career in the cloth trade. In 1717, he was sent to Exeter. In the early eighteenth century, Exeter was a hub in the European wool trade. Many continental merchants settled there to purchase woollens, which were dyed to local tastes, before export to home markets. The Vogdses sent Johann to Exeter to become their agent. However, because Johann had limited experience, it was decided he should first apprentice with a close business associate, Edmund Cock of Exeter, a serge maker and fuller. Johann performed so well that upon the termination of his apprenticeship, he was offered the position of clerk in the business. In 1722, Edmund Cock passed away.

[51] Buist, *At Spes Non Fracta*, 279.

[52] Buist, *At Spes Non Fracta*, 66, 243, 253–254.

[53] Austin, *Baring Brothers*, 10; Orbell, *Baring Brothers*, 2; Tearle, *Barings Bank*, 5, 14, 70.

[54] Ziegler, *The Sixth Great Power*, 13–14; Buist, *At Spes Non Fracta*, 40; Hidy, *The House of Baring*, 4.

Johann took over the business and was naturalised as a British citizen, henceforth being known as John Baring. He lost little time in seeking out new opportunities. One important step John took was to market his own goods through his German contacts, rather than rely on the services of middlemen. Quick success and profits enticed John to market the goods of other local manufacturers too, thus establishing himself as a merchant as well as a manufacturer. In 1729, John married Elizabeth Vowler (1702–1766), the daughter of a wealthy grocer and wholesaler of tea, coffee, sugar, and spices. The match was an indication of John's social rise and his integration into the social elite of Exeter. In 1748, John died of consumption.[55]

John left behind four sons and a daughter for Elizabeth to raise. He also left a considerable inheritance of £40,000. Elizabeth could have retired comfortably, but this was not in her character. She was determined to continue the business. For the immediate future, Elizabeth possibly formed a new partnership with several Exeter merchants under the name of Baring, Short, and Collyns.[56] To secure the long-term future of the business, Elizabeth set out to give her four sons the best possible education. The eldest son, John (1730–1816), was just eighteen years old when his father died. Elizabeth sent him to be educated in Geneva. Upon graduation, he travelled Western Europe to gain knowledge of local markets and to build a network of correspondents. In 1757, John settled in Exeter permanently.[57] The second son, Thomas (1733–1758), was kept in Exeter to learn the local Devon market. The third and fourth sons, Francis (1740–1810) and Charles (1742–1829), were sent to London for further education and to apprentice with a merchant. It is known that from 20 November 1755, Francis apprenticed with Samuel Touchet & Co., who traded on the West Indies and the Levant. Presumably, Charles took his apprenticeship there too, but if so, it was not for long. In 1758, on his wedding night, Thomas shot himself. Thereupon Charles was recalled to Exeter by his mother to take his place. Francis finished his

[55] B. Mallet, *Thomas George, Earl of Northbrook. A Memoir* (London: Longmans, Green and Company, 1908), 1–2; Orbell, *Baring Brothers*, 1–2; Ziegler, *The Sixth Great Power*, 13–15; Hidy, *The House of Baring*, 4–7.

[56] Ziegler, *The Sixth Great Power*, 16; Hidy, *The House of Baring*, 7.

[57] Orbell, *Baring Brothers*, 2; Ziegler, *The Sixth Great Power*, 17; Hidy, *The House of Baring*, 8.

apprenticeship in 1759, but he chose to remain in the employ of Samuel Touchet.[58]

In 1762, two events converged to reorganise the Baring firm. First, Elizabeth had now reached the respectable age of 60, and she was keen for her sons to step up in the firm. Second, Samuel Touchet's business was collapsing, bringing Francis' employment in doubt.[59] The moment would seem opportune for Francis to return to Exeter to take up a position alongside his brothers. However, he was reluctant to return, because he felt that Charles was already too firmly established. Thus, after some negotiation it was decided to establish two houses. The Exeter cloth business would continue as John & Charles Baring. A separate house was established in London, which was to purchase materials for Exeter, and look for new markets for its goods. It is sometimes assumed that Francis founded the London house, which grew into a bank of international repute, but that was not the case.[60] Baring's London agent and a close friend of the family, Nathanial Paice, was keen to retire. The Barings took up the offer to take over his firm.[61] The London house would go by the name of John & Francis Baring. The two houses were established on 1 January 1763 for a period of four years. In 1767, the interlocking partnerships were renewed for ten years, until 1 January 1777.[62] Despite the eldest brother, John, being the senior partner in both the Exeter house and the London house, he did not concern himself much with the business. John aspired to the easy-going life of an English country gentleman, and he had political ambitions. John contested the parliamentary constituency of Honiton in 1774, but he was defeated. In 1776, he won the election for Exeter. He remained an MP for Exeter until 1802, though he had to spend increasing sums in incentives and bribes to remain in his

[58] "Early Baring Firms, 1755–1811, by F.H. Baring, December 1912", UK-BA, House Correspondence [HC] 1/191; Orbell, *Baring Brothers*, 2–3; Ziegler, *The Sixth Great Power*, 17–18; Hidy, *The House of Baring*, 7.

[59] Tearle, *Barings Bank*, 200–201.

[60] Tearle, *Barings Bank*, 7.

[61] Orbell, *Baring Brothers*, 3; Ziegler, *The Sixth Great Power*, 18.

[62] "Early Baring Firms, 1755–1811, by F.H. Baring, December 1912", UK-BA, HC/ 1/191. The articles of agreement of the partnerships of 1762 and 1767 have not been found, but the accounts of the Baring firms, which shows their split are located in: UK-BA, NP1/A/14/1.

seat. The Exeter seat cost John about £25,000 throughout his career, and allegations of bribery and corruption continued to pursue him.[63]

Francis Baring showed great drive in expanding his business. Continuing the path his father had set, he established the London house as an agent for other Exeter cloth manufacturers through purchasing their raw materials and marketing their goods. From this agency business, Francis branched out into finance, conducting payments and settling bills on behalf of Exeter associates. Considering the embeddedness and prominence of Baring in the Exeter cloth trade, these steps were relatively straightforward, and they carried limited risk. But Francis was more ambitious. He sought to push his business beyond the constraints of the Exeter market. The trading business took on a new character when Francis started trading on commission and when he expanded his cargoes, occasionally in joint venture, to goods other than the needs and manufactures of the Exeter cloth trade. This was a risky step because it required reliable market intelligence and a good knowledge of a diversity of commodities and their quality. Francis took an even riskier step when he expanded the geographical scope of his financial services to include continental European houses, and when he increased the range of financial services by wading into acceptance credit. The success of the expansion of Francis' financial services depended on his ability to assess the creditworthiness of the houses he dealt with. This is difficult for houses with a long pedigree, and even more so for emerging houses.[64]

Francis' mother was not always happy with his independence and adventurism, and it seems with good reason.[65] In a memorandum on the early history of the Baring business, Francis writes that the London house did not make a profit for the first 14 years of its existence.[66] Francis' personal notebook, with annual overviews of profit and loss, corroborates the losses for most years. It furthermore shows that the London house remained afloat only because of an injection of £5,000, which Francis inherited from his mother in 1766, and close to £6,000, which he

[63] Ziegler, *The Sixth Great Power*, 18–19, 37.

[64] Ziegler, *The Sixth Great Power*, 19–20; Orbell, *Baring Brothers*, 3–5; Hidy, *The House of Baring*, 8, 12–16.

[65] Ziegler, *The Sixth Great Power*, 20–21.

[66] "My connections and conduct with my brother C[harles] B[aring] through life", UK-BA, NP1/D/1/2.

received through his wife.[67] According to Francis, the losses were due to his inexperience, a lack of caution, but most of all due to the association with the Exeter house.[68]

The relationship between the Exeter house and the London house was not equal. The Exeter house was the primary house. In 1763, it received the greatest share of the family capital. Moreover, the capital of the London house stood at the constant command of Exeter at a mere 30 days' notice, whilst the London house could not draw on the Exeter house. In principle, the arrangement need not stifle either business, but Charles inhibited good co-operation between both houses. Charles was vain, insecure, and he always felt a strong rivalry with both his brothers. Worse still, Charles was never a natural businessman. He was overly enthusiastic for new ideas, but he lacked proper judgement. Charles' character and his limited business acumen led to him enter into one ill-conceived venture after the other, for which he inevitably drew on Francis. Francis could not refuse, and so considerable capital that could have been employed profitably was instead drained through Charles. In 1776, the relationship between the Exeter house and the London house came to grief. Charles showed up unannounced in London with three associates to present Francis with an ambitious scheme for developing a wool spinning machine. Francis objected, because he doubted the prospects as well as the qualities of Charles' business associates. However, Charles overruled his brother and demanded £200–300 for some experiments, to which Francis conceded. Upon Charles' return two weeks later, Francis discovered that Charles had signed a partnership committing Baring to no less than £20,000. Seeing no room for compromise, Francis proposed to dissolve the interlocking partnerships.[69] With John's mediation, a dissolution was soon agreed. Per 1 January 1777, John & Charles Baring and John & Francis Baring would continue as separate entities. John, just

[67] "Sir Francis Baring's Notebook, 1763–1809", UK-BA, DEP/193/40.

[68] "My connections and conduct with my brother C[harles] B[aring] through life", UK-BA, NP1/D/1/2.

[69] "My connections and conduct with my brother C[harles] B[aring] through life", UK-BA, NP1/D/1/2; "Memorandum by Sir Thomas Baring on the Baring business in Exeter, 1716–1805", UK-BA, NP1/D/11/6.

having won the parliamentary seat of Exeter, remained a silent partner in both firms.[70]

Charles' conduct continued to tarnish the Baring reputation, and his ill-conceived ventures necessitated periodic financial injections by Francis, but as the relations between Charles and Francis have no direct bearing on the financing of the sale and purchase of Louisiana, we can leave the history of the Exeter house to focus on John & Francis Baring. Despite the losses in the early years of the London house, Francis later admitted that he felt the foundations of his house were laid in the years 1763–1777.[71] Not only had he gained valuable experience and knowledge of markets, but he also established a wide network of business relations spanning the European continent.[72] Once cut loose from Exeter, Francis allowed his relations with West Country houses to wither in favour of international business, and whilst Francis continued to trade, his banking activities, in particular the acceptance business, grew much faster.[73] Francis also became more involved in government and politics. In 1779, he became a director of the English East India Company (EEIC). Francis would hold various positions in the EEIC until his death.[74] In 1784, Francis sat in Parliament for Grampound in Devon, a rotten borough which cost him £3,000.[75] Francis hoped to return to Parliament in the elections of 1790. He bought the borough of Ilchester, Somerset from a certain Samuel Smith for £1,500, but Smith did not hold up his side of the bargain. Francis was not elected. Through a political contact, he was offered the borough of Chipping Wycombe, and later the borough of Calne.[76] Francis' contribution to government and politics was limited, but it did bring him three important benefits. First, Francis

[70] "Proposal by John Baring for dissolution of the houses, 1777", UK-BA, NP1/A/14/2/1; "Agreement to dissolution, 29 March 1777", UK-BA, NP1/A/14/2/2.

[71] J. Greig (ed.), *The Farington Diary*, 8 vols (London, 1926), VI: 137.

[72] Hidy, *The House of Baring*, 14.

[73] Ziegler, *The Sixth Great Power*, 28–33; Orbell, *Baring Brothers*, 10; Austin, *Baring Brothers*, 14–15.

[74] Orbell, *Baring Brothers*, 9–12; Ziegler, *The Sixth Great Power*, 39; R Hidy, *The House of Baring*, 19–20.

[75] Orbell, *Baring Brothers*, 9; Ziegler, *The Sixth Great Power*, 37.

[76] "Copy of Agreement between Francis Baring to Samuel Smith, London, 16 September 1789", UK-BA, HC/1/204/3/a; Ziegler, *The Sixth Great Power*, 37–38; Hidy, *The House of Baring*, 39.

gained new business. For example, in 1780, Francis' house was selected for marketing British loans to finance the war effort in the American War of Independence. The house would continue to place British war loans during the wars with France. In 1783, Francis obtained a contract for victualling the British armed forces in America.[77] Second, the governmental and political associations helped establish John & Francis Baring amongst the best houses in the City. For example, when the reputable house of Boyd, Benfield and Co. collapsed into administration, it was Francis Baring who was asked to mediate in the disputes that followed.[78] Third, the governmental and political positions broadened Francis' horizon. His work for the EEIC allowed Francis to see and seize opportunities in Asia. For example, he became aware of the Indian demand for cloth, and he redirected Devon manufacturers to that market through the EEIC, even though the Devon cloths were sold at a loss. Francis would also use his patronage at the EEIC to send four of his sons to Asia to learn about the local market.[79] Francis' work for the Pitt Administration during the American War of Independence also revealed to him the potential of the Americas. Much of Baring's prosperity and reputation can be traced back to their operations in the United States of America in the nineteenth century, but the first contacts were laid by Francis in this era.[80]

By the late 1780s, business was on a stable footing and growing, and so Francis turned his attention to planning for his succession. On 12 May 1767, Francis married Harriet Herring (1750–1804), a cousin of the Archbishop of Canterbury. They had twelve children, ten of whom lived to adulthood. Francis and Harriet's first three children were girls, Harriet (1768–1838), Maria (b. 1769), and Dorothy (1771–1839). They were not considered for a position in the firm, but they were part of Francis' succession strategy. Harriet married a London merchant, Charles Wall (1756–1815), who was in the employ of John & Francis Baring, and,

[77] Ziegler, *The Sixth Great Power*, 40–41; Hidy, *The House of Baring*, 18, 26–27; Austin, *Baring Brothers*, 11–12; Orbell, *Baring Brothers*, 9–10, 16–17.

[78] Orbell, *Baring Brothers*, 9; Ziegler, *The Sixth Great Power*, 42; Hidy, *The House of Baring*, 39.

[79] Ziegler, *The Sixth Great Power*, 40; Orbell, *Baring Brothers*, 19; Hidy, *The House of Baring*, 20, 44–45; "Sir Francis Baring's Notebook, 1763–1809", UK-BA, DEP/193/40.

[80] Orbell, *Baring Brothers*, 10; Austin, *Baring Brothers*, 14–15; Hidy, *The House of Baring*, 22.

as mentioned, Dorothy married Pierre César Labouchere. Maria married Richard Stainforth, but little is known of him. The youngest two children were Frances (1783–1825) and Lydia (1787–1843). They married Thomas Read Kemp and Philip Laycock Story respectively. Little is known of them too. Then there were the five sons, Thomas (1772–1848), Alexander (1773–1848), Henry (1777–1848), William (1779–1820), and George (1781–1854). In the late 1780s, the boys were still too young and inexperienced to be taken into the firm.[81] Francis thus promoted two employees to partner, James Francis Mesturas, the senior clerk of John & Francis Baring, and Charles Wall, Harriet's husband. The new partnership, renamed John & Francis Baring & Co., was established on 1 July 1788 for a period of seven years. Mesturas and Wall both took a $^{1}/_{7}$ share of the partnership. It is not explicated how the remaining $^{5}/_{7}$ share was divided between John and Francis, but John stayed in the background, and in 1796, his share of the profits was reduced to 25%. Francis' share of the profits was increased first to 50%, and in 1800 to 75%.[82]

For the longer term, Francis and Harriet groomed their sons for a position in the business. In 1790, Thomas was sent to Bengal to learn the local market. He returned to London around 1801. At this time, Francis' eldest brother, John, had reached the age of 70, and he felt the time ripe to retire from business. Thereupon, it was decided to reorganise the partnership of John & Francis Baring. John retired, and Thomas was made partner. The new firm was renamed Francis Baring & Co.. The act of partnership of 1801 has not been found, and so Thomas' share of the partnership and his position vis-a-vis the other partners cannot be established.[83] What is certain is that Thomas, despite his training, was not much interested in the family business. When Francis' health deteriorated in 1809, Thomas withdrew from the firm in anticipation of inheriting his father's estate and title.[84]

[81] "Sir Francis Baring's Notebook, 1763–1809", UK-BA, DEP/193/40; Orbell, *Baring Brothers*, 12.

[82] "Articles of Partnership John & Francis Baring & Co., 1 July 1788", UK-BA, NP1/A/15/1; Orbell, *Baring Brothers*, 19.

[83] "My connections and conduct with my brother C[harles] B[aring] through life", UK-BA, NP1/D/1/2; "Early Baring Firms, 1755–1811, by F.H. Baring, December 1912", UK-BA, HC/1/191.

[84] Ziegler, *The Sixth Great Power*, 40; Hidy, *The House of Baring*, 44–45.

Francis and Harriet's third son, Henry, was trained to become an expert in the tea trade. He apprenticed or worked for a tea trader under the name of Stockwell. Thereafter, Francis used his position at the EEIC to include Henry in Macartney's first Embassy from Britain to the Court of Peking.[85] Henry may have stayed in China for some time after to learn the local market. In 1804, Henry became a partner in the firm. His tenure was marked by scandals. Henry was an avid gambler, which did not do the reputation of the house any good. His private life was also tumultuous. Henry married Maria Bingham, the second daughter of William Bingham, an American senator and ostensibly the wealthiest man in the United States. The marriage was bad, but Henry turned a private matrimonial affair into a public scandal by divorcing his wife. Henry remained as a partner until 1823, but he was kept in the background.[86]

William was sent to learn the commodity trade in Amsterdam, and from there Francis used his position in the EEIC to find his son employ in Canton. William showed promise. He was diligent, learned quick, and he kept a dutiful correspondence with his father. However, his poor health prevented him from taking up a position in the firm. He died in 1820.[87] The fifth son, George, was a problematic child, though his problems are not entirely clear—some crucial pages that explicate his conduct are missing from the archives. From the writings that remain one can piece together a picture of a young man who could not control his passions. George entertained lavishly, he gambled, he drank too much, and he let himself in with loose women and prostitutes, who gave him "health disorder". His parents tried to raise George like his brothers, but George was

[85] "Francis Baring to Alexander Baring, London, 10 August 1790", UK-BA, NP1/B/13/2; "Robert Voûte to Francis Baring, Amsterdam, 19 June 1792", UK-BA, NP1/A/3/3; "List of members of Lord Macartney's embassy", UK-BA, NP1/C/2/2/6/1. The list notes "Young W. Baring", but the archivist assesses this to be Henry Baring. Possibly there was a last-minute swap.

[86] "Sir Francis Baring's Notebook, 1763–1809", UK-BA, DEP/193/40; "Francis Baring to William Bingham, 21 April 1802", UK-BA, NP1/B/3/1/1; Orbell, *Baring Brothers*, 19, 27; Ziegler, *The Sixth Great Power*, 40; Hidy, *The House of Baring*, 29, 45.

[87] "Robert Voûte to Francis Baring, Amsterdam, 19 June 1792", UK-BA, NP1/A/3/3; "David Lance to Francis Baring, Canton, 3 November 1803", NP1/B/3/4/2; "William Baring to Francis Baring, 5 August 1804", NP1/B/3/3/5; "William Baring to Francis Baring, Canton, 3 January 1806", NP1/B/3/3/6; "William Baring to Francis Baring, Canton, 25 January 1807", NP1/B/3/3/9; "Sir Francis Baring's Notebook, 1763–1809", UK-BA, DEP/193/40; "Henry Hope to Hope & Co., 14 August 1804", NL-SA, 735/464.

too headstrong. In 1801, George was removed from the temptations of London to be sent to a small, unnamed village in the Netherlands to learn the Dutch language, and, if possible, to learn the commodity trade. George, however, was unrelenting. He frequently deserted his studies to satisfy his passions in Amsterdam. After a raucous night at the residence of Maarten van der Goes Dirxsland, the Minister of Foreign Affairs of the Batavian Republic—Britain's enemy, in which George gambled away a large sum of money, Francis decided he could no longer allow his youngest son to tarnish the reputation of the house.[88] George was recalled to London. He joined Labouchere on a mission for Hope and Baring to Lisbon, before being sent to Calcutta to work as a supercargo for the EEIC, where he married a local woman against his father's wishes. In 1809, he established a trading house, which is known under the name of Dent & Co. However, George lost a lot of money in a speculation gone awry. He later joined the Church of England, but he found the life of a clergyman too tame. He became a priest in a sect, but the lavish lifestyle caused him to be declared bankrupt. He was rescued by his brothers, and he was packed off to live the rest of his days in Italy. George was never accepted into the firm.[89]

Francis' hope for the long-term future of his business lay with his second son, Alexander. In 1792, he was sent to apprentice with close business associates in Amsterdam, Hope & Co.. In Amsterdam, Alexander revealed a tendency towards leisurely pursuits rather than work. He would not finish the tasks for the day but would instead just pack up when his shift finished. Francis and John Williams Hope lamented this, but his mentor, Voûte, felt this youthful shortcoming was easily rectified. Henry Hope assessed Alexander to have little foibles which gained ground as he grew older, but he was clever enough when animated. In any case,

[88] "Robert Voûte to George Baring, 3 August 1801", UK-BA, NP1/A/9/7/1; "Francis Baring to Robert Voûte, 4 August 1801", UK-BA, NP1/A/9/5; "Robert Voûte to George Baring, The Hague, 7 August 1801", UK-BA, NP1/A/9/7/2; "George Baring to Robert Voûte, undated [August 1801]", UK-BA, NP1/A/9/7/2; "Robert Voûte to George Baring, 9 August 1801", UK-BA, NP1/A/9/7/2; "Robert Voûte to Francis Baring, 10 August 1801", UK-BA, NP1/A/9/7/1; "Robert Voûte to Francis Baring, 11 August 1801", UK-BA, NP1/A/9/7/2; "Robert Voûte to Francis Baring, The Hague, 26 October 1801", UK-BA, NP1/A/9/7/2.

[89] Ziegler, *The Sixth Great Power*, 47; A. Le Pichon (ed.), *China Trade and Empire: Jardine, Matheson & Co. and the Origins of British Rule in Hong Kong 1827–1843* (Oxford: British Academy, 2006), 67.

it appears that Hope knew how to animate Alexander. Alexander soon immersed himself in the business, and consequently, he was welcomed by his colleagues, most notably Pierre César Labouchere, his future brother-in-law.[90] Alexander learnt the trade in Amsterdam and was said to have become "a Dutchman in negotiation", which apparently meant that he was tough and shrewd, but never unreasonable.[91] Francis' decision to send Alexander to Amsterdam would have a lasting impact on the history of Baring, as well as on the financing of the sale and purchase of Louisiana. Because the history of Alexander Baring is just as much tied up with the House of Hope as it is with the House of Baring, we may first explore how the two houses became acquainted, before exploring Alexander's role in the financing of the sale and purchase of Louisiana.

The Hope-Baring Network

Bernard Mallet, the biographer of Francis Baring's great-grandson, Thomas George, the Earl of Northbrook, writes that Baring and Hope became acquainted at an early period of Francis' career. Hope had requested Baring to remit bills to a small amount on a commercial place in Europe. Francis executed the commission with great success, transmitting the returns at a higher rate than the course of the day. Hope was so pleasantly surprised that they requested Francis to remit a further £15,000. Francis had never received such a large order, and it was only through leaning heavily on his contacts that he managed to clear the commission. Francis' conduct impressed the Hopes so much that they decided to establish a constant business with Baring henceforth.[92] The tale of the origins of the Hope-Baring consortium has since become mainstream in the historiography.[93] The transaction is plausible, and the relationship is in line with the respective standings of the houses in the late eighteenth

[90] "Robert Voûte to Francis Baring, Amsterdam, 19 June 1792", UK-BA, NP1/A/3/3; "Robert Voûte to Francis Baring, Amsterdam, 4 June 1793", UK-BA, NP1/A/3/4; "Henry Hope to M.D.N. [Hope & Co.], 17 December 1803", NL-SA, 735/464; "Henry Hope to M.D.N. [Hope & Co.], 14 August 1804", NL-SA, 735/464.

[91] R.C. Alberts, *The Golden Voyage. The Life and Times of William Bingham, 1752–1804* (Boston: Houghton Mifflin Company, 1969), 270.

[92] Mallet, *Thomas George, Earl of Northbrook*, 3–4.

[93] Ziegler, *The Sixth Great Power*, 31–32; Hidy, *The House of Baring*, 14–15; Tearle, *Barings Bank*, 70–71.

century. Alas, the imprecise dating makes it impossible to identify with precision the origins of the Hope-Baring relationship. Orbell dates the first correspondence between Hope and Baring to 1766.[94] This means that the initial contact took place before 1766, which, considering that Francis' business did not really take off until the late 1770s, seems very early.

Rather than try to identify the moment when history was made, perhaps a better way to understand the origins of the Hope-Baring collaboration, or "the concern" as it is referred to in the Hope-Baring correspondence, is to view it as the result of a gradual entanglement of the parallel historical paths of two houses that had a similar outlook, business strategy, and ambition. Several entanglements of the history of Hope and the history of Baring can be found. A first entanglement runs through the cloth trade. Two connections in particular stand out. The first is centred on the Labouchere family. As mentioned, the Labouchere were cloth merchants who settled in Nantes, which was another important node in the European cloth trade. Part of the family relocated to the Netherlands, but the relationship with the Nantes branch remained strong. The father of the Dutch Laboucheres is Matthieu Labouchere.[95] Matthieu married Marie Madeleine Moliere. The couple had four sons. The first-born son, Abel Pierre, was a sickly child.[96] Not much is known of his life. The three other sons all apprenticed in their uncle's cloth trading business in Nantes. As mentioned, the second son, Pierre César, was recruited from his uncle's firm by Hope to manage their French desk. He worked closely with Alexander Baring in the Hope-Baring concern throughout his life, and he married Dorothy Baring. What is less well known is that the fourth brother, Samuel Pierre (1778–1867), conducted the French correspondence for Francis Baring. Samuel did not move to London. Rather he stayed in Nantes to translate the incoming and outgoing correspondence for Baring.[97] In 1808, John Dixon of Littledale & Dixon of Rotterdam,

[94] Orbell, *Baring Brothers*, 10.

[95] "Extraits des registres de l'Eglise parraoissielle [sic] Saint Pierre de la ville d'Orthès en Bearn, 21 April 1742", UK-BA, DEP/208/19/5.

[96] "Extrait des Registres de Bâtème de l'Eglise Wallone de la Haije", UK-BA, DEP/208/18/54; "Unknown to Pierre César Labouchere, 17 January 1797", UK-BA, DEP/208/19/18.

[97] "Extrait des Registres de Bâtème de l'Eglise Wallone de la Haije", UK-BA, DEP/208/18/55; Nolte, *Fifty Years*, 80.

a long-standing business associate of Hope, was recruited into Hope & Co.. Rather than dissolve Littledale & Dixon, the business was transferred to Samuel Pierre Labouchere.[98] In 1823, Samuel became a partner in Hope.[99] The third brother was Antoine Marie (1775–1829). Antoine did not enter into the employ of Hope or Baring. Rather, he remained in Nantes to take over the cloth trading business of his uncle.[100] However, Antoine, trading under the name of A.M. Labouchere & Trotreau, brings us to a second connection that links the histories of Hope and Baring, namely the Nolte family.

Vincent Nolte is known in the historiography for his prominent role in the economic and financial development of Louisiana, and the United States more broadly. However, the Nolte family history also has deep entanglements with the Hope-Baring network. As a young boy, Vincent's father, Johann Heinrich Nolte, was sent to Exeter to learn the Devon market. In Exeter, Johann moved in the same circles as other German immigrants, including the Barings. Johann and Francis Baring attended the same school. After graduation, Francis went to London, whilst Johann took up an apprenticeship in his uncle's house Otto Franck & Co. of Livorno. However, the two men remained lifelong friends, occasionally even taking holidays together. When Johann became a partner in Otto Franck & Co., the house became a key importer of dyestuffs for the Baring partnerships, thus becoming an integral part of the Hope-Baring network. The relationship remained strong after Johann relocated to his native Hamburg. Johann's son, Vincent, was initially apprenticed to Otto Franck & Co., but he was recalled by his father to extract him from the faltering business and to prevent a scandal resulting from Vincent's dalliance with the daughter of a local notable. Vincent then continued his training in the cloth trade with A.M. Labouchere & Trotreau. He performed well, and in 1804 he was recruited by Pierre César Labouchere as an American agent in one of the largest financial operations that Hope and Baring conducted, which was the operation to transport Mexican silver to Europe to pay for Spain's subsidies to Napoleon.[101]

98 "Memorandum of Agreement, 14 June 1808", UK-BA, DEP/208/11.

99 "Circular on the granting of the signature, 1 January 1823", NL-SA, 735/525.

100 "Extrait des Registres de Bâtème de l'Eglise Wallone de la Haije", UK/BA, DEP/208/18/58; Nolte, *Fifty Years*, 45–47.

101 Nolte, *Fifty Years*, 17–55.

A further entanglement between Hope and Baring runs through Robert Voûte. Voûte's connection to the Hopes has been mentioned. It is not known how Francis Baring became acquainted with him. It is likely that Voûte's father, Jean Jacques, who specialised in the trade of dyestuffs, tea, and coffee, traded with the Baring businesses. In any case, by the 1780s, Francis and Voûte had developed a close trading relationship. One of the scandals that continued to pursue Francis Baring throughout his political career was the accusation voiced in 1786 that Francis abused his privileged position at the EEIC to profiteer from the EEIC tea trade. Ziegler does not dispute the profiteering from the tea trade, but he argues that the trades were conducted by another specialist in the tea trade, Robert Voûte.[102] Whether Voûte acted independently or in collaboration with Francis Baring remains to be discovered.[103] What is clear is that the profiteering at the expense of the EEIC was no inhibition for Francis to continue working with Robert Voûte. In 1787, Baring joined Hope in the operation to corner the market for cochineal, which was set up and executed on the advice of Voûte.[104] And in 1793, Voûte was dispatched by both Hope and Baring to reorganise the associated Moscow trading house of G. Rowand & Co., whose ineptitude inhibited a smooth trade with the Baltics.[105] And the relationship between Francis and Voûte was not only professional. In fact, it may well be that Francis had a closer relationship with Voûte than he had with Henry Hope. For example, Francis relied on Voûte's advice and guidance in educating and training three of his five sons. When Alexander took up his apprenticeship with Hope, it was Voûte who advised and supervised him, and who reported on his progress to his father. William was sent to Amsterdam to learn the commodity trade under Voûte, and when George became untenable in London, he was packed off to the Netherlands, where Voûte attempted to control his passions by subjecting him to a strict educational regime.[106]

[102] Ziegler, *The Sixth Great Power*, 35–36.

[103] The starting place would be UK-BA, NP1/C/16 *Sir Francis Baring: Documents relating to the contract between the East India Co and Robert Voûte, merchant, for the provision of tea to the Company*.

[104] Buist, *At Spes Non Fracta*, 431–451.

[105] Buist, *At Spes Non Fracta*, 119–154.

[106] "Robert Voûte to Francis Baring, Amsterdam, 19 June 1792", UK-BA, NP1/A/3/3.

Reflecting on the origins of the Hope-Baring consortium, it is unlikely that one inadvertent interaction laid the basis for the lasting relationship. Rather, it is better to see both Hope and Baring as being part of the same network of houses in Western Europe, engaged in the cloth trade and later the broader commodity trade and financial services. Hope rose to the pinnacle of this network because it was one of the first houses to successfully branch out from trade to banking. Baring's role in this network was initially that of just another cloth trading business, interacting with houses like Labouchere and Otto Franck. Two developments contributed to Baring's rise to greater prominence. First, the dissolution of the interlocking partnerships, which freed Francis from the demands of Charles and allowed him to re-orient away from the Devon market. Second, Francis' employment in the EEIC, which revealed to him the opportunities of global trade for him to pursue presumably in collaboration with Voûte. Both developments brought Baring closer to Hope. Francis' competence and a similar business outlook drove both houses to seek to strengthen the relationship where possible.

The year 1794 was a turning point in the relationship between Hope and Baring. French Revolutionary ideals and criticisms always had a draw on a section on Dutch society, but in late 1794, the discussion turned to action when Dutch revolutionaries, the Batavians, collaborated with the forces of Revolutionary France to invade and conquer the Netherlands. In 1795, they ousted the House of Orange and installed a new regime. The Hopes, although politically inclined towards support for the Organist party, were pragmatists. They could have found an accommodation with the new regime. What induced them to leave was the economic uncertainty associated with regime change. In October 1794, Henry Hope and John Williams left Amsterdam for London. Pierre César Labouchere and Alexander Baring followed in early 1795. Paulus Taay, a trusted clerk, was placed in charge of the Amsterdam office, though greatly assisted by Robert Voûte, both with advice and financial support.[107]

Hope's departure was a sore point for the new Dutch regime. They did not like to see such an important merchant-banking house leave,

[107] "Henry Hope to Francis Baring, 3 October 1794", UK-BA, NP1/A/1/18; "Henry Hope to Francis Baring, 10 October 1794", UK-BA, NP1/A/1/21; "Procuration for Gregorius Cruys, Amsterdam, 15 January 1795", NL-SA/522; "Procuration for Paulus Taay, London, 10 August 1795", NL-SA, 735/523; Buist, *At Spes Non Fracta*, 48–51, 155.

let alone relocate to a rival power. The Batavian regime responded by seizing Hope assets in Amsterdam, both to set an example and to re-open communication with Hope. They succeeded in both aims. By and large, Amsterdam merchant-banking houses adapted to the new political climate and Hope opened communications so as to return to the Netherlands. Voûte was tasked with negotiating the terms of return. However, because both parties needed to be seen as having stuck to their guns, no compromise could be reached on the terms of Hope's return to Amsterdam just yet.

In Britain, Hope did not set up any financial operations, but because they did not want their funds to remain idle, they participated in Baring's operations. Baring made great use of Hope's capital, their knowledge, their guidance, and most of all their relations. Hope and Baring collaborated on several operations, including the marketing of British and American government loans. The largest Hope-Baring operation was the Portuguese diamond loan. From 1793, Portugal needed capital, initially to finance her war against Revolutionary France, and after her defeat in 1801, to pay France an indemnity of Fr.20 million.[108] Hope had much experience in the diamond trade, and they were thus the first point of call for the Portuguese crown. However, because they did not want to accept new business outside their home market, Hope refused twice, in 1796 and 1800. In October 1801, the need for capital became so dire that the Portuguese crown approached Baring. Francis was keen to accept, but he lacked the capital, the knowledge of the diamond trade, and the contacts to commit to a substantial financial operation. Francis thus turned to Henry Hope, who agreed to participate in the operation. Francis and Henry were quick to draft the outlines of the operation. Hope-Baring would lend £700,000 (about Fr.15 million) to the Portuguese crown, which would be repaid through the sale of Brazilian diamonds in London. As security, Portugal deposited diamonds totalling 40,000 carats in the Bank of England. After a provisional agreement was reached with the Portuguese envoy in London, Labouchere and George Baring travelled to Lisbon to hammer out the details of the sale of diamonds. On the insistence of Francis Baring, one major amendment was that, now that peace had returned to Europe, the diamonds would be sold, not in London, but in Amsterdam, where the diamond market was more developed. The

[108] Kerautret, *Documents diplomatiques*, I: 184–188, 201–204.

operation would be directed by Baring, but the ratio of participation, $^{2}/_{7}$ for Baring and $^{5}/_{7}$ for Hope, reveals Francis' reliance on Hope.[109]

The Portuguese diamond loan is reflective of the relationship between Hope and Baring at the beginning of the nineteenth century, as well as their response to the changing international environment. For the operation, Hope and Baring pooled their capital, contacts, and expertise on a range of commodities and markets. This was far beyond the co-operation one may expect of networked houses. The operation also reveals that Hope was still the senior partner in the concern, participating for 71%. This is in line with the custom ratio of participation that Hope and Baring adhered to, namely 75% for Hope and 25% for Baring.[110] The Portuguese diamond loan also shows how Hope and Baring responded to the changing European order. Since the outbreak of the Revolutionary Wars, a political divide was opening up in Europe, with France and her allies on one side, and the anti-Revolutionary and anti-Napoleonic coalitions on the other. This contentious political order was challenging to navigate for merchants and bankers because political obstacles could suddenly emerge to interrupt the flow of goods, capital, and information. Hope-Baring relied on Francis' contacts with the British establishment and Hope's integration into Dutch economic and financial networks to remain rooted in both political blocs, allowing them to spread risk, base their operations in the political environment most welcoming to their interests, and play off one party against the other when political obstacles were raised. This was a sure competitive advantage over peers.

The successful collaboration in London raised questions for the Hope and Baring partnerships. For Baring, two issues were at play. First, in 1802, Francis was 62 years old. He was ready to take a step back from business, but the absence of a suitable successor prevented his retirement. Second, Francis was always keenly aware of the prominence of Amsterdam in international finance, and his lifelong aspiration was to gain a foothold in the Amsterdam market. Hope's relocation to London raised the prospect of achieving this through a merger with Hope. The merger would also allow Francis to retire with relative peace of mind regarding the future of his business. Henry Hope was torn. On the one hand, he was

109 "Francis Baring to Hope & Co., London, 17 December 1802", NL-SA, 735/131; Buist, *At Spes Non Fracta*, 383–427; Orbell, *Baring Brothers*, 17–18.

110 "J[ohn] W[illiams] Hope to Francis Baring, 18 August 1804", UK-BA, NP1/A/4/58.

keen to return to Amsterdam. Despite the political unrest in the Netherlands, Henry felt that only the network of Amsterdam houses could provide the expertise and support necessary to navigate the challenging economic times towards success and profit. On the other hand, Henry wanted to maintain his London office to hedge against future political turmoil and uncertainty.[111] On 28 June 1802, Hope and Baring agreed that a partnership would be drawn up between Henry Hope, Alexander Baring, and Pierre César Labouchere to establish a new house under the name of Hope & Co. of Amsterdam. The partnership was backdated to 1 January 1802 and was to run for seven years. Labouchere was abroad on business for the Portuguese diamond loan, and so he appointed Francis Baring as his attorney. Presumably, Francis would have signed, but it never came to that because Alexander did not take up the offer.[112]

The forced relocation from Amsterdam in 1795 had cut Alexander's apprenticeship short. However, Alexander did not finish his training in London. Instead, he was sent to explore opportunities in the United States. Baring's early connections to the United States, and their involvement in American trade and finance are well known.[113] It is therefore often assumed that Alexander went to the United States at the behest of his father to become Baring's agent in America.[114] In fact, Alexander was Hope's agent in America. This is clear from a letter by Francis Baring in which he expresses his gratitude to Hope for releasing Alexander from work to conduct some business for Baring.[115] Baring and Hope's investment in Maine lands is even clearer proof of this. In 1786, the American senator and financier William Bingham acquired three million acres (12,141 km^2) of land in what was then known as the District of Maine for about $500,000, though with additional expenses for improvements. The transaction is referred to as the Bingham Purchase. Bingham

111 "Robert Voûte to Labouchere, The Hague, 24 July 1801", UK-BA, NP1/A/20/6; Buist, *At Spes Non Fracta*, 54–56, 68, 164, 389, 399, 666–667; Ziegler, *The Sixth Great Power*, 46.

112 "Act of Convention, 28 June 1802", UK-BA, DEP/208/15.

113 Hidy, *The House of Baring*, 21–23; Austin, *Baring Brothers*, 14–21; Tearle, *Barings Bank*.

114 Hidy, *The House of Baring*, 29; Austin, *Baring Brothers*, 15.

115 "Francis Baring to William Bingham, London, 31 August 1795", in *William Bingham's Maine Lands, 1790–1820*, ed. F.S. Allis Jr (Portland: The Anthoensen Press, 1954), 592–594.

hoped to make a profit by parcelling out the land for resale. However, the land was rugged, uncultivated, and remote. Demand was limited and Bingham made no substantial sales. Adding to his worries was a clause that obliged Bingham to establish 2,500 settlers on the land by 1803, or to pay a fine of $30 for each deficient settler. By the mid-1790s, Bingham's financial difficulties were such that he was forced to seek out European investors, including Hope and Baring. Baring's investment in Maine lands has always puzzled historians. They consider it unbecoming for Francis to tie up his capital in real estate.[116] It is indeed unbecoming. A more plausible explanation for Baring's investment in real estate is that he partook with Hope. As early as April 1793, Bingham had sent Hope a prospectus of the Maine lands.[117] At that time, one may presume that Henry was equally reluctant to tie up his capital in real estate. However, the calculus changed after the forced relocation to London. Hope did not want their capital to remain idle, and as compared to risky European financial operations, investment in American real estate that only returned profits in the long term may have been seen as a good alternative. So, on 23 September 1795, Hope dispatched Alexander to America to invest up to £125,000 ($555,000) in Maine lands.[118] Upon Alexander's arrival in Boston on 29 November, both parties engaged in theatrics to influence the price. Bingham dispatched an agent to accidentally bump into Alexander to inform him of the bright prospects of the District of Maine. Alexander made a show of meeting with other land agents to feign interest in other opportunities. Ultimately, a deal was struck. Hope and Baring purchased, at a ratio of participation of 75% for Hope and 25% for Baring, one million acres (4,046 km^2) of land for a sum of $401,000. This was considerably more than Bingham had paid, but Hope-Baring had acquired the best lands, thereby devaluing the remainder.[119]

[116] Ziegler, *The Sixth Great Power*, 63–65.

[117] Allis Jr, *William Bingham's Maine Lands*, 242; "Brochure met beschrijvingen van grond, klimaat en produktie van landerijen in het district Maine, Amerika, door William Bingham, 1793", NL-SA, 735/4188.

[118] "Alexander Baring to Henry Hope, Boston, 8 December 1795", UK-BA, NP1/A/24/1.

[119] "Extract of titles & further reflections on and concerning the Americans Lands in the District of Maine", NL-SA, 735/3754; Allis Jr, *William Bingham's Maine Lands*; Alberts, *The Golden Voyage*, 227–239, 268–284.

After the hard negotiations were concluded, the relationship between Alexander and Bingham became more amicable. Alexander was taken into the Bingham household, and it was not long before he fell in love with Bingham's eldest daughter, Anne Louisa (1782–1848). They married on 23 August 1798.[120] This was a favourable match for Bingham, as it added a personal bond to the business relationship. For Hope and Baring, the match meant that Alexander remained in America. Alexander used his time to integrate the Hope-Baring concern into American economic and financial networks. He traded in currencies and commodities, and generally, he made a good profit. Through Bingham's connections, Alexander also mingled with the political elite of the young American republic. It was not long before Alexander offered his services to the American government, who readily accepted. On behalf of the American government, Hope-Baring waded into the arms trade, and they marketed and traded government debt. In 1803, due to Alexander's services, Baring was rewarded with the office of financial agents in London for the United States.[121]

The reason for Alexander's refusal to enter into a partnership with Henry Hope and Labouchere was that he saw a future in the United States and wanted to remain there. Hope's reaction to the refusal is not known. Francis was exasperated. He felt that Alexander's once superior mind had been impaired by enervating habits in America and that he sacrificed the most brilliant prospects for the pleasures of the present. Most of all Francis lamented that Alexander failed to seize the object for which Francis had worked so hard, and which was now within reach—a merger with Hope.[122] In the event, Alexander's decision turned out well. As we shall see in the next chapter, having a man with contacts in Washington and an understanding of American politics was helpful in the operation to finance the cession of Louisiana.

So, at the last moment, the plans for the Hope partnership and the first step to a merger between Hope and Baring were changed. It was decided to split the Hope firm into two. One half was domiciled in London

120 "Sir Francis Baring's Notebook, 1763–1809", UK-BA, DEP/193/40.

121 "Alexander Baring to Labouchere, London, 15 November 1802", NL-SA, 735/131; Hidy, *The House of Baring*, 29–33; Orbell, *Baring Brothers*, 14–15; Austin, *Baring Brothers*, 15–17.

122 "Draft letter from Francis Baring to William Bingham, Bath, 19 January 1803", UK-BA, NP1/B/3/1/3.

under the name of Henry Hope (& Co.) of London. Its partners were Henry Hope, John Williams Hope, and two of Jan and Phillippina's sons, Thomas and Henry Philip. Adrian Elias was excluded. As mentioned, Thomas and Henry Philip were not much involved in the business. John Williams hoped to remain in London with Henry, but after Alexander's refusal he was sent to Amsterdam with Labouchere to establish a second office under the old name of Hope & Co. of Amsterdam. In practice, then, the London office was run by Henry alone. The Amsterdam partnership was backdated to 1 January 1802 and was to run for a minimum of seven years, with automatic annual extension if neither of the partners withdrew with one's year notice. Henry Hope of London provided Hcf.5 million for which they received $^{6}/_{7}$ share of Hope & Co., the remaining $^{1}/_{7}$ going to Labouchere, who did not put up any capital. John Williams was the primary partner, to be assisted by Pierre. However, Pierre was the driving force of Hope & Co.. It is important to emphasise that the split was artificial and meant to hedge against political risk. The partnership contract explicates that final decisions lay with Henry. This is not to imply that Hope & Co. was an office of an English banking house. Henry was keen for Hope to remain an Amsterdam house, and he included contractual safeguards to ensure this. For example, if conflicts arose in the house, it was stipulated that Amsterdam merchants would be appointed to mediate and rule on the dispute.[123]

The history of Hope and the history of Baring are so intertwined that it makes more sense to view the two houses as one consortium from 1795 to 1823, when the last of the Hope-Baring dynasty withdrew from the Hope partnership. On the eve of the transfer of Louisiana, the two men most readily associated with the financing of the sale and purchase of Louisiana, Francis Baring and Henry Hope were in London. In 1802, Francis was 62 years old, and Henry was 67 years old. Both had reached the age at which they hoped to withdraw from day-to-day business. Both men had faced difficulties in grooming their successors. Francis was unlucky with his children. Of his five sons, only two seemed suitable successors,

[123] "Anthony Charles to Henry Hope, Amsterdam, 7 September 1802", NL-SA, 735/477; "Power of Attorney for Henry Hope, Amsterdam, 30 September 1802", NL-SA, 735/477; "Adrian Elias Hope to Henry Hope, Amsterdam, 8 September 1802", NL-SA, 735/477; "Henry Hope to Adrian Elias Hope, London, 12 October 1802", NL-SA, 735/462; "Adrian Elias Hope to Henry Hope, Amsterdam, 19 October 1802", NL-SA, 735/477; Elias, *De vroedschap*, II: 934–935; Buist, *At Spes Non Fracta*, 56, 243; "Articles of Agreement, 5 October 1802", UK-BA, DEP/208/1.

but William was sickly, and Alexander preferred leisure to hard work and he was stubborn. Fortuitously, these traits had kept him in the United States where he established good political and economic contacts. Henry's nephews could not be interested in banking either. John Williams Hope was a good office manager, but he did not have the shrewdness, finesse, or drive to set up and execute complex financial operations. Much of the work to come thus rested on the shoulders of Henry's protégé and Francis' son-in-law, Pierre César Labouchere.

Alexander Baring by Sir Thomas Lawrence, undated, oil on canvas. Reproduced courtesy of the Baring Archive Limited. Portrait of Alexander Baring, 1st Lord Ashburton by Sir Thomas Lawrence [c1820]", UK-BA, PT/15.

P.C. Labouchere by an unknown artist, undated, oil on board. Reproduced courtesy of the Baring Archive Limited. Portrait of P.C. Labouchere by an unknown artist [c1800]", UK-BA, PT/31.

References

PRIMARY SOURCES

Archival Sources

The Netherlands, Stadsarchief Amsterdam [NL-SA]:
735 Archief van de Firma Hope & Co. met verwante archiefvormers
Amsterdam Office:
  Incoming Correspondence:
– 131: 1802–1803.
London Office:
  Outgoing Correspondence:

- 462: 1802–1809.
- 464: 1803–1806.

Incoming Correspondence:

- 477: 1800–1802.

Organisation of the firm:

- 520: Circular 1762.
- 521: Partners, 1782–1826.
- 522: Procuration Cruys, 1795.
- 523: Procuration Taay, 1795.
- 525: Circulars on Management, 1811–1938.
- 538: Contract Nicholas Baudouin, 1765–1772.

Personal Archives:

- 2903: John Williams: Prenuptial Agreement, 1782–1810.
- 2904: John Williams: Testament and Will.

Deposited Archives:

Common Fund of Original Louisiana Stock:

- 3754: Register of correspondence, 1803–1812.

Documentation:

- 4188: Prospectus of the Maine lands by William Bingham, 1793.

United Kingdom, The Baring Archive [UK-BA]

Northbrook Papers [NP]/1/A:

1. Correspondence between John & Francis Baring & Co., Hope & Co., John Williams and Henry Hope with Francis Baring, 1789–1809.
3. Correspondence between John & Francis Baring & Co., Hope & Co., John Williams and Henry Hope with Francis Baring, 1783–1806.
4. Louisiana Purchase Papers.
9. Northbrook Business Papers A9.
14. Northbrook Business Papers A14.
15. John & Francis Baring & Co., Articles of Partnership, 1788.
20. Northbrook Business Papers A20.
24. Volume of copies of correspondence. Alexander Baring with Sir Francis Baring, Hope & Co. and William Bingham: 1795–1796.

Northbrook Papers [NP]/1/B:

3. Letters from and papers concerning Henry, William and George Baring, 1802–1836.
13. The will of Jopseph Paice, 1773.

Northbrook Papers [NP]/1/C:

2. Notebooks compiled by Sir Francis Baring.
16. Documents relating to the contract between the East India Co. and Robert Voûte.

Northbrook Papers [NP]/1/D:

1. Papers concerning the affairs of John and Charles Baring in the Exeter House and the Devonshire Bank, Exeter.
11. Papers relating to the Larkbear firm, 1807–1902.
Deposits & Gifts [DEP]:
193/40. Sir Francis Baring's Notebook, 1763–1809.
208. Papers of the Labouchere Family, 1621–1822.
House Correspondence [HC]:
1. General.

Printed Primary Sources

Nolte, V., *Fifty Years in Both Hemispheres, or Reminiscences of the Life of a Former Merchant* (New York: Redfield, 1854).

SECONDARY SOURCES

Alberts, R.C., *The Golden Voyage. The Life and Times of William Bingham, 1752–1804* (Boston: Houghton Mifflin Company, 1969).
Allis Jr, F.S. (ed.), *William Bingham's Maine Lands, 1790-1820* (Portland: The Anthoensen Press, 1954).
Austin, P.E., *Baring Brothers and the Birth of Modern Finance* (London: Pickering & Chatto, 2007).
Bonney, R. (ed.), *Economic Systems and State Finance* (Oxford: Clarendon Press, 1995).
Bonney, R. (ed.), *The Rise of the Fiscal State in Europe, c. 1200–1815* (Oxford: Oxford University Press, 1999).
Bonney, R., "The Eighteenth Century. II. The Struggle for Great Power Status and the End of the Old Fiscal Regime", in *Economic Systems and State Finance*, ed. R. Bonney (Oxford: Clarendon Press, 1995), 315–390.
Breen, J.C., "De feestelijke stemming na de restauratie van 1787", *Maandblad Amstelodamum* 5 (1918), 89-91.
Buist, M.G., *At Spes Non Fracta. Hope & Co. 1770–1815. Merchant Bankers and Diplomats at Work* (The Hague: Bank Mees & Hope NV, 1974).
Elias, J.E., *De vroedschap van Amsterdam 1578-1795*, 2 vols (Amsterdam: N. Israel, 1963).
Gérard, M., *Messieurs Hottinguer. Banquiers à Paris*, 2 vols (Paris: Banque Hottinguer, 1968–1972).
Greig, J. (ed.), *The Farington Diary*, 8 vols (London, 1922–1928).
Hellie, R., "Russia, 1200–1815", in *The Rise of the Fiscal State in Europe, c. 1200–1815*, ed. R. Bonney (Oxford: Oxford University Press, 1999), 481–506.

Hidy, R.W., *The House of Baring in American Trade and Finance. English Merchant Bankers at Work 1763–1861* (Cambridge, MA: Harvard University Press, 1949).

Josselin de Jong, F. de, "Labouchère", *Nederland's Patriciaat* 49 (The Hague: Centraal Bureau voor Genealogie, 1963), 208–227.

Kerautret, M., *Documents diplomatiques du Consulat et de l'Empire*, 3 vols (Paris: Nouveau Monde/Fondation Napoléon, 2002–2004).

Labouchere Thorold, A., *The Life of Henry Labouchere* (London: Constable & Company, 1913).

Le Pichon (ed.), A., *China Trade and Empire: Jardine, Matheson & Co. and the Origins of British Rule in Hong Kong 1827–1843* (Oxford: British Academy, 2006).

Mallet, B., *Thomas George, Earl of Northbrook. A Memoir* (London: Longmans, Green and Company, 1908).

Molhuysen, P.C., P.J. Blok et al. (eds), *Nieuw Nederlandsch Biografisch Woordenboek*, 10 vols (Leiden: K.H. Kossmann, 1911–1937).

Orbell, J., *Baring Brothers & Co., Limited. A History to 1939* (London: Baring Brothers & Co., Limited, 1985).

Riley, J.C., *International Government Finance and the Amsterdam Capital Market 1740-1815* (Cambridge: Cambridge University Press, 1980).

Tearle, D., *Barings Bank, William Bingham and the Rise of the American Nation. A Transatlantic Relationship from the Revolutionary War through the Louisiana Purchase* (London and Jefferson, NC: McFarland & Co., 2010).

Valkenburg, C.C. van, et al., "Voûte", *Nederland's Patriciaat* 63 (The Hague: Centraal Bureau voor Genealogie, 1983), 420-482.

Voort, J. van der, *De Westindische plantages van 1720–1795. Financiën en handel* (Eindhoven: De Witte, 1973).

Ziegler, P., *The Sixth Great Power. A History of One of the Greatest of All Banking Families, the House of Barings, 1762–1929* (New York: Alfred A. Knopf, 1988).

Zylberberg, M., *Capitalisme et catholicisme dans la France moderne. La dynastie Le Couteulx* (Paris: Éditions de la Sorbonne, 2001).

Newspapers

Un radical d'outre mer', *Le Temps*, 23 January 1912.

CHAPTER 4

Financing the Sale and Purchase of Louisiana

Abstract This chapter examines how Hope and Baring developed and executed the financial operation to facilitate the cession of Louisiana. It discusses the various stages of the Louisiana operation: the origins of the operation, the financial contract, how Hope and Baring intended to mobilise resources to meet liquidity requirements, the ratification of the diplomatic treaty and conventions on the cession of Louisiana, the creation of Louisiana stock and certificates, the anticipatory payments to France, the political intervention by the Addington government that forced Baring to withdraw from part of the Louisiana operation, the re-allocation of Louisiana stock and the mobilisation of funds, the payments to France, and the redemption by the United States of America. The chapter concludes by quantifying the price paid by the United States of America, the sum received by France, and the profits made by the financial middlemen.

Keywords Financing the Louisiana Cession · Louisiana Purchase · Hope & Co. · Francis Baring & Co. · Pierre César Labouchere · Alexander Baring

Rumours of France's need for financing circulated widely on the continent. The rumours were likely triggered by Bonaparte's soliciting financial

M. E. Hay, *Transatlantic Finance in the Age of Revolutions*,
https://doi.org/10.1007/978-3-031-65232-5_4

mediation. Barbé-Marbois mentions that the First Consul had hoped for a French banker to mediate the transfer of Louisiana. He offered the operation widely, but no French house came forward. The financial operation was also offered to the Bank of France, but they refused, claiming that international financial operations were not within their remit.[1] In the Netherlands, Hope's associate Voûte picked up on rumours of a "new undertaking" of scale and risk by early March 1802. Likely this referred to an operation on Louisiana, but Voûte's letter has not been found and so it cannot be established with certainty.[2] Other Dutch houses also picked up on the rumours. Francis Baring mentions that two Dutch bankers by the name of "W.", most likely Wilhem and Jan Willink, an Amsterdam house with a long history of lending to the United States, were onto the scent of a financial operation on Louisiana.[3] One would expect similar rumours to have circulated in America. There are plenty of references to American loans or American business in the Hope-Baring correspondence, but it is difficult to link a reference to the Louisiana operation because of other operations under discussion. A first likely reference to the Louisiana operation is found in a letter from 15 November 1802, in which Alexander writes of wanting to inform Labouchere of "the Louisiana business".[4] The definite article infers previous discussions on the topic.

The first interaction that can be traced directly to the signing of the contract for the financing of the transfer of Louisiana dates to September 1802, when Daniel Parker, a longstanding correspondent of Hope in Paris, informed Labouchere of France's seeking financial mediation for the cession of Louisiana. Labouchere relayed this news to the partners in London.[5] What occurred in the following months is unclear. Hope-Baring had a lot on their plate: the merger, the relocation to the Netherlands, and the Portuguese diamond loan, which always required attention. An operation on Louisiana appears to have been discussed sporadically, but little was put to paper. Those ideas and proposals that

[1] Barbé-Marbois, *Histoire de la Louisiane*, 330–331.

[2] "Hope to Voûte, 2 March 1802", NL-SA, 735/128.

[3] "Francis Baring to Labouchere, 15 February 1803", UK-BA, NP1/A/4/4.

[4] "Alexander Baring to Labouchere, London, 15 November 1802", NL-SA, 735/131.

[5] "Draft letter by Francis Baring to J.W. Hope and H. Hope, 12 July 1803", UK-BA, NP1/A/4/55. "Francis Baring to Hope, 21 July 1804", NL-SA, 735/304; "Francis Baring to Henry Hope, Bath, 3 October 1804", UK-BA, NP1/A/4/59.

were put to paper were mostly destroyed later due to the perceived sensitivity of such a large operation in times of international tension.[6] The confusion of these months backfired on Hope and Baring. The lack of written records caused a nasty dispute to arise over the divisions of profits.

From January 1803, the discussions on a Louisiana operation became earnest. The partners explored the risks, contemplated mitigation strategies, and drafted an outline for an operation. The financing of the transfer of Louisiana carried two risks. First was international politics. The Revolutionary Wars had come to an end with the Treaty of Amiens of 25 March 1802. However, international tensions were building up once more, principally between Britain and France. War could affect the Louisiana operation by inhibiting the cession of Louisiana, and was Hope-Baring financially committed already, they could be stuck with financial losses. The second risk was financial. Mediating the transfer of Louisiana entailed one operation to lend the United States the funds to purchase Louisiana and a second operation to pay France for the sale of Louisiana. Both operations had risks of their own. The risk of the American operation is related to the perception of American credit standing. As a young nation, this was not firmly established. Moreover, the United States might require further financing in the future. Additional debt issues would dilute outstanding bonds, including any related to Louisiana. These risks were amplified because the American repayments would be drawn out over a long period, ensuring ample time for unhelpful American financial decisions to bear down on the operation. The principal risk in the French operation related to the payment plan that France demanded. There was a fear that either the size or speed of French demands could outstrip Hope-Baring's liquidity. It should be noted that whilst diplomatically France and the United States were directly linked through treaty transferring Louisiana, from a financial point of view the two operations to finance the sale and purchase of Louisiana were not linked. One could take one operation without the other. However, were one to opt for both operations, there was the additional risk of aligning the timeline of the French operation with the timeline of the American operation. Hope-Baring would have to pay out France in a very short period, whilst having to await American payment for a long, uncertain period. The divergence between the timeline of the French operation and the timeline of the American

[6] "Francis Baring to Labouchere, 15 February 1803", UK-BA, NP1/A/4/4; "Alexander Baring to Labouchere, London, 23 July 1804", NL-SA, 735/304.

operation could be bridged through a third financial operation, the operation to mobilise resources. The principal risk of this operation related to market conditions in London and Amsterdam. Resource mobilisation was easier in good economic times than in times of economic downturn, and here international politics had a great impact. International tension and war could negatively affect investor sentiment, reduce the volume of transactions, interrupt trade, and limit market access. Not only would this depress prices, but it could limit or inhibit the remitting of funds. So, in mediating the transfer of Louisiana Hope-Baring needed to price for the risk of war, to price American credit risk, and to align payments to France with projected liquidity, and, ideally, execute all operations before hostilities resumed.

The principal architects of the operation were Labouchere and Francis Baring, with Henry Hope advising Francis in London. A first outline was drafted by Labouchere on 30 January 1803. Pierre felt that the resumption of war was imminent. This greatly increased the risks, and therefore he proposed to demand a higher interest rate from the Americans than they were accustomed to offer, 6% rather than 5%, and to stagger the payments to France at Fr.1 million France per month until the end of 1806 (at this time Hope-Baring assumed that the transfer would cost Fr.40 million, or $8 million). The French payment schedule was ambitious but could be achieved if the Portuguese diamond loan was on track.[7] The Portugal operation is discussed in depth by Buist.[8] For the Louisiana operation, it is important to know that the Portugal operation progressed in leaps and bounds. Portugal repaid Hope-Baring through diamonds that were sold in Amsterdam. However, the Portuguese envoy had insisted on signing off on every minor transaction, which held up business considerably. Francis and Henry considered war unlikely to resume until the Spring of 1804, if at all. There was thus a bit more time. From London, the biggest doubts regarded liquidity. Francis and Henry felt that the Portugal operation was stagnant, and this might force Hope-Baring to choose but one of the two operations. Francis trembled at the magnitude of the American operation, and if forced to choose, he preferred the French operation. Henry felt that the French

[7] "Labouchere to Alexander Baring, 30 January 1803", UK-BA, NP1/A/4/3; "Labouchere to Alexander Baring, 30 January 1803", NL-SA, 735/5.

[8] Buist, *At Spes Non Fracta*, 383–427.

operation was risky. However, he conceded to Francis that the French operation could be done under any circumstance. The American operation, however, could be conducted only if the Portugal operation was on track. As the Portugal operation was run out of Amsterdam, they reverted to Pierre's advice on whether to take on both operations, or only the French operation. Francis did propose a new payment plan for France in which the payments were larger and sped up. He feared that too slow a release to France could cause Hope-Baring to miss out on the business.[9] In a response of 24 February, Labouchere indicated that he preferred to have both operations. The risk of insufficient liquidity to meet French payments could be addressed through two measures. First, Hope-Baring must insist on distanced payments. Second, the Hope-Baring concern could be expanded to include associated houses in Amsterdam and London. The risk of American operation could be addressed through increasing the price. Labouchere felt that Washington wanted one banking consortium to do the whole American operation. By threatening to take only part of the operation, he felt they could extract a higher price.[10]

By March 1803, the partners agreed to the outlines of the Louisiana operation. Hope-Baring opted to take both the French operation and the American operation, though the latter only on the conditions that the stock which was to be created was fully transferable, that interest and principal was payable in Amsterdam and/or London, that neither the transfer of stock nor the payment required American ministerial or notarial consent, and that the Americans provided adequate security which was to be deposited in Europe.[11] Despite the broad agreement, some details remained unsettled, most notably on the French payment plan and whether or not to expand the consortium for additional liquidity. The partners were aware of these loose ends, but they decided to leave the matters for their negotiator to decide on the spot. This was unwise. Both issues became embroiled in the dispute over profits.

[9] "Francis Baring to Labouchere, 15 February 1803", UK-BA, NP1/A/4/4.

[10] "Labouchere to Francis Baring, 24 February 1803", NL-SA, 735/5.

[11] "Labouchere to Francis Baring, 1 March 1803", NL-SA, 735/5; "Labouchere to Alexander Baring, 2 March 1803", UK-BA, NP1/A/4/6; ibidem, NL-SA, 735/5; "Francis Baring to Labouchere [and Alexander Baring], 21 April 1803", UK-BA, NP1/A/4/7; "Labouchere to Francis Baring, 28 April 1803", UK-BA, NP1/A/4/8.

Alexander Baring was chosen to close the deal in Paris and then to travel the Washington to hammer out the details of the American operation.[12] Alexander was not chosen because he was the best negotiator. He was simply in line for the next job. Both Henry Hope and Francis Baring were of age and unwilling to undertake such an arduous task. John Williams was probably not capable of undertaking the task. Besides, he was occupied with the re-establishment of the Amsterdam office. And so, Hope-Baring had only two negotiators available: Alexander and Pierre. In selecting the negotiator Hope-Baring would alternate between the two. Alexander was employed for the Maine lands, and Pierre did the Portuguese diamond loan. As Alexander was up next, he was selected for the Louisiana operation. Pierre later took up the even larger business of the Spanish subsidy.

The Financial Contract

The sum that the United States paid for Louisiana was Fr.80 million. Fr.20 million consisted of French debt to American citizens that the United States assumed. This was a domestic affair. What remained to be financed was Fr.60 million. The French budget for Year XI (23 September 1802–23 September 1803) was about Fr.632 million. The receipts for Louisiana thus amounted to slightly under 10% of annual expenses, making a considerable, but not significant one-off payment.[13] However, as France sold Louisiana in anticipation of war, it makes more sense to understand the sum in the context of French war finances. Nicolas François Mollien, the head of the French *caisse d'amortissement* and later Minster of the Treasury, assessed that the average annual maintenance cost of a single French soldier in times of war was Fr.700 per year.[14] The sale of Louisiana could thus allow Bonaparte to field a contingent of about 85,000 men for 1 year. This is a substantial contribution to the war effort. The Americans bought Louisiana for $11.25 million. At the time, American public finances were in a good state. For 1804 the American

[12] "Power of Attorney for Alexander Baring from Francis Baring & Co., 3 May 1803", NL-SA, 735/3754; "Power of Attorney for Alexander Baring from Hope, 5 May 1803", NL-SA, 735/3754.

[13] Branda, *Le prix de la gloire*, 575.

[14] N.F. Mollien, *Mémiores d'un Ministre du Trésor public, 1780–1815*, 3 vols (Paris: Guillaumin et Co., 1898), I: III-XIX.

Secretary of Treasury, Albert Gallatin, anticipated ordinary fiscal revenue at $10.4 million. With expenditure at $9.8 million, the American Treasury ran a healthy surplus of $600,000.[15] Notwithstanding the surplus, the price of Louisiana was greater than the annual ordinary fiscal revenue and thus there never was any doubt that America required financing.

The negotiations on the financial operations to transfer Louisiana took place simultaneous to the diplomatic negotiations. In fact, it is quite likely that the diplomatic negotiations were informed by Hope-Baring's financial considerations. In the treaty and conventions of 30 April 1803, America and France agreed on detailed terms of payment. The United States would pay France $11.25 million in 6% interest-bearing stock. The use of the term stock might be confusing to the modern reader. In modern parlance, stocks are financial securities that represent part-ownership of a company or enterprise, including a claim on assets and earnings. However, the contracting parties employed the term in the broader sense to include both stock in the modern sense and what now is referred to as bonds, financial securities that represent an investment in the debt issued by a government or company. The stock could be issued unrecorded or recorded. Unrecorded stock was issued as obligations to the bearer with coupons. Recorded stock was issued either as book-entry stock, whereby ownership was recorded in the debt books of the issuing authority, in this case, the American Department of Treasury, or as certificates of stock, whereby the debt holder is given a physical piece of paper that represents the holder's ownership. Hope-Baring opted for the latter because it best balanced security with transferability.[16] Whilst the American payment consisted of what is now referred to as bonds, this study adheres to the name employed by the contracting parties, stock or Louisiana stock. Interest on the Louisiana stock was payable biannually in Amsterdam, London, or Paris. Redemption was annually at a rate of no less than $3 million per year, starting 15 years after the exchange of the ratifications. These terms make sense in light of another contract, which was signed by Alexander and Barbé-Marbois that same day, with which France immediately transferred the Louisiana stock to Hope-Baring for a sum of Fr.52 million. In return for the Fr.8 million discount, Hope-Baring committed to accelerated payments: they would pay Fr.6 million

[15] "Report by Albert Gallatin, October 1803", UK-BA, NP1/A/4/17.

[16] "Alexander Baring to Francis Baring, 21 October 1803", UK-BA, NP1/A/4/19.

in month 1, and then Fr.2 million monthly until completion, with the last payment falling in month 24.

Hope-Baring had not agreed to a starting date for payments to France. Instead, payment was made dependent on the reception of the certificates of stock to the sum of $11.25 million. The certificates would be created within three months after the ratification of the diplomatic treaty and conventions for the cession of Louisiana and the fulfilment of the transfer of Louisiana. The certificates were divided into three equal tranches. Alexander would travel to Washington to receive the first tranche and return them to Hope-Baring's custody in Europe. The other two tranches would be dispatched to Europe by a representative of the American government, who would deposit them with a trustee, who was to be the American Minister Plenipotentiary at Paris, Livingston. Payments would commence within 30 days of official notice being received of Alexander having in his possession the first tranche of certificates and of the second and third tranches being dispatched to Europe. The payments to France would be made in bills of exchange. Blank bills of exchange to the sum of Fr.52 million were also deposited with Livingston in Paris. Upon commencement of the payments, Livingston transferred one-third of the bills of exchange to the French treasury. Once the first third of payments was completed, Livingston would transfer the second tranche of American certificates to Hope-Baring, and the second third of the bills of exchange to the French treasury. Upon completion of this part of the operation, the final tranche of certificates and the last bills of exchange would be released. Considering the steps to be taken, Alexander did not expect payments to France to commence until January 1804, or December 1803 earliest.[17]

[17] "Engagement souscrit par Mr Alex. Baring fondé de pouvoir de Maisons Franc. Baring & co. de Londres, et Hope & co. d'Amsterdam, relativement à la négociation d'un fonds américan, montant à 11,250,000 Piastres [Dollars]", NL-SA, 735/1911; ibidem, USA-LoC, *Louisiana Miscellany*, 15, or "Contract for the purchase of transfer to H&Co & Fr.B. & Co. of 11,250,000 Dollars 6pct Amer. Stock from the French Gov., 2–3 May 1803", NL-SA, 735/3754; "Template bill of exchange, 2 May 1803", NL-SA, 735/3754; "Proces verbal de la livraison des lettres de change, 3 May 1803", NL-SA, 735/1911; "Analysis of the engagement made by A.B. [Alexander Baring] at Paris in the name of H[ope] & Co. and F[rancis B[aring] & Co. with the Treasury with the concurrence & by desire of the American Ministers, 1803", NL-SA, 735/1909; ibidem, NL-SA, 735/3754; "Barbé-Marbois to Livingston and Monroe, 4 May 1803", NL-SA, 735/3754; ibidem, USA-LoC, *Louisiana Miscellany*, 15. "Livingston to Madison,

The financial contract was a good balance of interests. France received full payment in 24 months and the United States had the benefit of deferring payment for 15 years, whilst already taking possession of Louisiana. The risks of the financial operations were borne by Hope-Baring, but they had minimised their exposure through four provisions. First, payment was conditional upon the ratification and execution of the diplomatic treaty and conventions regarding the cession of Louisiana. Second, with Livingston as trustee of the American certificates and the bills of exchange to France, the United States had a continued stake in the financial operation. Three, payments to France were staggered over two years. Four, Hope-Baring was never exposed to more than one-third of the liabilities to France.

The Resource Mobilisation Operations

The operation to mobilise the funds to pay France was decided between the partners. Neither France nor the United States were directly involved. In short, funds could be mobilised by selling the Louisiana stock and using the proceeds to pay France, by keeping the Louisiana stock and allocating revenue from other operations towards France, by employing trade credit to allow France to acquire goods and resources, or by a combination of the above. Each strategy had its benefits and drawbacks. Selling the stock would allow for a quick and easy resolution of the operation, freeing time and resources for other operations. However, one would miss out on the lucrative interest payments. Keeping the stock secured the interest payments, but it meant that capital would be tied up for a lengthy period. Any risk emanating from the United States also remained with the concern. Employing trade credit effectively merged the financial operation with commercial operations more broadly. Benefits were that no capital need be mobilised, new business would be infused into Hope-Baring's commercial networks, and additional commissions could be made on trading operations. However, employing trade credit would make the operation much more complex and involve much more paperwork.

The operation for mobilising funds does not seem to have been set, probably because some flexibility in meeting challenges and demands as they emerge is always needed. The talk of having the Portugal operation

30 July 1803", *State papers*, 224–225; "Livingston and Monroe to Barbé-Marbois, 28 May 1803", NL-SA, 735/3754.

on track indicates that Hope-Baring hoped to pay France with at least some revenue from other operations, but presumably, the scale of the Louisiana operation was such that Hope-Baring could not but employ all avenues for raising funds. It is clear that mobilising funds was devolved to the various stakeholders as showed in Table 4.1.

Several observations can be made. First, there is no distinction between Hope & Co. of Amsterdam and Henry Hope & Co. of London. They are treated as one house. It is unclear why. There is an impression that Henry Hope was reluctant to participate in the Louisiana operation because of wanting to retire from active business. Second, $5 million was domiciled in Amsterdam, and $6.25 million was domiciled in London. This may be considered a reflection of the perceived demand of both markets. Third, Baring took $5,375,000, Hope took $2,875,000, and the Hope-De Smeth-Willink consortium took $3 million, or a ratio of participation of 47.8% for Baring, 25.5% for Hope and 26.7% for the consortium of Amsterdam houses. The ratios are difficult to interpret as they reflect a combination of factors: ambition, the strategy for mobilising resources, and the extent of financial and commercial networks. In any case, the ratios of participation changed considerably, and so they will be discussed below. The reference of the Hope-De Smeth-Willink consortium requires elaboration. As mentioned, during the discussion on a potential operation on Louisiana, Labouchere advised that the risk of constrained liquidity could be addressed by expanding the Hope-Baring consortium to include

Table 4.1 Allocation of the Louisiana stock

Tranche	*Holder*	*Domicile*
First tranche		
$1,250,000	Hope-De Smeth-Willink consortium	Amsterdam
$2,500,000	Francis Baring & Co.	London
Second tranche		
$1,750,000	Hope-De Smeth-Willink consortium	Amsterdam
$2,000,000	Hope & Co. and Francis Baring & Co.	London
Third tranche		
$2,000,000	Hope & Co. and Francis Baring & Co.	Amsterdam
$1,750,000	Hope & Co. and Francis Baring & Co.	London

"List of certificates of Louisiana six per cent stock", NL-SA, 735/3754; ibidem, NL-SA, 735/3756.

partners in Amsterdam and London.[18] Francis did not follow up on the advice.[19] Hope included the house of Raymond and Theodoor de Smeth and the house of Jan and Wilhem Willink.

De Smeth and Willink were both Amsterdam merchant-banking houses of the second order, below the likes of Hope. Unfortunately, the business archives of both houses are lost, and so very little is known. Only an incomplete picture can be pieced together based on a scattering of sources. The Willinks had their roots in the east of the Netherlands. A certain Jan Willink is registered as a merchant in the city of Deventer, from where he moved to Amsterdam in 1698. His grandsons Wilhem (1750–1841) and Jan (1751–1826) renamed the firm to carry their names and built it into a house of standing. Willink had a reputation for conspicuous consumption and maximising profits whilst eschewing hard work. This was frowned upon in Amsterdam, where frugality, keeping the costs of business low, and hard work were valued. Outside the Netherlands, however, these traits gave the Willinks an aura of creditworthiness. The Willinks are best known for operations in America, including the Dutch loans to America after independence, and the real estate investments through the Holland Land Company. By 1803, the partnership had expanded to include Jan and Wilhem's sons, Jan Willink Janszoon and Wilhem Willink Junior. The third son of Wilhem, also Jan, was established as a merchant in New York.[20]

A little more is known about the De Smeths. The origins of the family lay either in Cologne or Brussels—the family moved between these places several times. The founder of the Dutch branch is Joost de Smeth (1587–1662). Joost was a registered merchant in Cologne, but he moved to Amsterdam shortly before passing away. His son, also Joost de Smeth (1626–1704), continued the business with a Dutch associate to become Egidio van den Bempden & Joost de Smeth. The firm traded in silk on England, Spain, Italy, and the Levant. Later they branched out into financial services. Under Joost's son, Pieter (1665–1724) the business prospered. Pieter became the first of the family to be elected to office

[18] "Labouchere to Francis Baring, 24 February-1 March 1803", UK-BA, NP1/A/4/5.

[19] "Francis Baring & Co. to Hope & Co., 15 October 1803", NL-SA, 735/300.

[20] P. van Eeghen, "Willink", *Nederland's Patriciaat* 36 (The Hague: Centraal Bureau voor Genealogie, 1950), 368–378; Van Winter, *Het aandeel van den Amsterdamsche handel*, I: 59–87, 223–334.

in the political-economic institutions of Amsterdam, which is an indication of his social rise as well as his acumen as a merchant-banker. Pieter's untimely death in 1724 threatened the existence of the firm. Fortunately, Pieter's second wife, Helena Gertruy Colonius (1681–1735) continued the business. She recruited her two young sons, Raymond (1706–1784) and Theodoor (1710–1772), to become Widow Pieter de Smeth & Sons. In 1736, after the passing of Helena, the brothers renamed the firm Raymond & Theodoor de Smeth & Co.. After a trusted associate, Alexander Hurter, retired in 1746, the firm simply became Raymond & Theodoor de Smeth. The house is mostly known for its loans to Russia, placing Hcf.17 million in 1769–1782.[21] However, De Smeth were replaced as bankers to Russia by Hope, and since then, the house appears to have reduced their active issuing operations in favour of entering local politics. Financial operations seem to have been limited to underwriting loans oriented on France. Consequently, De Smeth developed good contacts with French houses, in particular, the house of Hottinguer, who ostensibly was not to be approached by Amsterdam houses without referral by De Smeth. In 1803, the firm was run by Theodoor's son Pieter (1753–1810), and an associate, Willem Gerrit van de Poll.[22]

The how and why of De Smeth and Willink joining with Hope to market the Louisiana stock in Amsterdam is obscured by a lack of sources. One can take Labouchere's word that Hope felt necessitated to invite the houses to ensure adequate liquidity for the payments to France. There could also be more to the matter. Francis preferred no other houses to join. If additional funds were needed, Baring would provide these. Hope's broadening of the concern against their partner's wishes, and with it the opening of the books and the sharing of the profits, could relate to several underlying dynamics in the Amsterdam market. First, it may be that Hope had difficulty in re-establishing the office in Amsterdam. Hope's departure from Amsterdam had left a vacuum for others to fill. One may imagine that Amsterdam houses were not keen to see a

[21] "Genealogy De Smeth", The Netherlands, Hoge Raad van Adel, Archief van de Hoge Raad van Adel, III/D/497; Elias, *De vroedschap*, II: 796–800; "Notarial act regarding the bequeathal of the common fund of Original Louisiana Stock, 3 August 1804", NL-SA, 735/1900.

[22] "Labouchere to Francis Baring, 24 February 1803", NL-SA, 735/5.

powerful house return and favour British partners over Amsterdam partners. De Smeth and Willink were embedded in the political and economic institutions of Amsterdam, and they could well frustrate Hope's return to Amsterdam. Henry Hope, at least, justified the broadening of the concern to prevent public opinion in Amsterdam being turned against Hope-Baring's Louisiana operation.[23] It may also be that the Amsterdam operation was broadened to stifle competition. As mentioned, Francis suspected that Willink was on the scent of an operation. Labouchere suspected that De Smeth was onto something in Paris.[24] With Willink's relations to the United States and De Smeth's relations with French houses, there was a potential for the two houses combining to pitch a rival operation to Paris and Washington. Hope could have invited De Smeth and Willink to join to prevent that competition. Finally, the inclusion of the two houses may relate to the structure of Amsterdam's credit market. In contrast to markets like London, where stock was usually resold on the secondary market, in Amsterdam stock was often consolidated into a common fund, and derivatives were issued on the Amsterdam market. In such operations, it was customary to broaden the consortium of lenders, each of whom would have their own underwriters, who tended to their own clients in their own markets. In such a manner, all would share in the business and the profits, and all markets could be tapped. A comment by Francis Baring, in which he acknowledged that Hope might need to "[…] consolidate a certain amount of […] certificates & found thereon a subordinate loan in the Dutch manner", lends credence to this interpretation.[25] Of course, possibly all three dynamics fed into the decision to include De Smeth and Willink.

The Ratification of the Treaty and Conventions

[23] "Henry Hope to Francis Baring, 3 July 1803", NL-SA, 735/464.

[24] "Labouchere to Francis Baring, 24 February 1803", NL-SA, 735/5; "Labouchere to Alexander Baring, 9 August 1804, NL-SA, 735/304.

[25] "F. Baring to Labouchere [and Alexander Baring], 21 April 1803", UK-BA, NP1/A/4/7.

No sooner had the financial contract been concluded than problems arose. Within three weeks of signing the treaty, Franco–British relations broke down and hostilities resumed.[26] The renewal of hostilities put pressure on the French role in the cession of Louisiana. On the one hand, the war with Britain was sure to test France to her limits. All the nation's resources would need to be harnessed to emerge victorious. In this light, the payments for Louisiana would be welcome sooner rather than later. On the other hand, the possibility that Britain would seek to impede France from taking possession of Louisiana could not be ignored. If France could not take possession, she could not cede the territory to the United States, and the whole arrangement would unravel. So, with the aim of concluding the transfer of Louisiana to the United States as soon as possible, on 22 May 1803, Bonaparte ratified the treaty and two conventions.[27] If Bonaparte hoped for an equally swift ratification on the part of the United States, he was to be disappointed.

The treaty and conventions did not arrive in America until 14 July 1803. Congress was adjourned, but Jefferson convened a Special Session of Congress on 17 October 1803, in which he spoke on the transfer of Louisiana and introduced the treaty and conventions for consideration.[28] With 24 yeas and 7 nays, the Senate gave its constitutional sanction that same day. The treaty and conventions then passed to the House, where a lively debate erupted. For a large part, the debate centred on constitutional arguments. In the early nineteenth century, the American republic was a project still in the works. The constitution was a framework for government that still needed to be elaborated into a working system. To start, the constitution was unclear on whether treaty-making powers lay exclusively with the executive. And so the adherents of a strict interpretation of the American constitution challenged the acquisition of Louisiana on account of Jefferson's misappropriating treaty-making powers. Neither did the constitution contain provisions for the acquisition of territory. And so it was wholly unclear if the United States could annex Louisiana,

[26] A. Mikaberidze, *The Napoleonic Wars. A Global History* (Oxford: Oxford University Press, 2020), 122–172; C.D. Hall, *British Strategy in the Napoleonic War 1803–15* (Manchester: Manchester University Press, 1992), 102–103.

[27] Barbé-Marbois, *Histoire de la Louisiane*, 335–339.

[28] "Madison to Livingston and Monroe, 29 July 1803", *State papers*, 222–224; "Message from the President of the United States, 17 October 1803", *State papers*, 251–253.

and if so, how the new territory would be governed. Moreover, there was the question of whether the Louisianans had a right to be given a say in their future, or whether their liberty could be subjected to the needs and interests of the United States. Concern over the impact on domestic politics also fed into the debate. The states on the eastern seaboard feared that the acquisition of Louisiana would shift the political centre of gravity westwards to their detriment, and the Federalist Party feared that the inhabitants' inclination towards the Democratic-Republicans would upset the existing political balance between the two parties. A final line of argument contested the contents of the treaty. First was asked whether the price of Fr.80 million was not too much for a territory with so few resources. Second, it was questioned whether the acquisition of Louisiana resolved the problem it sought to address. The principal aim of acquiring Louisiana, in particular the port of New Orleans, was to grant the Western Territories a commercial outlet and thereby thwart any possibility of an independent state being established in North America outside the United States. The treaty acquired New Orleans, but the acquisition also included a vast territory west of the Mississippi that was certain to attract American colonists, thereby once more giving rise to the possibility of uncontrolled, and uncontrollable, state-formation outside the United States. Or, in other words, the problem of the possibility of an independent state emerging on the fringes of the United States was not resolved, but merely moved further west. A related issue regarded the Floridas. The American government had hoped to acquire all territory east of the Mississippi, including the Floridas, which it believed had been, or would be, ceded to France. However, Spain retained the Floridas. Some in the opposition now argued that, as a result, the port of New Orleans was vulnerable to foreign attack, in particular from the Floridas. The two issues above combined, when voices went up for the trans-Mississippi West to be exchanged with Spain for the Floridas. By and large, these challenges to the treaty were easily seen off, not in the least because the Jefferson Administration held a majority in both the House and the Senate.[29]

[29] "Alexander Baring to Hope & Co., Baltimore, 28 September 1803", NL-SA, 735/300; ibidem, NL-SA, 735/302; Barbé-Marbois, *Histoire de la Louisiane*, 344–350; Kastor, *The Nation's Crucible*, 35–52; E.S. Brown, *The Constitutional History of the Louisiana Purchase 1803–1812* (New York: Cosimo, 2005).

There was but one objection that had a bearing on the financial operation, and that regarded the Franco-Spanish agreement on the retrocession of Louisiana underpinning the Franco-American treaty of 30 April. Doubts existed over whether Louisiana had been retroceded to France, and whether France had legal proof of this. Were this not the case, France could not legally transfer the territory to the United States. To guard against this eventuality, on 31 October 1803 the House decided to ratify the treaty and conventions and to agree in principle to the creation of the stock with which France was to be paid. However, the stock was not to be created nor transferred until Washington had received confirmation that the territory had been taken possession of. To that purpose, an expedition was sent out.[30]

The House's concerns were not without merit. Since the formal retrocession of Louisiana at Aranjuez on 21 March 1801, France had neglected to send an expedition to take possession of the territory. Louisiana remained under Spanish administration and with war resumed, it was unlikely that France could successfully dispatch an expedition any time soon. France's imbroglio offered Spain an opportunity to press for political advantage. Spain seized the moment to refuse to recognise the cession of Louisiana to France, ostensibly because France had agreed not to cede the Louisiana Territory to any other nation than Spain. There is no mention of any such obligation in any of the Franco-Spanish treaties, so it is difficult to determine if France made any such commitment or not. It is not improbable that Spain seized on the transfer of Louisiana to advance her European interests. Per Treaty of Aranjuez, Spain had exchanged Louisiana for the Grand Duchy of Tuscany, but European powers were reticent to recognise Spanish possession. Spain may well have resisted recognising the transfer of Louisiana until she felt France exerted herself

[30] Bush, *The Louisiana Purchase*, 72–85; "Alexander Baring to Hope & Co., Baltimore, 10 October 1803", NL-SA, 735/300; "Alexander Baring to Francis Baring, 21 October 1803", UK-BA, NP1/A/4/19; "Madison to Monroe, 24 October 1803", *State papers*, 260–261; "Act enabling the taking of possession of Louisiana, 31 October 1803", NL-SA, 735/484; "Madison to Barbé-Marbois, 4 November 1803", *State papers*, 264; "Madison to Livingston, 9 November 1803", *State papers*, 264–265; "An act authorising the creation of a stock, to the amount of $11,250,000 for the purpose of carrying into effect the convention of the 30th April 1803 [...] between the United States of America and the French Republic [...], Washington, 10 November 1803", NL-SA, 735/1912; ibidem, NL-SA, 735/484.

satisfactorily to help gain that recognition.[31] Whatever Spain's true intentions, they would not be known until the American expedition arrived in Louisiana to take possession.

The Anticipation

After the treaty and conventions were signed, both Monroe and Alexander continued to linger in Paris. Monroe put out feelers in preparation for the possible acquisition of the Floridas. Alexander wrapped up some business related to the Maine lands.[32] By early June, the American negotiators became aware of French discontent over the possibility of a drawn-out ratification in Washington and a subsequent delay in the start of payments to France. Monroe and Livingston feared that if French discontent grew too strong, France might reconsider the cession of Louisiana.[33] To bind France to the transfer of Louisiana, on 7 June 1803, Monroe offered an advance payment, or anticipation, of Fr.10 million. However, Barbé-Marbois refused the offer. Monroe then decided to depart for Spain to continue his mission, when he received notice that Rufus King, the American ambassador to the court of St. James, had left London without appointing a chargé d'affaires. Monroe was appointed his successor in London. He left France on 17 July 1803.[34] Around that time, Barbé-Marbois revived the idea of an anticipation. He requested Fr.2 million in trade credit in America, and a credit line of Fr.8 million. On 30 July 1803, Alexander and Barbé-Marbois agreed to allow France to draw Fr.2 million on Hope's associates Willings & Francis of Philadelphia for a commission of 2½%. The credit line was dropped, because Hope wanted the sum made available in Amsterdam and they could not agree on an exchange rate with Barbé-Marbois.[35] With the matter seemingly

31 "Alexander Baring to Francis Baring, Washington, 21 October 1803", UK-BA, NP1/A/4/19; "Alexander Baring to Hope & Co., Washington 5 November 1803", NL-SA, 735/152; Fugier, *Napoléon et l'Espagne*, I: 189–197; Barbé-Marbois, *Histoire de la Louisiane*, 345–346.

32 "Hope to Francis Baring, 3 June 1803", NL-SA, 735/300.

33 "Livingston and Monroe to Madison, Paris, 7 June 1803", *State papers*, 209–214.

34 McGrath, *James Monroe*, 245–247.

35 "Hope to Willings & Francis, 20 May 1803", NL-SA, 735/5; "Propositions faites an Ministre du Trésor public par Mr. Alexandre Baring, fondé de pouvoir de la maison Hope d'Amsterdam, 30 July 1803", NL-SA, 735/1911; "Barbé-Marbois to Willing &

concluded, Alexander left for London to report on his travails before setting off to the United States to receive the first tranche.

By mid-August 1803, Barbé-Marbois renewed his calls for a credit line. Hope was willing to open negotiations on the condition that America provided security.[36] The American negotiators had been given the authority to apply up to $2 million for securing the cession of Louisiana. Monroe was now inclined to pledge this sum as a security for an anticipation to France, and he drafted and signed a guarantee, which he forwarded to Livingston in Paris for his co-signature. However, Livingston refused to sign. On the face of it, the dispute hinged on whether or not the negotiators had the authority to apply the $2 million after the treaty on the transfer of Louisiana was concluded. Livingston argued that, since France was already committed to ceding Louisiana, the money could not be touched. Monroe argued that the need to keep Franco-American relations amicable outweighed any overstepping of authority and any possible financial risk. On a deeper level, the dispute flowed from a rivalry between Monroe and Livingston, rooted in the latter's need for recognition.[37]

The rivalry had great ramifications for the cession of Louisiana. The longer the dispute lasted, the more discontented France grew. And the more discontented France was, the greater the chances that the diplomatic agreement on the transfer of Louisiana collapsed. The impact of the dispute on the financial operation followed from that. A collapse of the diplomatic treaty would mean that all effort to develop the financial operation was wasted. Yet, any financier would conclude that if the United

Francis, 13 September 1803", in *Willing Letters and Papers, Edited with a Biographical Essay of Thomas Willing of Philadelphia (1731–1821)*, ed. T. Willing Balch (Philadelphia: Allen, Lane and Scott, 1922), 158–160; "Alexander Baring to Hope & Co., Paris, 1 August 1803", NL-SA, 735/302; "Monroe to Livingston, 20 August 1803", *The Writings of James Monroe*, IV: 63–69; "Alexander Baring to Francis Baring, Philadelphia, 26 November 1803", UK-BA, NP1/A/4/26; "Hope & Co. to Barbé-Marbois, 16 January 1804", NL-SA, 735/6.

[36] "Barbé-Marbois to Hope & Co., Paris, 23 August 1803", NL-SA, 735/300; "Hope to Francis Baring & Co., 30/31 August. 1803", NL-SA, 735/302; "[Labouchere] to Alexander Baring, 31 August 1803", NL-SA, 735/299; "Labouchere to Barbé-Marbois, 1 September 1803", NL-SA, 735/134.

[37] "Anonymous [Dan Parker] to Alexander Baring, 12 September 1803", UK-BA, NP1/A/4/69; "Monroe to Livingston, 20 August 1803", *The Writings of James Monroe*, IV: 63–69; "Monroe to Livingston, 9 October 1803", *The Writings of James Monroe*, IV: 78–92; Brecher, *Negotiating the Louisiana Purchase*, 80–105.

States was willing to jeopardise the diplomatic treaty, their commitment was hesitant at best. There was no sense in extending credit on that basis. On 15 October 1803, Hope-Baring suspended all discussion of a further anticipation to France until clarity on the American commitment to the treaty emerged.[38]

Livingston's intransigence soon became untenable, yet his ego did not permit him to concede at once. By early November, Livingston indicated that he was willing to co-sign the guarantee if Monroe clarified some outstanding issues.[39] By 14 November, Livingston conceded to signing the guarantee in principle.[40] Finally, on 2 December 1803, Livingston transferred the American guarantee of $2 million, signed by both him and Monroe, to Hope for an anticipation to France to be made.[41] Livingston declared that "certain reasons" determined him to comply.[42] It may well be that the reasons were prompted by a note from Madison, in which he expressed his disapproval of the money intended for securing the cession not having been applied.[43]

Livingston's change of mind persuaded Labouchere to travel to Paris to negotiate the details of an anticipation. The deal was done quickly. On 8 December 1803, Labouchere and Barbé-Marbois agreed on a further anticipation of Fr.8 million. The divisive issue of the exchange rate was resolved through disbursing about one-half of the sum in Amsterdam: Fr.3.33 million in bills on Hope & Co., and about half in Paris: Fr.2.5 million in credit on Charles Joseph Baguenault de Puchesse, a Paris associate of Hope, and Fr.1.6 million in French paper—bank notes and drafts on the Cashier General of the Public Treasury. Another Fr.352,800 was

[38] "Francis Baring & Co. to Hope & Co., 15 October 1803", NL-SA, 735/300; "Hope & Co to Francis Baring & Co., 25 October 1803", NL-SA, 735/300.

[39] "Barbé-Marbois to Hope & Co., 4 November 1803", NL-SA, 735/300; "Hope & Co. to Francis Baring, 9 November 1803", NL-SA, 735/299; "Labouchere to Barbé-Marbois, 10 November 1803", NL-SA, 735/5.

[40] "Livingston to Henry Hope, Paris, 14 November 1803", NL-SA, 735/480; "Labouchere to Barbé-Marbois, 14 November 1803", NL-SA, 735/5; "Labouchere to Barbé-Marbois, 14 November 1803", NL-SA, 735/134.

[41] "Livingston to Labouchere, 2 December 1803", UK-BA, NP1/A/4/34; "Livingston to Henry Hope, Paris, 2 December 1803", NL-SA, 735/480.

[42] "Livingston to Henry Hope, Paris, 14 November 1803", NL-SA, 735/480.

[43] "Monroe to Madison, 25 November 1803", *The Writings of James Monroe*, IV: 99–107.

disbursed in trade credit to Jean Calamis, an associate of Hope in Livorno. The remainder, Fr.213,867, was Hope's commission.[44] Livingston was authorised to discharge the equivalent sum of bills from the first third of payments to France.[45] The payments were met from revenue from the Portugal operation and other sources of revenue in Amsterdam.[46] The anticipation, together with the trade credit that had been disbursed via Willings & Francis, was secured on an American guarantee which was transferred to Hope the following day.[47]

The anticipation was a good step towards concluding the transfer of Louisiana. The release of funds by the United States was the clearest sign yet that the American government was determined to bring the treaty to a conclusion. France's acceptance of the anticipation meant that she was firmly involved too. The American and French financial commitment thus reduced the overall risk to the financial operation, and Hope pocketed a handsome commission. And even if the Franco-American treaty fell through, the American guarantee ensured that Hope-Baring would not be left with financial losses.

The Certificates

44 "Propositions made to the Minister of the [French] Public Treasure by PC Labouchere, agent of the house of Hope & Co of Amsterdam", UK-BA, NP1/A/4/35; "Labouchere to Francis Baring, 8 December 1803", UK-BA, NP1/A/4/33; "Procès verbal de remise de 52,000,000 francs de lettres de change, tirés sur le maison Hope, d'Amsterdam, en éxécution de l'engagement de Mr. Alexandre Baring du 13 Floréal an XI [3 May 1803]/Procés verbal de la livraison des lettres de change", NL-SA, 735/1911.

45 "Labouchere to Livingston, Paris, 7 December 1803", NL-SA, 735/6.

46 "Labouchere to Alexander Baring, Amsterdam, [end of July 1803]", UK-BA, NP1/A/4/14.

47 "Livingston to Labouchere, 9 December 1803", UK-BA, NP1/A/4/34; "Livingston to Henry Hope, Paris, 9 December 1803", NL-SA, 735/480; "Labouchere to Livingston, Paris, 9 December 1803", NL-SA, 735/6.

On 14 August 1803, Alexander left England to receive the first tranche of the certificates.[48] In the haste of concluding the transfer of Louisiana, several aspects of the American payment remained undefined or unclear.[49] These aspects were important because they determined the risk and margins of the American operation, as well as the ability to mobilise resources.

Broadly speaking there were three interrelated issues. First was the proprietorship and transferability of the stock: in whose name would the stock and certificates be made out, and would stock be transferable without reference to a notary or an American official? Proprietorship of the certificates was important because it offered legal protection and gave the holders a key role in the payment of interest and principal. Simultaneously, easy transferability of the stock was desired as it increased the appeal of the stock and facilitated resource mobilisation. Second was interest payments. Key questions remained unanswered, such as when would interest commence, who would mediate the interest payments, where would interest payments be made, and could interest payments be transferred from one market to another. The answers to these questions determined how much and with whom interest accrued. The final issue was the exchange rate. Trade and communication between Europe and America were still so slow-paced that it was near impossible to anticipate exchange rate fluctuations. Thus, this needed to be negotiated. In addition to these anticipated issues, confusion emerged over the terms of redemption of the Louisiana stock.

On 25 September 1803, Alexander arrived in America to open negotiations. Alexander's instructions have not been found in the archives. Fortunately, the risks of a transatlantic crossing in the Fall were not lost on Hope-Baring, and they took precautions for safeguarding the American payment by nominating an American agent, Robert Gilmor, as a stand-in in case Alexander was prevented from arriving. From Gilmor's instructions, one can learn that Hope-Baring desired the certificates to

[48] "Alexander Baring to Hope & Co., London, 9 August 1803", NL-SA, 735/299; "Power of attorney for Alexander Baring by Hope & Co., 20 July 1803", USA-LoC, *Louisiana Miscellany*, 15; ibidem, USA-NA, RG/56; "Power of attorney for Alexander Baring by Francis Baring & Co., 12 August 1803", USA-LoC, *Louisiana Miscellany*, 15; ibidem, USA-NA, RG/56.

[49] "Alexander Baring to Hope & Co., Paris, 6 June 1803", NL-SA, 735/299.

be made out in their names only: $5 million for Hope and $6.25 million for Baring, though with the possibility to alter the proportions within the first two years to have the ability to respond to market volatility resulting from the resumption of hostilities. On interest, Hope-Baring were not concerned with the dates of biannual payment, but they did insist interest commence "from the signature of the treaty in Paris".[50] It is unclear whether this refers to the signing of the treaty and conventions on the cession of Louisiana (30 April/2 May 1803), or the French ratification (22 May 1803). Hope-Baring also demanded that interest payments in Amsterdam were paid exclusively through Hope and interest payments in London were paid exclusively through Baring for which they were to receive a ½% commission, though any stockholder was to be given the opportunity to receive interest in America. The exchange rate was to be set at par, which was Hcf.2.5 and 4 shillings and sixpence sterling to the dollar. The sense was that most of these issues could be hammered out easily. The only issue likely to be contested was the proposed starting date for interest. It was probable that Washington insisted on interest commencing from the ratification in America. The point was to be pressed through offering a concession. Hope-Baring had become aware that Washington was keen to drop Paris as a location for interest payments, ostensibly because Franco-American commercial relations were too restricted to accommodate large monetary flows. Alexander could agree to this if interest were to commence from the French signature. Whilst dropping Paris was presented as a concession to the United States, in fact, it suited Hope-Baring because they had less ability to shape that market than Amsterdam or London.[51]

From the internal correspondence, it becomes clear that Alexander was dispatched to America without full consensus on the issue of proprietorship of the certificates. It will be recalled that Hope of Amsterdam had included De Smeth and Willink in the Amsterdam resource mobilisation operation. The Amsterdam consortium now demanded that the names of De Smeth and Willink be included on the certificates so that they enjoyed benefits and legal protection equal to the other parties. However, London resisted the demand. Henry Hope pointed out that there was an interval

[50] "Francis Baring to Robert Gilmor, 15 August 1803", UK-BA, NP1/A/4/16.

[51] "Francis Baring to Robert Gilmor, 15 August 1803", UK-BA, NP1/A/4/16; "Labouchere to Francis Baring, 28 April 1803", UK-BA, NP1/A/4/8.

between the drawing up of the certificates and the moment when it was clear whether the Hope-De Smeth-Willink resource mobilisation operation was successful. During this interval, risk and responsibility rested solely with Hope, and therefore it was logical that the legal protections lay with Hope too. Besides, the certificates with appropriate powers of attorney could always be deposited with the Amsterdam consortium once they were received in Europe.[52] It was at this unresolved point of the discussion that Alexander was sent off.[53] One week later, Labouchere reported that the prospects of the Amsterdam resource mobilisation operation looked good, and he pressed for De Smeth and Willink to be included on the certificates.[54] London conceded, and on 9 September 1803 Alexander's instructions were updated.[55]

The communication would not have reached Alexander until mid-October earliest, by which time negotiations with the American Secretary of the Treasury, Albert Gallatin, had started. The exchange rate was agreed at par, which was Hcf.2.5, 4 shillings and sixpence sterling, and Fr.5.33 to the dollar, though it was not specified whether the agreed exchange rates were set for the entirety of the loan. The transfer of stock and the altering of the proportions between Amsterdam and London was also discussed, but Washington would go no further than keeping the issues under consideration. American reluctance to give in on these points is unclear. Possibly Gallatin was concerned with American credit standing in general, and he wanted a grip on American government paper.[56] The proposal to commence interest from the French signature was resisted outright. The make-up of the certificates was left until all issues were agreed on. It is at this meeting that Alexander and Gallatin noticed that confusion had emerged over the American redemption payments, presumably because of informal reference to payment "in threes". The original

[52] "Labouchere to Francis Baring, 8 August 1803", NL-SA, 735/5; "Labouchere to Alexander Baring, 9 August 1803", NL-SA, 735/5; "Henry Hope to Hope & Co., 9 August 1803", NL-SA, 735/464; "Francis Baring to Hope & Co., 17 August 1803", NL-SA, 735/299.

[53] "Alexander Baring to Hope & Co., London, 9 August 1803", NL-SA, 735/299.

[54] "Labouchere to Alexander Baring, 23 August 1803", NL-SA, 735/299.

[55] "[Henry Hope or Francis Baring] to Alexander Baring, 9 September 1803", NL-SA, 735/299.

[56] "Francis Baring to Gallatin, 20 April 1804", UK-BA, NP1/A/17/8/2; "Baring to Hope, 9 March 1804", NL-SA, 735/302.

contract mentioned a minimum redemption of $3 million per year, suggesting at least four instalments. However, the Amsterdam consortium had taken "in threes" to mean that redemption would be made in three instalments at a rate of $3.75 million.[57] The issue was difficult to address because Alexander did not know whether the Amsterdam consortium had made financial plans based on this interpretation, and so he pressed for looser terms of redemption. However, at this point, Gallatin was not inclined to deviate from the original contract.[58]

By the third week of October, two communications induced Alexander to push the negotiations to a conclusion. First was his updated instructions. Second was the news of France and the United States having formally exchanged ratifications of the 30 April treaty and conventions.[59] In the meeting that followed, Gallatin was quick to accept adding the names of De Smeth and Willink to the certificates. However, he was unwavering on interest. Gallatin declared Washington would only allow interest to commence after America had taken possession of Louisiana. Alexander pressed this point hard, but ultimately, he conceded, adding with some chagrin that "[…] the foolishly exalted opinion the secretary [Gallatin] and the people here generally have of the value of their funds made them unaccommodating […]".[60] Interest payments would be made on 1 January and 1 July annually. Lists of proprietors would be draw up on each date for interest payments to be made by the next date.[61] The payment of interest based on a list of proprietors was an elegant solution to the interrelated issues of the transferability of stock and the altering of the proportions between Amsterdam and London. Hope, Baring, and the Amsterdam consortium could remain the proprietors by holding on to the certificates, and so interest payments would accrue with them. In case they wished to alter the proportions between Amsterdam and London, or to transfer stock to the market, they could do so on their own accord and settle interest independently. The issue of the exchange rate was again

57 "Henry Hope to John Williams Hope, 20 December 1803", NL-SA, 735/464.

58 "Alexander Baring to Hope & Co., 10 October 1803", NL-SA, 735/300.

59 "Madison to Monroe, 24 October 1803", *State papers*, 260–261.

60 "Alexander Baring to Francis Baring, 21 October 1803", UK-BA, NP1/A/4/19.

61 "Alexander Baring to Francis Baring, 21 October 1803", UK-BA, NP1/A/4/19; "Alexander Baring to Hope & Co., Washington, 5 November 1803", NL-SA, 735/152; "Alexander Baring to Hope & Co., [?] March 1804", NL-SA, 735/152.

raised. Gallatin offered "par for the whole payable in 1, 2, 3 years".[62] It is unclear whether this refers to interest payments or redemption payments. In practice, it appears that interest payments were done in Europe, whilst redemption payments were done in America. This was a good balance of the exchange risks: the United States bore the risk of exchange on interest payments, whilst Hope-Baring bore the exchange risk for the redemption payments. The confusion over the redemption terms was resolved by over-ruling the original clause with a new phrase allowing the United States to redeem the stock in four equal annual instalments starting 15 years after the exchange of ratifications, "and also shorten the period fixed by the convention for its reimbursement".[63] This modification of the original contract meant that Washington had more flexibility in deciding when to redeem the stock. Two issues are not further mentioned in the sources. One, the issue of who would mediate interest payments and the associated ½% commission. Because America made interest payments to certificate holders and not to stockholders, it is assumed that Hope-Baring did not receive a commission. Of course, were they to transfer stock to the market, they could charge stockholders a fee themselves. Two, Paris is no longer listed as a place for interest payments. No interest payments would be made in Paris, and so it is safe to assume that Gallatin saw through Hope-Baring's ruse to employ the issue as a concession. Paris was simply dropped. With all affairs now settled, the date of the second, conclusive round of negotiations, 21 October 1803, was taken as the formal starting point of the American operation. On 10 November 1803, an act of Congress authorised the creation of the stock.[64] The certificates would now be drawn up, with the date of interest payment left blank.[65] Once confirmation of the possession of Louisiana reached Washington, the dates would be filled in and the certificates would be released.

[62] "Alexander Baring to Francis Baring, 21 October 1803", UK-BA, NP1/A/4/19.

[63] "An act authorizing the creation of a stock, to the amount of $11,250,000 for the purpose of carrying into effect the convention of the 30th April 1803 [...] between the United States of America and the French Republic [...], Washington, 10 November 1803", NL-SA, 735/1912; ibidem, NL-SA, 735/484.

[64] "An act authorizing the creation of a stock, to the amount of $11,250,000 for the purpose of carrying into effect the convention of the 30th April 1803 [...] between the United States of America and the French Republic [...], Washington, 10 November 1803", NL-SA, 735/1912; ibidem, NL-SA, 735/484.

[65] "Alexander Baring to Francis Baring, Philadelphia, 26 November 1803", UK-BA, NP1/A/4/26.

In Louisiana, Spanish resistance to the cession was not as strong as was feared. On 30 November, the Spanish governor of Louisiana retroceded the territory to France.[66] On 20 December 1803, France formally ceded Louisiana to the United States.[67] However, it was not until 16 January 1804 that Jefferson was informed of this.[68] It was only now that Jefferson authorised Gallatin to finalise the certificates. Gallatin ordered the stock to be registered in the books of the Treasury, and for the dates of interest payment to be filled in.[69] The first tranche of the certificates was now transferred to Alexander.[70] The second and third tranches were dispatched to Livingston in Paris.[71]

The Political Storm

Just when the affairs in America were on track for payments to start, what was referred to as "the political storm" was brewing in Britain.[72] The Addington government was well aware of the pending transfer of

[66] "Pichon [French chargé d'affaires at Washington D.C.] to Barbé-Marbois, Georgetown, 19 December 1803", FR-AN, AF/IV/1681/A.

[67] "Articles of Exchange of Possession, New Orleans, 20 December 1803", *State papers*, 286–288; Bush, *The Louisiana Purchase*, 79–91; [Barbé-Marbois, *Histoire de la Louisiane*, 352–359.

[68] "Message from President Jefferson to Congress, 16 January", USA-NA, RG/46.

[69] "Jefferson to Gallatin, Washington, 16 January 1803", USA-LoC, *Louisiana Miscellany*, 15; "Alexander Baring to Gallatin, 16 January 1804", USA-NA, RG/56; "Gallatin to Joseph Nourse, 16 January 1804", USA-LoC, *Louisiana Miscellany*, 15; ibidem, USA-NA, RG/56; "Alexander Baring to Gallatin, Washington, 16 January 1804", USA-LoC, *Louisiana Miscellany*, 15.

[70] "Receipt of the first third of capital stock, 16 January 1804", USA-LoC, *Louisiana Miscellany*, 15.

[71] "Authorisation of the delivery of the second and third parts of the stock, 20 January 1804", USA-LoC, *Louisiana Miscellany*, 15; "Gallatin to Pichon, Washington, 20 January 1804", USA-LoC, *Louisiana Miscellany*, 15; "Pichon to Gallatin", Georgetown, 20 January 1804", USA-LoC, *Louisiana Miscellany*, 15; "John B. Nicholson", USA-NA, RG/56; "Alexander Baring to Hope & Co., New York, 28 January 1804", NL-SA, 735/152; "Gallatin to Joseph Nourse, 7 February 1804", USA-LoC, *Louisiana Miscellany*, 15; ibidem, USA-NA, RG/56; "James Leonard's acknowledgement of receipt of last two thirds of stock, 13 February 1803″, USA-LoC, *Louisiana Miscellany*, 15; ibidem, USA-NA, RG/56.

[72] "Henry Hope to John Williams Hope, 20 December 1803", NL-SA, 735/464; "John Williams Hope to Francis Baring, 29 June 1804", UK-BA, NP1/A/4/53, ibidem, NL-SA, 735/304.

Louisiana. London did not object to the transfer itself, but since war with France had resumed, Prime Minister Henry Addington did become increasingly uneasy about a British house remitting vast sums to Paris, which were sure to be applied to the war effort.

By the third week of June 1803, Francis Baring was called in by both Addington and Robert Jenkinson, Lord Hawkesbury, the Secretary of State for Foreign Affairs, to inform them of the details of the financial operation. Francis' notes for the meeting show that he gave an honest account, though perhaps slightly emphasising Alexander's role in negotiating the price down, implying a service to Britain. Both Addington and Hawkesbury were satisfied and approved of Baring's conduct.[73] The matter remained dormant for some months, but the intervention unsettled both Henry Hope and Francis.[74] On 10 November 1803, Francis was called in once more. Both verbally and in writing, Francis set out in detail the French operation, the American operation, and the resource mobilisation operations, thereby stressing the pivotal role of the Amsterdam consortium. Francis' elaborations were of little importance, for the British government had turned decidedly against the financial operation.[75] Baring was ordered to refrain from remitting funds to Paris. On 22 November 1803, Francis informed Hope of Amsterdam of his withdrawal from the French operation.[76] This letter has puzzled historians. To pull out at this point was certain to scuttle the financial operation, which was something a renowned banker like Francis Baring was unlikely to do. Therefore the letter is interpreted as a token protest only, and consequently disregarded.[77] The matter is not helped by a ruse developed by Francis Baring to mislead the British government. Formally, Baring applied to Hope for his share of the payments to France to be

[73] "Account of events by Sir Francis Baring, 19–30 June", UK-BA, NP1/A/4/13; Perkins, "England and the Louisiana Question", 294.

[74] "Henry Hope to Francis Baring, 3 July 1803", NL-SA, 735/464.

[75] "Note on the Louisiana operation by Francis Baring, 10–12 November 1803", UK-BA, NP1/A/4/23; "Francis Baring to Henry Addington, 12 November 1803", UK-BA, NP1/A/4/22; "Francis Baring to Henry Addington, 15 November 1803", UK-BA, NP1/A/4/24.

[76] "Francis Baring to Hope & Co., 22 November 1803", UK-BA, NP1/A/4/25; "Francis Baring to Labouchere, 22 November 1803", NL-SA, 735/302.

[77] Ziegler, *The Sixth Great Power*, 71–72; Hidy, *The House of Baring*, 34; Tearle, *Barings Bank*, 161.

returned to London. Informally, Baring intimated that his share of the receipts in the Portuguese diamond loan, which was to be remitted to London, could be maintained on the continent for use in the Louisiana operation.[78]

The British government was not fooled. Francis was informed that "His Majesty's government would not be satisfied in allowing any subjects of this country to facilitate [...] pecuniary arrangements as may subsist between other foreign powers & the government of France". Baring was ordered not to remit any funds to France and to withdraw all his funds from the continent.[79] Francis had little option but to comply. On 19 December 1803, Francis conveyed his withdrawal from the continent to Hope.[80] It is important to emphasise that this marks a deviation from previous agreements. Whilst payments to France were always to be made from Amsterdam, they were to be made from the concern's funds. Now Baring withdrew their share of the concern's funds, leaving Hope with only their funds. Not having received acknowledgement of his writing, Francis reiterated his intention in a second letter.[81] Hope's reply came on 26 December 1803. In the letter, Hope expressed disappointment at the injudicious conduct of the British government, and Francis' conforming to it. Baring's remittances to France would be stopped, but the associated costs would be for Baring's account only. Furthermore, Francis was forbidden from trading in the Louisiana stock without Hope's consent.[82]

The significance of this last comment becomes clear from an updated overview of the apportionment of Louisiana stock. Baring's withdrawal from the continent forced all of the labour and risk of the French operation onto Hope. This was unexpected and unwanted, and it forced a

78 "Francis Baring to Hope & Co., 22 November 1803", NL-SA, 735/302; "Template response marked A", NL-SA, 735/302; "Template response marked B", NL-SA, 735/302; "Hope & Co. to Francis Baring, Amsterdam, 6 December", UK-BA, NP1/A/4/31.

79 "Henry Addington to Francis Baring, Downing Street, 16 December 1803", UK-BA, NP1/A/4/28.

80 "Francis Baring to Hope & Co., 19 December 1803", UK-BA, NP1/A/4/37.

81 "Francis Baring to Hope & Co., 23 December 1803", UK-BA, NP1/A/4/38; "Francis Baring to Labouchere, 25 December 1803", NL-SA, 735/300.

82 "Hope & Co. to Francis Baring, Amsterdam, 26 December 1803", UK-BA, NP1/A/4/40.

rethink of the entire operation.[83] To price for this risk, the Louisiana stock, originally intended to be allocated as shown in Table 4.1, was reallocated. The $2 million, domiciled in Amsterdam in Hope & Baring's name was transferred to the Amsterdam consortium.[84] The $6.25 million domiciled in London—$2.5 million in Baring's name and $3.75 million in Hope and Baring's name—was lumped together. Baring maintained $1 million, $550,000 was transferred to Henry Hope of London, and $1.5 million was transferred to Hope of Amsterdam. In turn, Hope of Amsterdam ceded $1.2 million to Henry Hope, bringing his allocation up to $1.75 million. In the months that followed, Henry Hope gradually increased his allocation to $2.5 million and Francis' share was later increased with $50,000.[85] After Baring's withdrawal from the French operation, the allocation of Louisiana stock was as per Table 4.2.

So, the political storm unleashed by the Addington government forced Baring to withdraw from the French operation. Not only did this compel Henry Hope of London to step in, but, to accommodate for the additional risk to his associates, Francis was obliged to transfer most of the Louisiana stock in his name. This altered the ratios of participation

Table 4.2 Allocation of the Louisiana stock per agreement of 12 January 1804

	Holder	*Domicile*
$5,000,000	Hope-De Smeth-Willink consortium	Amsterdam
$1,050,000	Francis Baring & Co.	London
$2,500,000	Henry Hope & Co.	London
$2,700,000	Hope-Baring concern	London
$11,250,000		

[83] "John Williams Hope to Francis Baring, 18 August 1804", UK-BA, NP1/A/4/58.

[84] "Henry Hope to Hope & Forster, 24 February 1804", NL-SA, 735/464; "Power of Attorney from Francis Baring for Hope & Co., 27 March 1804", NL-SA, 735/1900; "Rittenhouse, agent of the commissioners of the sinking fund of the United States of America [to Hope-De Smeth-Willink], 1 February 1808", NL-SA, 735/1900; "Transfer of Power of Attorney from Hope-Baring to Hope-De Smeth-Willink", 27 June 1804″, NL-SA, 735/1914; "Certificaten van Amerikaanse 6pct fondsen berustende onder Hope & Comp., R.&T. de Smeth en Wilhem & Jan Willink, als Bewaarders en Directeuren van een gemeeschappelijk Bezit van vijf millioenen Dollars van gemelde fondsen", NL-SA, 735/3757.

[85] "List of certificates of Louisiana six per cent stock", NL-SA, 735/3754.

to 21.2% for Baring, 34.4% for Hope, and 44.4% for the Amsterdam consortium. Or, in other words, the intervention by the British government turned what was a Hope-Baring operation into primarily a Hope operation.

Mobilising the Resources

Resource mobilisation is a continuous process. The wheels were set in motion as soon as it became likely that Hope-Baring would finance the transfer of Louisiana, and the operation remained in flux until payments were concluded. However, early 1804 was a turning point. The French operation was agreed upon, all parties were committed through the anticipation to France, news from America was encouraging, and British political intervention had forced Hope-Baring to make choices on the allocation of Louisiana stock. The time to shift from planning to executing the resource mobilisation operations had arrived.

Operations in London were uneventful. Henry Hope held onto his allocation of $2.5 million. The Louisiana stock was shared amongst the nominal partners of Henry Hope & Co. of London, Henry himself as well as Thomas and Henry Philip, but some stock flowed to the broader family, including Henry's sister and her family, and John Williams. Over the years, Louisiana stock would be used to settle internal payments, including with Baring, but no stock was sold to mobilise resources for paying France. Francis shared his allocation of Louisiana stock amongst his family too. Francis' three sons, Thomas, Alexander, and Henry, as well as Francis' son-in-law, Pierre César Labouchere, each received $100,000. Charles Wall, Francis' son-in-law and a partner in Francis Baring & Co., received $150,000. Francis kept $200,000 for himself and the Bingham family received $300,000. The $2.7 million allocated to the concern was sold to meet broader liquidity demands in London. Some $200,000 made its way into the hands of Raymond & Theodoor de Smeth, who kept it separately from the Amsterdam consortium. $500,000 was sold by Alexander in the United States. The stock was sold slightly under par, and the proceeds were used to cover Alexander's expenses whilst in America and to settle with Willings & Francis the Fr.2 million that Hope drew for the anticipation to France.[86] The remaining $2 million was marketed for

[86] "Alexander Baring to Hope & Co., London, March 1804", NL-SA, 735/152.

resale. Formally, Hope-Baring consolidated the Louisiana stock into a new stock for which they issued a prospectus.[87] Interest payments would be made through Baring in London, and redemption trailed the Louisiana stock by one year to allow for the funds to be remitted to London. In reality, Baring simply sold tranches of stock via brokers when the concern required liquidity. Francis soon lost track of where the stock ended up. Interest payments were made to the brokers.[88] The archives reveal several inquiries for this stock. Daniel Parker, who had tipped off Labouchere on France's need for financing for the cession of Louisiana, applied for $250,000. It is likely that he received at least $200,000, but there is no definitive proof.[89] Another consortium of Amsterdam houses, consisting of N.&J.&R. van Staphorst, Ketwich & Voombergh, and Willem Borski, acquired a tranche which they consolidated into a common fund for resale on the Amsterdam market. However, neither the capital sum nor the details of the operation are known.[90]

The Amsterdam operation was set up "in the Dutch manner". On 4 May 1804, Hope, De Smeth, and Willink consolidated the $5 million allocation of Louisiana stock into a new stock entitled "a common fund

[87] "Prospectus for the Louisiana 6% Loan, London, undated [before 1 January 1804]", UK-BA, NP1/A/17/2; ibidem, UK-BA, NP1/A/4/45.

[88] "Prospectus for the Louisiana 6% Loan, London, 3 April 1804", UK-BA, NP1/A/17/2; ibidem, UK-BA, NP1/A/4/45; "List of American Stock", UK-BA, NP1/A/4/64; "List of certificates of Louisiana six per cent stock", NL-SA, 735/3754; "Calculations of funds advanced by Francis Baring & Co. for account L[ouisiana]", UK-BA, NP1/A/4/48; "General estimate and settlement for the Louisiana stock, [undated]", UK-BA, NP1/A/4/63; "Hope to Baring, 22 June 1804", NL-SA, 735/6; "Amount of American stock, dividends on which are paid through Baring Brothers & Co., 1 January 1807", UK-BA, NP1/A/17/15.

[89] "Daniel Parker to Labouchere, Paris, 12 March 1804", NL-SA, 735/1911; "Hope & Co. to Daniel Parker, 19 March 1804", NL-SA, 735/6; "Daniel Parker to Labouchere, Paris, 26 March 1804", NL-SA, 735/1911; "Hope & Co. to Daniel Parker, 30 March 1804", NL-SA, 735/6; "Hope & Co. to Daniel Parker, 2 April 1804", NL-SA, 735/6; "Daniel Parker to Labouchere, Paris, 4 June 1804", NL-SA, 735/1911; "Daniel Parker to Hope & Co., Paris, 18 June 1804", NL-SA, 735/134; "Daniel Parker to Hope & Co., Paris, 18 June 1804", NL-SA, 735/134; "Alexander Baring to [Daniel Parker], 28 June 1804", NL-SA, 735/134; "Labouchere to Alexander Baring, 8 December 1804", NL-SA, 735/300.

[90] "Onderlinge conventie tusschen N.&J.&R. van Staphorts, Ketwich & Voombergh & Willem Borski, 29 July 1805", NL-SA, 735/2869.

of Original Louisiana Stock" to the sum of Hcf.12.5 million.[91] The shares in this stock, at Hcf.1,000 apiece, would be offered to the public at 5½% interest, payable in Amsterdam. The difference between the 6% interest of the Louisiana stock and the 5½% interest that the consortium paid out—½% interest—was deposited in a reserve fund. This fund was used to buy up shares that may have found their way to the market to prevent the price of shares from dropping too much or too quickly. Interest payments were annual, rather than biannual, and they slightly trailed the Louisiana stock, commencing on 1 January 1805 and running to 1 January 1822 inclusive. Redemption mirrored the original stock. Once a Louisiana share from the Amsterdam allocation was redeemed, a corresponding share, chosen by lot, of the Amsterdam stock would be redeemed too.[92] This stock was also referred to as Louisiana stock, by the contracting parties. It shall be referred to as the Amsterdam derivatives to distinguish it from the original Louisiana stock.

The Amsterdam consortium opened pre-inscriptions for a 10% down payment in August 1803—prior to the plan of participation, or prospectus, being published.[93] Probably, Hope-De Smeth-Willink wanted to test the market for demand to strengthen their claim for the certificates to be made out in their names, and for a larger allocation of the Louisiana stock. The shares were marketed widely, including in Belgium and Germany, and demand was high.[94] Within a month, by September 1803, the consortium had secured the remaining Fr.7.5 million of the first tranche, for when payment came due.[95] Demand remained high, and Amsterdam derivatives generally traded above par.[96] They only dropped

[91] "Contract of the Hope-De Smeth-Willink consortium, 4 May 1804", NL-SA, 735/3756.

[92] There exist various drafts of the "plan of participation" in the Dutch, British and French archives. The definitive plan of participation is the version of 1 June 1804: "Plan van deelgeeving in een gemeenschappelijk bezit van origineele Americaansche Fondsen", NL-SA, 735/1893; "Acte van Aandeel, 1 June 1804", NL-SA, 735/1893.

[93] For receipts, see: "Kwitanties van verrekeningen betreffende aandelen in Amerikaanse fondsen, 1803", NL-SA, 735/3751.

[94] "Labouchere to Sir Francis Baring, 8 August 1803", NL-SA, 735/5.

[95] "[Francis Baring & Co.] to Hope & Co., 20 September 1803", NL-SA, 735/300; "[Labouchere] to Alexander Baring, 4 October 1803", NL-SA, 735/299; "Francis Baring & Co. to Hope & Co., 15 October 1803", NL-SA, 735/300.

[96] "Hope & Co. to Baguenault, 15 March 1804", NL-SA, 735/6.

slightly in 1811–1816, when the economic strain of continuous warfare was felt.[97] From 1 January 1805 to 1 January 1819, the consortium only purchased 1,349 shares of a stock of 12,500, or 10.8%, to maintain the price.[98]

In sum, Baring's withdrawal affected the resource mobilisation plans. Baring's share of the Louisiana stock was limited to slightly over $1 million, which he distributed amongst his family. Henry Hope & Co. had not intended to become financially involved in the Louisiana operation. However, after Baring's withdrawal, they accepted $2.5 million in Louisiana stock, which was kept in the portfolio by the Hope family and associates. Of the remaining $2.7 million, only $500,000 was indirectly employed for mobilising funds for the Louisiana operation. The rest was sold to meet liquidity demands in London if and when they arose. It was the Amsterdam allocation, which was increased from $3 million to $5 million after Baring withdrew, that was employed for payments to France.

The French Payments

The French chargé d'affaires at Washington, Louis-André Pichon, had kept Paris dutifully informed of twists and turns of the ratification and exchange of the treaty and conventions and of Alexander's negotiations with Gallatin on the American payment.[99] Hoping to supplement French coffers sooner rather than later, Barbé-Marbois occasionally referred to the progress in the diplomatic and financial negotiations to implore Hope to commence payments to France.[100] However, Hope resisted any further anticipations. They stuck to the letter of the treaty, meaning that

97 "Ingekogte Aandelen ten profijte van de deelneming uit het gereserveerde ½ pct van de interest jaarlijks en verdere interest", NL-SA, 735/3757; "Hope & Co. to Francis Baring, 15 October 1803", NL-SA, 735/299; "Henry Hope to John Williams Hope, 20 December 1803", NL-SA, 735/464.

98 "Ingekogte aandelen ten profijte van de deelneeming uit het gereserveerde ½ pct van de interest jaarlijks en verdere interest", NL-SA, 735/3757.

99 "Pichon to Barbé-Marbois, Georgetown, 19 December 1803", FR-AN, AF/IV/1681/A; "Pichon to Barbé-Marbois, 3 January 1804", NL-SA, 735/134.

100 "Hope & Co. to Barbé-Marbois, 29 December 1803", NL-SA, 735/6; "Labouchere to Barbé-Marbois, 29 December 1803", NL-SA, 735/6.

payments to France would not commence until within 30 days of an official notice being received of Alexander having in his possession the first tranche of certificates and of the second and third tranches being dispatched to Europe.

After receiving the first tranche of certificates on 16 January 1804, adverse winds kept Alexander in America until early February.[101] He arrived in Falmouth in the first week of March and was in London with the certificates on 9 March 1804. Alexander was now supposed to travel to Paris to organise the French payments, but unfortunate events kept him in England. Alexander's father-in-law, William Bingham, had been touring Europe when he got seriously ill at the end of January 1804. He passed away at Bath on 6 February 1804. Bingham's death revealed his business to be in chaos. There was no order to his papers, Bingham had not drawn up a will until his deathbed, and the legality of it was doubted. Someone would need to bring order to Bingham's estate as soon as possible. This person could be none other than Alexander. So, at the last moment, Alexander refrained from travelling to Paris. Labouchere would take his stead.[102]

Labouchere was quick to set the payments to France in motion. On 15 March 1804, Pierre wrote to Barbé-Marbois to acknowledge the arrival of Alexander with the first tranche of certificates. Formally, payment would have to wait until word of the second and third tranches had been received by Livingston in Paris, but Labouchere indicated a willingness to commence payments on the following terms: Fr.6 million on 20 April 1804, and then Fr.500,00 every seven to eight days until completion on 6 March 1806. Barbé-Marbois was receptive to commencing payments, but his ideas on the payments had evolved since the first contract.[103]

[101] "Alexander Baring to Hope & Co., New York, 28 January 1804", NL-SA, 735/152; "Francis Baring & Co. to Hope & Co., 10/21 February 1804", NL-SA, 735/300.

[102] "Henry Hope to John Williams Hope, 14 January 1804", NL-SA, 735/464; "Wall to Labouchere, 7 February 1804", NL-SA, 735/300; "Francis Baring & Co. to Hope & Co., 9 February 1804", NL-SA, 735/300; "Hope & Co. to Barbé-Marbois, 16 February 1804", NL-SA, 735/6; "Francis Baring & Co. to Hope & Co., 13 March 1804", NL-SA, 735/299.

[103] "Hope & Co. to Barbé-Marbois, 15 March 1804", NL-SA, 735/6.

Pierre decided to travel to Paris to hear out Barbé-Marbois' wishes and to negotiate new terms.[104]

Labouchere arrived in early April. The first point of discussion was the payment of the first third, for which the certificates were in London. It will be recalled that Hope had provided an anticipation of Fr.10 million against the first third. Only Fr.7.5 million remained to be settled. On 20 April 1804 an agreement was reached in which Hope allowed France to draw Fr.4 million in Paris from their associate Baguenault and Fr.3.5 million on Hope in Amsterdam. Both sums were available immediately. In exchange for accelerating the payments, Hope received a discount, commission, and interest fee of Fr.173,256.[105]

With the first third of payments settled, Pierre opened negotiations on the outstanding Fr.34.5 million. It was agreed that the sum would be split into three. Fr.15 million would be paid in French obligations of the Receiver General of Finance: Fr.5 million by 17 September 1804 and Fr.10 million by 22 October 1804. A further Fr.5,825,000 would be settled in promissory notes at a rate of Fr.1 million per month, starting on 20 May 1804 and concluding with a final payment of Fr.825,000 on 22 October 1804. The first two promissory notes were paid through Baguenault in an assortment of French paper. The details of the four remaining promissory notes would be determined prior to the call date. Fr.12 million was to be paid in trade credit on the Baltic ports at a rate of Fr.1.5 million a month from 20 May 1804 to 21 December 1804. France used the trade credit to obtain materials for her naval shipbuilding programme. The commercial and financial transactions that followed from Hope's trade credit on the Baltic ports were referred to as "*les operations du nord*". They were the first time that Hope waded into Napoleonic war financing, and they laid the foundation of a collaboration between Hope

104 Hope & Co. to Barbé-Marbois, 2 April 1804", NL-SA, 735/6; "Hope & Co. to Sémonville [French ambassador at The Hague], 2 April 1804", NL-SA, 735/6; "Hope & Co. to Sémonville, 4 April 1804″, NL-SA, 735/6.

105 "Hope & Co. to Baguenault, 1 March 1804", NL-SA, 735/6; "Hope & Co. to Baguenault, 15 March 1804", NL-SA, 735/6; "Réglement de compte arrêté le 20 Avril 1804 entre le Trésor Public at la Maison Hope", NL-SA, 735/1911; "Liquidation du 1er tiers des lettres de change fournier par les maisons Baring et Hope, pour prix du fonds Américain", FR-AN, AF/IV/1681/A; "Bordereau des valeurs à remettre à Mr Hope & Co. contrepareille somme qu'ils remmetrent [...], 20 April 1804", NL-SA, 735/1911. "Payment Schedule, 20 April 1804", NL-SA, 735/1911.

and the Napoleonic regime that lasted throughout Napoleon's rule.[106] Of the second and third tranches, Fr.1,675,000 remained unexpended. This sum was deposited into an account from which reciprocal costs and fees were paid. Most of this sum was transferred to Hope for accelerating the payments as compared to the first terms of payment.[107] Meanwhile, on 25 April 1804, the second and third tranches of the certificates arrived with Livingston in Paris, who transferred them to Hope all at once.[108] With Hope's demands for security satisfied, Barbé-Marbois submitted the new terms of payment to Bonaparte for his accord. The First Consul agreed on the condition that all unpaid sums, principally the trade credit, could be drawn in Paris.[109] Labouchere's consent marked the end of the negotiations. The original terms of payment were voided, and Hope was discharged of any further obligations to Paris.[110]

Thus, by 21 December 1804, in just nine months, and less than 20 months after the signing of the treaty and conventions on the transfer of Louisiana, France received full payment for the cession of Louisiana to the United States. Hope made the payments principally through the sale of Amsterdam stock, which converted to Fr.26,875,000. The remainder, minus the Fr.10 million anticipation and commission fees, was paid from other sources of revenue. This would have been relatively easy to accommodate as the Fr.12 million on Baltic ports and the sums via Baguenault merged payments with broader commercial operations. No money need trade hands. These were book-only transactions.

[106] "Labouchere to Alexander Baring, Amsterdam, [end of July 1803]", UK-BA, NP1/A/4/14.

[107] "Propositions faites au Ministre du Trésor public par Mr Labouchere, associé de la maisone Hope & Co d'Amsterdam, 21 Avril 1804", NL-SA, 735/1911; ibidem, FR-AN, AF/IV/1681/A; "Annexe au Traité […] pour régler définitivement le mode de paiement des deux derniers tries du fonds américain, crée pour la cession de la Louisiane", NL-SA, 735/1911; ibidem, FR-AN, AF/IV/1681/A; "Compte d'interêts réciproques", FR-AN, AF/IV/1681/A; "Hope & Co. Francis Baring & Co., 22 June 1804", NL-SA, 735/6.

[108] "James Leonard to Gallatin, 12 May 1804", USA-NA, RG/56; "Confirmation of receipt of final two thirds of stock by Livingston, 25 April 1804", USA-NA, RG/56.

[109] "Barbé-Marbois to Bonaparte, Paris, 25 April 1804", FR-AN, AF/IV/1681/A; "Barbé-Marbois to Bonaparte, Paris, 26 April 1804", FR-AN, AF/IV/1681/A; "Barbé-Marbois to Bonaparte, Paris, 27 April 1804", FR-AN, AF/IV/1681/A.

[110] "Barbé-Marbois and Labouchere to Livingston, Paris, 27 April 1804", NL-SA, 735/1911; "Livingston to Henry Hope, Paris, 27 April 1804", NL-SA, 735/480; "France discharges Hopes and Barings from their obligations, 28 April 1804", USA-LoC, *Louisiana Miscellany*, 15; USA-NA, RG/56.

Redemption

It will be recalled that per the diplomatic agreement of 30 April 1803, the United States was to redeem the Louisiana stock annually at a rate of no less than $3 million per year, starting 15 years after the exchange of the ratifications. However, confusion over the terms of redemption arose between the Amsterdam consortium and the London houses. The London houses conformed to the terms of redemption as per original contract. The Amsterdam consortium understood redemption to be in three instalments, rather than in instalments of $3 million. To allow the Amsterdam consortium to align the timeline of redemption of their derivative stock with the timeline of redemption of the Louisiana stock, during the October 1803 negotiations, Alexander and Gallatin agreed that redemption would be in four instalments commencing on 21 October 1818 or earlier, leaving the sums of redemption purposefully open.

Few sources have been found to shed light on the American redemption of Louisiana stock. A source that has been disclosed points to a considerable deviation of the redemption terms as originally envisaged. The source is a statement of the redemption of the Louisiana stock by the American Treasury Department. The statement was requested by Winston and Colomb for their study on the financing of the Louisiana Purchase. The data is included in his study, but no reference has been added, so it has not been possible to corroborate the source. The data has been collated in Table 4.3.

The table shows that there are three redemption payments in 1812, 1813, and 1817 to the sum of $958,300. From 1818, there were four uneven redemptions. There are two further unscheduled small redemption payments in 1822 and 1823. The payments in 1822–1823 could well be to fulfil an outstanding sum resulting from the settling of accounts. The payments in 1818–1821 are in line with the latest terms of redemption, though hefty payments in 1818 may indicate that the United States was hoping to reduce the debt as soon as possible. The three payments of 1812, 1813, and 1817 mark a significant deviation from the original terms of redemption. It is not clear why they occurred. It could be that the United States employed the looser wording agreed on 21 October 1803 to redeem prior to schedule. In any case, any deviation from the contract would have to be agreed upon by Hope-Baring. Without the

Table 4.3 The Redemption of Louisiana Stock

Year	*Redeemed*
1812	$218,200.00
1813	$108,300.00
1817	$631,800.00
1818	$4,909,575.00
1819	$1,471,058.72
1820	$1,771,173.78
1821	$2,132,102.50
1822	$5,290.00
1823	$2,500.00
	$11,250,000.00

Winston and Colomb, "How the Louisiana Purchase Was Financed", 199

full correspondence relating to redemption available, it is impossible to quantify the costs and profits for all parties involved. However, a cache of letters from the Hope archives provides insight into the dynamics and challenges of loosely defined terms of redemption, as well as the costs and profits involved.

The Hope archives show that on 28 April 1818, William Crawford, the American Secretary of the Treasury, informed Hope that Washington intended to redeem the entire stock allocated to the Amsterdam consortium, half on 21 October 1818, and half on 21 October 1819.[111] The notification of redemption caught the Amsterdam consortium slightly off guard. They had not anticipated such large payments from America at such short notice, and they had not the arrangements in place for remitting the funds to Europe. At the last moment, they appealed to Alexander Baring to remit the payments to Europe. Baring committed to do so by 21 June 1819 and 21 June 1820 for a commission of 1½% and a significantly discounted exchange rate (the correspondence mentions 41 cents to the florin, but this seems excessive. Possibly, it was 41 stuivers to the dollar). In any case, the price was high, and the

[111] "Crawford [Secretary of the Treasury] to Hope & Co., 28 April 1818", NL-SA, 735/1910.

Amsterdam consortium only reluctantly agreed.[112] Towards the deadline of payment of the first instalment there was a minor amendment. Presumably to keep the costs down, as was allowed per contract, a holder of Amsterdam stock travelled to the United States to receive his reimbursement to the sum of Hcf.387,000 in person. The remainder was remitted by Baring via the Boston associate John Richards.[113] Upon receipt, Hope-De Smeth-Willink redeemed a corresponding half of the Amsterdam stock.[114]

The redemption of the second instalment did not proceed as intended. In May 1819, Washington was forced to conclude that it had only sufficient liquidity to cover 54% of the redemption of the second half of the Louisiana stock allocated to Amsterdam. However, having set in motion the redemption, there was no option but to pay it out in full. To bridge the lack of liquidity, the president and directors of the Bank of the United States appointed a representative, Thomas Cadwalader, to negotiate a loan in Europe.[115] The houses that Cadwalader chose to approach were Baring of London and Hope of Amsterdam. Alexander and Labouchere agreed to lend Washington $2 million at 6% interest for a period of three years commencing on 21 October 1819. The loan was secured on $2.5 million in transferable 5% interest-bearing United States bonds.[116] The loan negotiations took up some time and so the deadline of 21

[112] "Alexander Baring to Hope & Co., 16 July 1818", NL-SA, 735/1910; "Labouchere to Hope-De Smeth-Willink, 6 August 1818", NL-SA, 735/1910; "Hope & Co. to Labouchere, 21 August 1818", NL-SA, 735/1910; "Baring Brothers & Co. to Hope-De Smeth-Willink, 14 September 1818", NL-SA, 735/3756.

[113] "Alexander Baring to John Richards, Amsterdam, 19 September 1818", NL-SA, 735/1910; "Le Roy Bayarde to Hope & Co., 6 October 1818", NL-SA, 735/1910; "Memorandum of agreement between The President & Directors of the Bank of the United States and John Richards, 18 December 1818″, NL-SA, 735/1910.

[114] "Notarial act of the redemption of half of the Amsterdam stock, 19 May 1819", NL-SA, 735/1892.

[115] "Power of attorney for Thomas Cadwalader, 3 May 1819", NL-SA, 735/1910.

[116] "Baring Brothers & Co. to Hope-De Smeth-Willink, 20 June 1819", NL-SA, 735/1910; "Articles of agreement between President, Directors and Company of the Bank of the United States and Alexander Baring of Baring Brothers & Co. and Pierre César Labouchere of Hope & Co., 5 July 1819", NL-SA, 735/1910; "Resolution of the President & Directors of the Bank of the United States, 27 August 1819", NL-SA, 735/1910; "Certificate of debt, 20 October 1819", NL, SA, 735/1910; "Instrument of assignment, 20 October 1819", NL, SA, 735/1910; "Richards to Hope & Co., 23 October 1819", NL-SA, 735/1910.

October 1819 for the redemption of the second instalment was missed. Only the 54% for which the United States had liquidity was redeemed. The remaining 46% was pushed forward to the third redemption deadline of 21 October 1820.[117]

In the meantime, Hope had transferred to their associates and brokers the bonds that the United States had provided as security.[118] The funds acquired in this manner were subsequently made available to Washington under the loan agreement. Washington employed the funds to pay Hope for the outstanding Louisiana stock of the Amsterdam allocation. With the Amsterdam allocation of the Louisiana stock now fully redeemed, the Amsterdam consortium redeemed the outstanding Amsterdam derivatives, and the common fund of Original Louisiana Stock was liquidated.[119]

In sum, 50% of the Amsterdam allocation of Louisiana stock was redeemed on 21 October 1818, 27% (54% of the second half) was redeemed on 21 October 1819, and 23% was redeemed on 21 October 1820. About 74% of the Amsterdam allocation was redeemed via Baring's mediation. Hcf.387,000 was picked up in person. And 23% of the Amsterdam allocation was redeemed in Amsterdam with funds that Hope and Baring lent to the United States. Reflecting on this episode of the Louisiana operation, one cannot but conclude ill-defined terms of redemption were costly. The United States hoped to save on interest through redeeming as soon as possible. However, she lacked the liquidity, forcing Washington to borrow money from Baring and Hope to pay Hope-De Smeth-Willink. The affair was costly to Hope too. The expense of remitting funds from America was great. This was only partially offset by the revenue from the new loan to America. The principal beneficiary of this deviation to the terms of redemption was Baring. That said, the fact that more than 15 years after the conclusion of the treaty on the cession

[117] "Jan Willink to Hope & Co., 9 July 1819", NL-SA, 735/1910; "Baring Brothers & Co. to Hope-De Smeth-Willink, 20 June 1820", NL-SA, 745/1910; "Overview of the redemption of Louisiana stock, [1820]", NL-SA, 735/1910.

[118] "Overview of transactions of the second reimbursement, undated", NL-SA, 735/1910.

[119] "Liquidation of the Commission of keepers and directors of the common fund [of Original Louisiana Stock], 23 May 1822", NL-SA, 735/1910; "Announcement of the Commission of keepers and directors of the common fund of Original Louisiana Stock", NL-SA, 735/1498.

of Louisiana, the contracting parties found each other with so much ease testifies to the trust and confidence that had been built over the years.

On Balance

It is often stated that the United States paid $15 million for the Louisiana Territory, $11.25 million to France, and $3.75 million in claims of American citizens on France.[120] This is incorrect. The $11.25 million is only the principal sum for the financial operation that Hope-Baring developed. Because the United States did not possess the means to purchase Louisiana outright, she was forced to rely on financial mediation, and because American credit standing was not set, financial mediation could only be had at a hefty 6% interest, or $675,000 annually. Establishing the sum of interest for the duration of the loan is complicated because it is not known whether redemption proceeded as per original intention, or as per schedule proposed by Winston and Colomb. Table 4.4 gives interest payments as per the original redemption schedule. Table 4.5 gives the interest payments per Winston and Colomb's schedule. Adding the interest to the principal gives a sum of $25,227,570 to $25,662,653 as the price that the United States paid for the acquisition of Louisiana. The interest is higher than the consensus in American historiography of about $8.5 million. Presumably this is because of different redemption schedules or the inclusion of second and third-order operations. This sum carries one qualification. The exchange rate is not known for all interest payments. The United States remitted the interest payments to Europe to be paid at par in local currencies as per the October 1803 agreement. However, were the market rate to deviate from the negotiated rate, the difference would be borne by the United States. This would affect the purchase price.

The United States paid a high price for Louisiana, but arguably no investment in a promising future for the young republic was too high. The United States acquired access to the Gulf of Mexico for the Western

[120] For example: Hidy, *The House of Baring*, 33; Ziegler, *The Sixth Great Power*, 70; Austin, *Baring Brothers*, 206, n42; Peterson, *Thomas Jefferson*, 760; Branda, *Le prix de la gloire*, 256; Pagé, *L'Amérique du Nord*, 77; Kennedy, *Mr. Jefferson's Lost Cause*, 183; Lyon, *The Man Who Sold Louisiana*, 121; McGraw, *The Founders and Finance*, 241–242; Orbell, *Baring Brothers*, 15; Tearle, *Barings Bank*, 160. Some do include the interest: Bush, *The Louisiana Purchase*, 68.

Table 4.4 Interest payments per original redemption schedule

	Allocation	*Share of Louisiana Stock*	*$*	*Hcf.*	*£*	*Fr.*
Francis Baring & Co.	$1,050,000	9.33%	998,534	2,496,335	224,693	5,325,182
Henry Hope & Co.	$2,500,000	22.22%	2,377,461	5,943,653	534,982	12,679,000
Hope-Baring Concern	$2,700,000	24.00%	2,567,658	6,419,145	577,781	13,693,320
Amsterdam Consortium	$5,000,000	44.44%	4,719,000	11,797,500	1,061,881	25,166,427
Total	*$11,250,000*	*100.00%*	*10,662,653*	*26,656,633*	*2,399,337*	*56,863,929*

Table 4.5 Interest payments per Winston and Colomb's redemption schedule

	Allocation	*Share of Louisiana Stock*	*$*	*Hcf.*	*£*	*Fr.*
Francis Baring & Co.	$1,050,000	9.33%	925,440	2,313,600	208,245	4,935,372
Henry Hope & Co.	$2,500,000	22.22%	2,203,428	5,508,570	495,821	11,750,882
Hope-Baring Concern	$2,700,000	24.00%	2,379,702	5,949,255	535,486	12,690,951
Amsterdam Consortium	$5,000,000	44.44%	4,719,000	11,797,500	1,061,881	25,166,427
Total	*$11,250,000*	*100.00%*	*10,227,570*	*25,568,925*	*2,301,433*	*54,543,632*

Territories, which helped consolidate the union. She also acquired a vast stretch of land from which thirteen new states were created in whole or in part, though of course, it would take considerable time, effort, and investment to utilise the full potential of the acquired territory. Moreover, from a financial perspective, the terms on which Washington dealt were not excessive. Acquiring Louisiana meant wading into European politics. This was not easy for a state that was still finding its feet internationally. At various times, American conduct strained or even imperilled the diplomatic agreement: Washington was slow in ratifying the treaty and conventions, Washington was slow in creating the stock and certificates, and Livingston and Monroe's quarrel raised doubts over American commitment to the transfer of Louisiana. Bankers like Hope and Baring, who had a financial stake in the success of the diplomatic agreement, also played an important diplomatic role, acting as shock absorbers and ironing out compromises to keep agreements alive. The price to pay for this service was a higher interest rate. Washington seems to have been aware of this.

France did not receive the price Washington paid. France chose not to keep the Louisiana stock, but she transferred it to Hope-Baring for Fr.52 million. In addition, there were deductions for amending and accelerating the payments. For first anticipation, Hope-Baring deducted 2½% of the credit on Willings & Francis, Fr.50,000, and Fr.213,867 for the Fr.8 million advanced per 8 December 1803 contract. A further Fr.173,256 was deducted from the remaining portion of the first third of the payments to France. Labouchere charged up to Fr.1,675,000 in fees, commission, and interest for the amended and accelerated payment of the second and third instalments to France. The deductions add up to Fr.2,112,123, or perhaps Fr.2 million if one allows for reciprocal interest on the Fr.1,675,000 account. So, France would have received Fr.50 million.

The sum that France received might seem disappointingly small, but it is important to emphasise three things. First, in no way was Bonaparte, or France, deceived. Bonaparte could have retained the Louisiana stock and received the principal and interest on the Louisiana operation in full (Fr.104.5-106.9 million), but, in the broader international context of renewed animosity with much of Europe, the considered decision was taken to sacrifice revenue for the sake of speed. If France's international agency in the years to come may be held as a yardstick for the wisdom of that decision, it must be argued that the decision to dispose of the Louisiana stock promptly was a good one. Two, the Fr.50 million that France received was the exact sum that Bonaparte initially demanded in exchange for Louisiana. From this point of view, the transaction could be understood as having panned out precisely as intended. Three, through disposing of the Louisiana stock, Bonaparte established a good working relationship with international high finance, particularly with Amsterdam high finance. In fact, one could argue that the Louisiana operation marked a return of France to the international capital market. In the years to come the Napoleonic regime would be in dire need of financial mediation to finance the Napoleonic wars and to remit plundered and extracted wealth from across Europe to Paris. The close relationship with Hope was key to the success of Napoleonic war financing—at least for as long as Napoleon kept winning. In this context, the sacrifice of income from the Louisiana stock in the short term was more than cancelled out by the easy access to the capital market in the medium to long term. Or, put differently, the decision to dispose of the Louisiana stock was an investment by Napoleonic France in the relationship with international finance. It does not matter much whether the decision was taken wittingly or unwittingly, the financial operation regarding the transfer of Louisiana re-established France's reputation on the credit market, at least in the eyes of Amsterdam financiers.

The profits for Hope and Baring can only be established by approximation, but it was high enough for Francis Baring to want it to be kept secret from Washington.[121] It is important to realise that the Louisiana operation consisted of an American operation and a French operation, and that profits could be made on both. In addition, there were various resource mobilisation operations. Each party developed a different strategy for their allocation of stock. The profitability of each operation depended not only on when the stock was disposed of, but also at what price and whether fees or commission were charged or granted.

The profits on the American operation consisted of the interest payments on the loan. Based on the latest allocation of stock, one can calculate the interest received by the various holders as per Tables 4.4 and 4.5. The redemption dates of the Amsterdam allocation are known, and so it has been possible to calculate with precision the interest accrued on this allocation. The interest on the other allocations has been calculated as if they were redeemed pro rata.

As mentioned, Hope-Baring disposed of the $2.7 million of the London allocation to meet the liquidity demands of the concern. Francis administered the allocation, but he did not actively market the Louisiana stock. The stock was simply sold. The dates of sale are unknown, but it seems the stock was disposed of relatively quickly. By 31 December 1805,

121 "Francis Baring to Labouchere, Bath, 9 October 1804", UK-BA, NP1/A/4/67.

Baring had disposed of $1.5 million already.[122] The price of sales is not known, but it appears that the London allocation of Louisiana stock often sold under par, or with commissions awarded.[123] If one accepts that the limited interest received was balanced out by the discounts and fees, the profits on this portion of the London allocation would have accrued with the purchasers of the stock.

The Amsterdam allocation was disposed of in the Dutch manner. The Louisiana stock was consolidated into a fund, and derivatives were marketed in Amsterdam. It is not known how much of the derivative stock was sold, and how much was retained by Hope-De Smeth-Willink. Because of the need to meet French payments from Amsterdam exclusively, it seems there was a pressure to sell off as much stock as possible, most likely all of it. The fragmentary evidence that exists of the pre-inscriptions supports this idea. Due to the establishment of the reserve fund we also know that the price of Amsterdam derivatives was maintained above par for most of the duration of the loan, save a few years in the 1810s. So, on average, the Amsterdam consortium would not have made losses on the sales, possibly even some profits, though it is impossible to establish how much. The interest payments would have flowed to the purchasers of the Amsterdam derivatives, minus the ½% that was deposited into the reserve fund to buy up derivatives that had made their way to the market. Hope-De Smeth-Willink purchased a total of 1,349 derivatives. In theory, the Amsterdam consortium could have resold the derivatives once the price stabilised, but it seems purchased derivatives were kept off the market. Interest accrued with the consortium, which deposited the revenue in the reserve fund. Upon liquidation of the fund, each holder of Amsterdam derivatives was awarded a premium of Hcf.55.75.[124]

Of the sum of interest on the Louisiana loan, less than 10%, £208,245–£224,693, was profit for Francis Baring and family. The Hope family in London made £495,821–£534,982. In addition, there were indirect profits from operations that followed from the Louisiana loan, such as in the case of the redemption of the Amsterdam allocation. Baring of

122 "List of certificates of Louisiana six per cent stock", NL-SA, 735/3754.

123 "Rough calculations", UK-BA, NP1/A/4/44.

124 "Notarial act of the redemption of half of the Amsterdam stock, 19 May 1819", NL-SA, 735/1892; "Announcement of the liquidation of the common fund of Original Louisiana Stock", NL-SA, 735/1498.

London and Hope of Amsterdam made $360,000 in interest, which was presumably shared equally between Hope and Baring. Possibly there were additional commissions for payment. Baring also earned on remitting the American funds to Amsterdam: a commission of $55,428 plus a possible discount of $665,136. Such profits could be added to the profits of the Louisiana operation. However, it could also be argued to leave out these sums, in particular, because the overview of second order operation is incomplete, and it is difficult to establish where a second order operation ends, and where a subsequent operation begins. An important qualification to the sums cited is that the exchange rate is not known for all redemption payments. The redemption payments were made in America, and any cost following from a deterioration of the exchange rate, as well as the costs of remitting funds to Europe were borne by Hope, Baring, and the Amsterdam consortium. This could reduce profits, as the redemption of the Amsterdam allocation shows.

The profits of the French operation consisted of the discounts, commissions, and fees for accelerating payments to France. One can establish with certainty that Hope-Baring received at least Fr.8 million in discount on the price at which they took over the Louisiana stock from France. Hope received approximately another Fr.2 million for accelerating payments, making about Fr.10 million in profits on the French operation. What remains unanswered, is the division of profits on the French operation between Hope and Baring. Due to the speed with which the operations were developed and executed, the exaction division of profit had never been agreed upon. Baring's withdrawal further complicated the matter. It placed the execution and risk of the French operation solely with Hope, who expanded the partnership with De Smeth and Willink. This change mid-way through the operation opened the door for the Amsterdam consortium to claim a greater share of the profit. What ensued was a disagreement between Francis Baring and Hope and associates that strained relations to breaking point. The disagreement is revealing of different dynamics of London and Amsterdam credit networks, and of the changing relationship between London and Amsterdam as centres of international finance. The topic merits discussion in depth. This publication is focussed narrowly on the Louisiana operation, and so the examination of the disagreement over profits must wait until a future publication.

References

PRIMARY SOURCES

Archival Sources

The Netherlands, Stadsarchief Amsterdam [NL-SA]:
735 Archief van de Firma Hope & Co. met verwante archiefvormers
Amsterdam Office:
Outgoing Correspondence:
– 5: 1798–1803.
– 6: 1803–1805.
Incoming Correspondence:
– 128: 1801–1811 and undated.
– 131: 1802–1803.
– 134: 1802–1817.
– 152: 1803–1811.
Correspondence with Baring:
– 299: 1803–1805.
– 300: 1803–1805.
– 302: 1803–1810.
– 304: 1804.
London Office:
Outgoing Correspondence:
– 464: 1803–1806.
Incoming Correspondence:
– 480: 1802–1803.
– 484: 1803–1805.
Business:
Bills of Exchange:
– 1498: Accounts with R.&Th. De Smeth and Tourton Ravel & Co., 1812–1813.
International Government Lending:
– 1892: Receipts, 1792–1818.
– 1893: 1803–1819.
– 1900: Incoming correspondence on Russian and American loans, 1799–1845.
– 1909: America: Notes by Alexander Baring of negotiations in Paris, 1803.
– 1910: America: incoming correspondence on management of American stock, 1803–1811.
– 1911: America: archives relating to the Louisiana operation, 1803.
– 1912: America: American ratification of the Louisiana loan, 1803–1804.

– 1914: Procuration to deal with Office of Treasury, 1804.
Personal Archives:
– 2869: Borski: Archives relating to American stock, 1805–1879.
Deposited Archives:
Common Fund of Original Louisiana Stock:
– 3751: Receipts, 1803.
– 3754: Register of correspondence, 1803–1812.
– 3756: Archives regarding to share purchases, 1804–1819.
– 3757: Financial Administration, 1804–1819.
The Netherlands, Hoge Raad van Adel:
– III/D/497: De Smeth.
United Kingdom, The Baring Archive [UK-BA]
Northbrook Papers [NP]/1/A:
4. Louisiana Purchase Papers.
17. Northbrook Business Papers A17.
United States of America, Library of Congress [USA-LoC]:
Louisiana Miscellany:
15 Papers in relation to the purchase of Louisiana, 1803–1804.
United States of America, National Archives [USA-NA]:
- Record Group 56: *General Records of the Department of the Treasury, Documents relating to the Purchase of Louisiana.*
France, Archives nationales [FR-AN]:
Archives du pouvoir exécutief, 1789–1815 [AF], IV Secrétairerie d'état impériale et cabinet de Napoléon 1er:
- 1681/A: Relations extérieures: États-Unis, An VIII-1813.

Printed Primary Sources

Barbé-Marbois, F., *Histoire de la Louisiane et de la cession de cette colonie par la France aux États-Unis de l'Amérique Septentrionale; précédée d'un discours sur la constitution et le gouvernement des États-Unis* (Paris: Firmin Didot, 1829).

Mollien, N.F., *Mémoires d'un Ministre du Trésor public, 1780-1815*, 3 vols (Paris: Guillaumin et Co., 1898).

Monroe, J., *The Writings of James Monroe, including a collection of his public and private correspondence now for the first time printed*, ed. S.M. Hamilton, 7 vols (New York: G.P. Putnam's Sons, 1898–1903).

[United States Department of State], *State papers and correspondence bearing upon the purchase of the territory of Louisiana* (Washington, DC: Government Printing Office, 1903).

SECONDARY SOURCES

Branda, P., *Le prix de la gloire. Napoléon et l'argent* (Paris: Fayard, 2007).

Brecher, F.W., *Negotiating the Louisiana Purchase: Robert Livingston's Mission to France, 1801–1804* (Jefferson, NC: McFarland & Company, 2006).

Brown, E.S., *The Constitutional History of the Louisiana Purchase 1803-1812* (New York: Cosimo, 2005).

Buist, M.G., *At Spes Non Fracta. Hope & Co. 1770–1815. Merchant Bankers and Diplomats at Work* (The Hague: Bank Mees & Hope NV, 1974).

Bush, R.D., *The Louisiana Purchase. A Global Context* (New York and London: Routledge, 2014).

Eeghen, P. van, "Willink", *Nederland's Patriciaat* 36 (The Hague: Centraal Bureau voor Genealogie, 1950), 368-378.

Fugier, A., *Napoléon et l'Espagne, 1799-1808*, 2 vols (Paris: Félix Alcan, 1930).

Hall, C.D., *British Strategy in the Napoleonic War 1803-15* (Manchester: Manchester University Press, 1992).

Hidy, R.W., *The House of Baring in American Trade and Finance. English Merchant Bankers at Work 1763–1861* (Cambridge, MA: Harvard University Press, 1949).

Kastor, P.J., *The Nation's Crucible. The Louisiana Purchase and the Creation of America* (New Haven, CT: Yale University Press, 2004).

Kennedy, R.G., *Mr. Jefferson's Lost Cause. Land, Farmers, Slavery, and the Louisiana Purchase* (Oxford: Oxford University Press, 2003).

Lyon, E.W., *The Man Who Sold Louisiana. The Career of François Barbé-Marbois* (Norman, OK: Oklahoma University Press, 1942).

McGrath, T., *James Monroe. A Life* (New York: Dutton, 2020).

McGraw, T.K., *The Founders and Finance. How Hamilton, Gallatin, and Other Immigrants Forged a New Economy* (Cambridge, MA: Belknap Press of Harvard University Press, 2012).

Mikaberidze, A., *The Napoleonic Wars. A Global History* (Oxford: Oxford University Press, 2020).

Orbell, J., *Baring Brothers & Co., Limited. A History to 1939* (London: Baring Brothers & Co., Limited, 1985).

Pagé, S., *L'Amérique du Nord et Napoléon* (Paris: Nouveau Monde/Fondation Napoléon, 2003).

Perkins, B., "England and the Louisiana Question", *Huntington Library Quarterly* 81/3 (May, 1955), 279–295.

Peterson, M.D., *Thomas Jefferson and the New Nation: a Biography* (Oxford: Oxford University Press, 1975).

Tearle, D., *Barings Bank, William Bingham and the Rise of the American Nation. A Transatlantic Relationship from the Revolutionary War through the Louisiana Purchase* (London and Jefferson, NC: McFarland & Co., 2010).

Willing Balch (ed.), T., *Willing Letters and Papers, Edited with a Biographical Essay of Thomas Willing of Philadelphia (1731–1821)* (Philadelphia: Allen, Lane and Scott, 1922).

Winston, J.E., and R.W. Colomb, "How the Louisiana Purchase Was Financed", *The Louisiana Historical Quarterly* 12/2 (Apr., 1929), 189–201.

Winter, P.J. van, *Het aandeel van den Amsterdamschen handel aan den opbouw van het Amerikaansche Gemeenebest* (The Hague: Martinus Nijhof, 1927–1933).

Ziegler, P., *The Sixth Great Power. A History of One of the Greatest of All Banking Families, the House of Barings, 1762–1929* (New York: Alfred A. Knopf, 1988).

CHAPTER 5

Conclusion

Abstract The conclusion reflects on the development and execution of the financial operation to facilitate the transfer of Louisiana from France to the United States. It argues that the operation was improvised and rushed, and that the role of Baring was less prominent than is often assumed. Furthermore, the conclusion discusses the impact of the Louisiana operation on the history of the House of Hope and the House of Baring. For Hope, the Louisiana operation facilitated a return the Amsterdam capital market and it established a good relationship with the Napoleonic regime. For Baring the Louisiana operation was disappointing on the short term. Baring was isolated from the continent that was experiencing a boom in demand for capital. But Baring did learn from their collaboration with Hope, contributing to the merger of Hope and Baring in 1813.

Keywords Financing the Louisiana Cession · Louisiana Purchase · Hope & Co. · Francis Baring & Co. · Pierre César Labouchere · Alexander Baring · Napoleonic War Financing

The successful financing of the sale and purchase of Louisiana had a significant impact on history, on the history of the United States, the history of France, the history of geopolitical rivalry in the Americas, the history

M. E. Hay, *Transatlantic Finance in the Age of Revolutions*, https://doi.org/10.1007/978-3-031-65232-5_5

of transatlantic and international finance, the history of the London and Amsterdam capital markets and the relationship between the two, and the evolution of Dutch and British credit networks. In line with the modest aim of this publication, the conclusion will be limited to reflecting on the financial operation that was developed to facilitate the transfer of Louisiana from France to the United States and the impact of the Louisiana operation on the House of Hope and the House of Baring.

A first observation is that the Louisiana operation was a rushed job. One would expect reputed merchant-banking houses like Hope and Baring to have set up and executed a meticulous financial operation, but nothing was further from the truth. There was no clarity on all the major aspects of the financial operation, the French payment plan, the American redemption, the resource mobilisation operations, whether to expand the consortium, and the division of profits. Additional uncertainty was allowed to creep into the operation in the form of political risk following the resumption of hostilities in Europe. The fact that Hope-Baring accepted the business on this insecure basis and brought it to a successful and profitable conclusion testifies as much to the confidence and professionalism of the two houses as to the realities of transatlantic finance.

Second, the historiography assumes that the financial operation to facilitate the transfer of Louisiana was developed and executed by Baring of London, or principally by Baring of London. The reason for this assumption seems to be Alexander Baring's role in the negotiations in Paris and Washington. However, Alexander was not a partner in his father's house. The relationship between Francis and Alexander was always strained and Alexander did not become a partner in Baring until after his father retired in 1804.[1] At the time of the Louisiana operation, Alexander was a free agent, who worked on commission in America. Principally he worked for Hope. He did conduct business for his father, but only if and when released by Hope. For the Louisiana operation, Alexander worked for the Hope-Baring concern, but his expenses were charged to Hope's account, not to Baring's account.[2] Alexander, then, was a Hope man, more than a Baring man. Of course, Alexander did not complete his

[1] Orbell, *Baring Brothers*, 19, 26–27; Ziegler, *The Sixth Great Power*, 51–54; Hidy, *The House of Baring*, 37–48.

[2] "Calculations of funds advanced by Francis Baring & Co for account L[ouisiana]", UK-BA, NP1/A/4/48.

Louisiana commission. After successfully negotiating the financial contract in Paris and the American payment in Washington, he was prevented from negotiating the start and schedule of the French payments due to the unfortunate death of his father-in-law. It was Pierre César Labouchere of Hope who stood in for Alexander to conclude this important part of the operation. Stepping back from the historiography and focussing on the primary sources further brings into perspective Labouchere's role in the Louisiana operation. There are no studies dedicated to Labouchere or his work, and thus he remains obscured by history. But the archives of Hope and Baring show that it was Labouchere who first caught wind of an operation on Louisiana, and subsequently most decisions on the development of the financial operation were delegated to him by Henry and Francis. If Alexander was the principal negotiator of the Louisiana operation, Labouchere was the architect and troubleshooter. A final event that sheds a new light on Baring's role in the Louisiana operation is of course Baring's withdrawal from continental operations under pressure from the Addington government. Not only did this mean Baring had to withdraw from the French operation, but his allocation of the Louisiana stock was curtailed, and Francis' disposal of Louisiana stock became conditional on Hope's consent. The vacuum left by Baring was filled by Henry Hope & Co., and by Amsterdam associates of Hope. The ratio of participation in the American operation thus became 21.2% for Baring and 78.8% for Hope and associates. The ratio of participation for the French operations was 100% for Hope and associates. As to the resource mobilisation operations, Hope-De Smeth-Willink mobilised the resources for payments to France. Francis Baring only managed a small allocation on account of the concern, and part of this was disposed of by Alexander in America. The rest was sold off like any other stock. In light of the above, one cannot but conclude that the financial operation to facilitate the transfer of Louisiana was not a Baring operation, but principally a Hope operation, which was developed in the Dutch manner, with local Amsterdam associates.

Third, the price that the Americans paid for the Louisiana territory is significantly higher than conventionally assumed, and the profits made by the financial mediaries are greater than acknowledged. The figures do carry one important qualification, which is that the exchange rates are not known for all interest and redemption payments. Any deviation from the agreed exchange rates would affect the price that the United States paid and the profits that Hope, Baring, and the Amsterdam consortium made. One could come to a more precise calculation if one knew the market exchange rate of all the payments. However, the dates of redemption have not been established. In any case, it is felt that any amendment would not have too great an effect on the sums cited.

Hope, Baring, and the Louisiana Operation

The Louisiana operation was a key moment in the history of Hope for two reasons. First, the operation facilitated Hope's return to the Netherlands. After the French invasion and conquest of the Netherlands in 1794–1795, Hope made a considered decision to leave Amsterdam. However, Henry always intended for Hope to return because he felt that only the interrelated network of Amsterdam merchant-banking houses could ensure success in business. Hope's structuring of the Amsterdam resource mobilisation operation in the Dutch manner, in collaboration with other Amsterdam houses, ensured that the business and profits were shared broadly and that relations were re-established. This paved the way for Hope's return. Hope's involvement in the Louisiana operation, in particular the full assumption of the payments to France, also brought the house into close contact with the Napoleonic regime. In the historiography, Napoleon is presented as an old regime man, who preferred strict monetarism over experiments with paper currencies, who rejected banking and large-scale borrowing in favour of fiscal discipline, and who was reluctant to rely on the capital markets because he detested financiers.[3] This may be true with regard to French financiers, but the Napoleonic Empire was more than France. It came to encompass a large part of Europe, including the Netherlands, which was gradually integrated into the empire with Amsterdam becoming the third capital of the empire. The Napoleonic regime had a good relationship with Amsterdam financiers, first and foremost with Hope. The seeds of the relationship were sown

[3] M. Marion, *Histoire financière de la France depuis 1715*, 6 vols (Paris: Rousseau & Co., 1914–1931), IV: 246–250, 334–341; J. Gabillard, "Le Financement des Guerres Napoléonniennes et la Conjoncture du Premier Empire", *Revue économique* 4/4 (July, 1953), 549–552; F. Crouzet, *La grande inflation. La monnaie en France de Louis XVI à Napoléon* (Paris: Fayard, 1993), 399, 530–539; L. Bergeron, *France under Napoleon* (Princeton: Princeton University Press, 1981), 41–44; G. Ellis, *The Napoleonic Empire* (London: Macmillan, 1991), 33–39; S. Woolf, *Napoleon's Integration of Europe* (London: Routledge, 1991), 138; M.D. Bordo and E.N. White, "A Tale of Two Currencies. British and French Finance During the Napoleonic Wars", *The Journal of Economic History* 51/2 (June, 1991), 314–315.

with the Louisiana operation. The original terms of payment delivered to France funds needed for the upcoming war, but Hope's assumption of the full payment to France sped up remittances, and it directly involved Hope and their associates in French war financing by releasing funds via the Baltic ports. Hope's professionalism and co-operation were rewarded with further business. In 1805, a botched financial operation developed by the French financier Jean-Gabriel Ouvrard to deliver Spanish subsidy payments to Paris brought the Napoleonic empire to the brink of a financial crisis. Ouvrard was relieved of his position, and Napoleon appointed Hope & Co. to bring the Spanish subsidy payments back on track. Hope did so by developing an intricate operation that remitted South American silver via the United States and London to the continent.[4] This successful collaboration induced the Napoleonic regime to rely increasingly on Hope and Amsterdam financiers for mediating large imperial financial operations. For example, French satellite states and allies were encouraged to run their loan operations via Amsterdam, such as was the case with Spain, Portugal, and Naples.[5] The Napoleonic regime also relied on Amsterdam mediation for the remittance of indemnity payments, such as with the Habsburg indemnity of 1809.[6] The convergence of Dutch financial interests and the interests of the Napoleonic regime, rooted in Hope's role in the financing of the sale and purchase of Louisiana, raises interesting questions about the Dutch involvement in Napoleonic war financing and the financial integration of Europe under the Napoleonic regime, 1799–1813, as well as the trend and speed of the decline of the Amsterdam capital market and the reorientation of Dutch credit networks, 1795–1815. However, before any conclusions can be drawn,

[4] A. Lévy, *Un grand profiteur de guerre sous la Révolution, l'Empire et la Restauration* (Paris: Calmann-Lévy, 1929), 121–221; J. Savant, *Tel fut Ouvrard* (Paris: Fasquelle, 1954), 111–162; J. Wolff, *Le financier Ouvrard (1770–1846)* (Paris: Tallandier, 1992), 69–140; O. Wolff, *Ouvrard. Speculator of Genius* (London: Barrie and Rockliff, 1960), 71–124; R. Herr, *Rural Change and Royal Finances in Spain at the End of the Old Regime* (Berkeley: University of California Press, 19891989), 141, 145–146; Bonney, "The Eighteenth Century", 158–171; Buist, *At Spes Non Fracta*, 279–380, Riley, *International Government Finance*, 169–174; C. Marichal, *Bankruptcy of Empire. Mexican Silver and the Wars between Spain, Britain and France, 1760–1810* (Cambridge: Cambridge University Press, 2007), 158–171.

[5] Buist, *At Spes Non Fracta*, 292–427; J.A. Davis, *Naples and Napoleon. Southern Italy and the European Revolutions 1780–1860* (Oxford: Oxford University Press, 2006), 177.

[6] Kerautret, *Documents diplomatiques*, II: 140, 455.

further research is needed, both on the cases mentioned above and on other cases in which Hope and Amsterdam financiers may or may not have been involved. What is clear from a letter by Labouchere, at least, is that Hope looked upon the Louisiana operation as an opportunity to promote themselves and to establish a business relationship with the Napoleonic regime.[7]

The Louisiana operation was important yet frustrating for Baring. The operation was to be Baring's entry into large-scale international government lending, and it was developed and to be executed with the leading European house in international finance, Hope. Great profits, recognition, and future business were to be expected. Yet, reality turned out differently. Addington's intervention forced Baring to withdraw from the continent, reducing Baring's role. Francis received only a small allocation of the Louisiana stock, which, always opposed to co-opting other houses to market the stock, he chose to sell on the market with limited profit. The expectation of a strengthened position in international finance, from which more business could come, was also dashed. For the immediate term, Baring's response to the forced withdrawal from the continent was twofold. First, Baring aligned their interests to those of the British government by marketing British debt to allow London to subsidise her allies. Second, Baring turned to the Americas. In the short term, this decision did not pay off, not least due to the tension and conflict that existed between Britain and the colonial power in South America, Spain, and between Britain and the United States culminating in the War of 1812. Yet, solid foundations were laid that meant a good return on investment in the later nineteenth century.[8] However, the lure of international government finance remained, and the lessons of how Hope marketed the Louisiana stock were learned. This was not a lesson that was put to paper, but it can be learnt from Baring's future conduct, which was closely tied to Alexander's management.

After a long and distinguished career, and with an ailing health, Francis Baring retired in 1804 at the age of 64. The opportunity was taken to reorganise the firm. Francis' sons Thomas, Alexander, and Henry, and his son-in-law Charles Wall each took a 25% stake in the new business, which

[7] "Labouchere to Alexander Baring, Amsterdam, [end of July 1803]", UK-BA, NP1/A/4/14.

[8] Ziegler, *The Sixth Great Power*, 47–48, 54–58, 71–74; Hidy, *The House of Baring*, 24–37, 48–53; Orbell, *Baring Brothers*, 16–17.

was renamed Baring Brothers & Co. by 1807. As mentioned, Henry was a troubled man. He was kept in the background until being pushed out in 1823. Thomas was never much interested in business. He remained a partner, but he had his mind set on his father's estate and title. In 1809, Francis' poor health caught up with him. He passed his estate and title to Thomas, who formally withdrew from the business. Charles Wall took this opportunity to retire too. Francis Baring passed away several months later.[9] Two clerks, Thomas Nixson and John Deacon, were promoted to restricted partners, but the business was firmly under Alexander's control.[10] In order to understand how Alexander applied the lessons from the Louisiana operation, one must return to Hope.

In the aftermath of the Louisiana operation, the Hope partnership was tumultuous. It will be recalled that after Alexander rejected a partnership in Hope, two houses were established, one in London and one in Amsterdam. Henry Hope, John Williams Hope, and two of Jan and Phillippina's sons, Thomas and Henry Philip, were partners in the London house. The London house took a $^{6}/_{7}$ share in the Amsterdam house, with the remaining $^{1}/_{7}$ going to Labouchere. Per articles of agreement of 1802, the partnership ran for seven years, until 31 December 1808. On 7 March 1808, the partnership was extended for a further seven years, thus running to the end of 1815. However, Labouchere was developing a desire to withdraw from active banking, and so the contract included provisions to ameliorate him. Pierre was allowed to withdraw from the partnership after five years rather than seven, and he was allowed to start withdrawing capital. Though, as an enticement to stay, Pierre's share in the partnership was increased from $^{1}/_{7}$ share to $^{8}/_{49}$ share.[11] Labouchere's urge to retire was stronger than anticipated. In June 1808, Pierre secured the possibility to retire by the end of 1811.[12] To ensure the continuity of the firm, John Dixon, a longstanding associate of Hope was recruited. He received a $^{6}/_{49}$ share of the firm.[13] It was at this time

[9] "Henry Hope to Alexander Baring, 12 September 1810", NL-SA, 735/465.

[10] "Early Baring Firms, 1755–1811, by F.H. Baring, December 1912", UK-BA, HC/1/191; Orbell, *Baring Brothers*, 19, 26–27; Ziegler, *The Sixth Great Power*, 51–54; Hidy, *The House of Baring*, 37–48.

[11] "Memorandum of Agreement, 7 March 1808", UK-BA, DEP/208/13.

[12] "Memorandum of Agreement, Amsterdam, 4 June 1808", UK-BA, DEP/208/12.

[13] "Memorandum of Agreement, Amsterdam, 4 June 1808", UK-BA, DEP/208/9.

that John Dixon transferred his firm, Littledale & Dixon of Rotterdam, to Samuel Pierre Labouchere.[14]

The next few months are unclear. It appears that John Williams Hope deserted his post in Amsterdam to be with Henry, who was now growing old. John Williams did not formally withdraw from the partnership, but his first-born son, Henry Junior, was given power of procuration and took his father's stead.[15] Henry Junior was not made out for banking. He returned to London no later than the end of 1810. Around this time, John Dixon suffered a stroke. He recovered but could not return to work. Much of the business thus reverted to Labouchere, who was hoping to retire. Pierre established a new management by granting the power of attorney to Pierre Firmin Lestapis, Adriaan van der Hoop, and William Gordon Coesvelt. All three men were close associates of Hope.[16]

Then, on 25 February 1811, Henry Hope passed away. Labouchere chose this moment to withdraw from the partnership. John Williams consented to terminate the Hope partnership on 31 December 1811.[17] By the beginning of 1812, Pierre had retired from Hope and relocated to England. However, Hope's affairs kept pulling him in. John Williams could not manage the strain of being the sole active partner. From London, he took the decision to liquidate the Amsterdam house. Labouchere felt this decision untimely. Market conditions in Amsterdam had deteriorated considerably, and so liquidation would mean considerable financial and reputational loss. So, Pierre intervened to countermand the order to liquidate. John Williams reluctantly agreed. This state of affairs lasted until the death of John Williams on 12 or 18 February 1813.[18] John Williams' share of the partnership passed to his estranged wife, Ann Hope, who sold the share to the remaining two partners,

[14] "Memorandum of Agreement, 14 June 1808", UK-BA, Dep/208/11.

[15] "Powers of Procuration for Labouchere, Henry Hope Junior, and John Dixon, [1 January] 1809", NL-SA, 735/524; ibidem, NL-SA, 735/525.

[16] "Powers of Procuration for Labouchere, Henry Hope Junior, John Dixon, and Pierre Firmin Lestapis, [1 January] 1810", NL-SA, 735/524; "Powers of Procuration for Labouchere, Coesvelt, Adriaan van der Hope and Lestapis, [1 January] 1811", NL-SA, 735/524; ibidem, NL-SA, 735/525; Buist, *At Spes Non Fracta*, 64–65, 357, 367.

[17] "Memorandum of Agreement, 15 April 1811", UK-BA, DEP/208/10.

[18] "Summons *Bestuur der Registratie van de Domeinen*, 22 October 1813", NL-SA, 735/1910; "Abstract of the Will to the inheritance in fee simple of Penrose in the Parish of Cornelly in the County of Cornwall, copy of 25 July 1859", NL-SA, 735/2904.

Thomas Hope and Henry Philip Hope, for a sum of £183,509.[19] Not having been active in banking for many years, Thomas and Henry Philip were unsure what to do with the business. It is at this moment that Alexander Baring offered to buy out the brothers for £253,521. The brothers agreed.[20]

The price that Alexander paid for Hope was very high. For example, it was higher than the profits that Baring made on the Louisiana operation. This begs the question of what Alexander purchased. Hope still had a good reputation, but the house had conducted very little business in the past years, and two important financial operations, the Russian loans and the Spanish subsidy payments, were stagnant or loss-making. Buist describes Hope as a near-empty shell.[21] The fact is that Hope still had at least one valuable asset: their network. Of course, all merchant-banking houses had their networks. What set Hope apart is the systematic manner in which information was gathered, organised, and applied to business. From August 1778, Hope started compiling profiles of merchant-banking houses that they engaged with or heard of, including on the partners and managers, the firm's capitalisation, its credit standing, its relations, and its reputation amongst peers. Initially, these profiles were based on snippets drawn together from correspondence. Later, Hope actively solicited information from associates. For example, before establishing a relationship with a new house, Hope would request information from that house on associates and rivals. The quality of the information determined whether and to what extent Hope pursued a relationship with that house. The notes were carefully copied, indexed, and archived into books. For the period 1778–1819, there are four volumes of about 350 pages each that cover houses in every corner of the Western hemisphere.[22] It was this information, or what is better-termed trade intelligence, that allowed Hope to establish and grow the solid network that allowed only them to conduct large-scale financial-commercial operations.

19 "Agreement Anne Hope & Thomas and Henry Philip Hope, 17 July 1813", NL-SA, 735/521.

20 "Deed of Assignment and Transfer, from Thomas Hope and Henry Philip Hope to Alexander Baring, 3 September 1813", NL-SA, 735/527; Buist, *At Spes Non Fracta*, 65–68, 246–247, 375–376, 424–427.

21 Buist, *At Spes Non Fracta*, 65–68.

22 "Handelsinlichtingen [Trade Intelligence], 1778–1819", NL-SA, 735/1404–1407.

The major difference between Hope and Baring in the Louisiana operation was how they mobilised resources. Hope, together with De Smeth and Willink, marketed the stock through their credit network. Francis Baring was reluctant to invite other houses into the operation. He preferred selling the Louisiana stock on the secondary market. Francis perceived Hope's approach as a reflection of limited market power and a capitulation to rivals. In fact, it should be seen as a reflection of the smooth working of a carefully nurtured credit network, which was built through intelligence gathering, but which was kept vital through the periodic infusion of new business. It is felt that Alexander recognised that Hope's true value lay in the considered nurturing of their networks, and that this was what he was willing to pay for. No hard evidence has been found, but it is only from 1815, after Alexander's purchase of the Hope partnership, that Baring started to collect trade intelligence, and archive it in a fashion similar to Hope.[23]

It was some time before Alexander employed Hope's network. In late 1813, Alexander felt that European market conditions were too uncertain for large international operations. However, after the defeat of Napoleon and the prospect of a new order for Europe negotiated at the Congress of Vienna, Alexander deemed the time right to take the next step. In June 1814, at a meeting in Tunbridge Wells, Alexander Baring and Pierre César Labouchere decided to re-establish Hope & Co. of Amsterdam per 1 January 1815. Alexander and Pierre took a $^{5}/_{6}$ share in the business, for which they put up Hcf.1.25 million. The funds were drawn from the liquidated Hope partnership. Alexander did not involve himself in the business. Labouchere became the principal partner. Two former managers of the Amsterdam house, Van der Hoop and Lestapis, were rehired for a commission of $^{1}/_{8}$ share of the annual profits each. The third manager of the old house, Coesvelt, was kindly invited to retire, though he was allowed to invest Hcf.250,000 for $^{1}/_{6}$ share of the new house. A further Hcf.250,000 was provided by Jérôme Sillem. Sillem was a senior partner in Matthiessen & Sillem of Hamburg, but he had worked on commission for Hope in the past. He was now recruited to become the second partner after Labouchere. The contract with Sillem has not been found, but it is presumed he took a $^{1}/_{7}$ share in the business.[24] It was in this

[23] "Reports on Business Houses", UK-BA, HC/16.

[24] "Circular on the aborted liquidation of Hope & Co., 1 January 1815", NL-SA, 735/524; ibidem, NL-SA, 735/525; "Contract A. van der Hoop, 4 March 1815", UK-BA,

capacity, as chief of Baring Brothers. & Co. of London and as a silent partner in Hope & Co. of Amsterdam, both houses firmly embedded in the Hope-Baring international credit network, that Alexander Baring, together with Pierre César Labouchere, entered onto the market for international government lending to secure an operation that earned Baring the predicate of the Sixth Great Power for their financial prowess, the French indemnity loans of 1817–1818. The loans were developed and executed in a Dutch manner.[25] So, it seems Alexander not only became a Dutchman in negotiation, but also a Dutchman in developing large international financial operations.

Limitations and Further Research

This publication has several limitations. First, there are two issues directly related to the Louisiana operation that have not been explored, Hope's payment to France through offering credit on Baltic ports, which directly involved Hope in French war financing, and the conflict over the division of the profits of the French operation. Both issues require substantial discussion and contextualisation. Their examination would have fitted into this monograph, but it would have taken it beyond its stipulated length. Both issues also speak to the broader topic of the changes to international finance during the Age of Revolutions, in particular, the shift of the centre of international finance from Amsterdam to London, which is

DEP/208/18/99; "Contract P.F. Lestapis, 4 March 1815", UK-BA, DEP/208/18/68; "Contract W.G. Coesvelt, 2 June 1815", UK-BA, DEP/208/18/70; "Contract between Alexander Baring and Labouchere, 17 July 1815", UK-BA, DEP/208/8; "Circular on granting of signature, 1815″, NL-SA, 735/524; Buist, *At Spes Non Fracta*, 68–69, 174–175, 264–270.

[25] C. Haynes, *Our Friends, the Enemies. The Occupation of France after Napoleon* (Cambridge, MA: Harvard University Press, 2018), 42, 214–224, 281–284; K. Oosterlinck, L. Ureche-Rangau & J.-M. Vaslin, "Waterloo: a Godsend for French Public Finances?" *EHES Working Papers in Economic History* 41 (July, 2013); E.N. White, "Making the French Pay. The Costs and Consequences of the Napoleonic Reparations", *European Review of Economic History* 5/3 (Dec., 2001), 337–365; Z. Xiaolan, "La Crise économique française de 1816 à 1817: La dernière crise d'Ancien régime?", *Revue française d'histoire économique* 2/2 (2014), 86–108; J. Greenfield, "Financing a New Order: The Payment of Reparations by Restoration France, 1817–1818", *French History* 30/3 (2016), 376–400; A. Nicolle, *Comment la France a payé après Waterloo* (E. de Boccard: Paris, 1929).

the topic of a future study. For this reason, both issues have been pushed forward.

Second, the American side of Hope-Baring's Louisiana operation merits further research, two issues in particular. One, the redemption of the Louisiana stock can be investigated to establish with precision the exchange rate of all transactions, the price that the United States paid, as well as the profits that Hope and Baring made. It is not felt that any research finding would challenge the conclusions of this study, but a precise figure is always preferable to a range. Such a study would span two decades and involve exploring a range of second and third-order operations. It is a study of itself. Two, Alexander disposed of $500,000 Louisiana stock in the United States. One could explore how the stock was employed by American merchants and financiers. Whilst the sum might not be great, the transfer of stock took place at an interesting time when European trade and finance were strained because of the Revolutionary and Napoleonic wars. The cession of Louisiana shows that American politicians seized on European disengagement in the Americas to expand and fortify their interests. It would be interesting to see if American merchants and financiers also seized on European economic disengagement to fortify their positions. This topic has been left to a time when the American archives can be explored in depth.

A limitation of what has been examined is that the Louisiana operation has been discussed in relative isolation. Whilst necessary for clarity, it must be emphasised that the Louisiana operation was but one operation of various ongoing operations. In addition to regular trade, which always took up a good bit of time, there was the Portuguese diamond loan, the Maine lands business, the Russian loans, and the forthcoming business that was in preparation, including the Spanish subsidy payments. All operations were connected, and to lift just one operation from the web of interconnected operations, distorts the picture. For a full appreciation of the Louisiana operation, the other operations need to be examined with equal depth.

On the history of Baring and Hope, one could conclude that much work remains to be done. The history of Baring could benefit from more in-depth study into how operations were developed and executed, similar to how Buist has done for the early history of Hope, and how this publication has done for the Louisiana operation. In addition, the early history of Baring would merit further investigation, including Francis' management, the roles of his children, and the Baring-Voûte connection and its importance in the rise of the house of Baring. As to the history of Hope, there are known unknowns and unknown unknowns. A known lacuna in the history of Hope is the post-1815 era. Because of the restructuring of the house, 1815 is a logical endpoint of study. Yet, a history from 1815 onwards would reveal much about how Hope dealt with the relative demise of Amsterdam as a centre of international finance. The period up until 1815 is relatively well served, but there are some topics that require further study, such as the Spanish war subsidy operation, and Hope's role in Napoleonic finance more broadly.

The last comment is reserved for the archives. Both Hope and Baring had a central role in international trade and finance in the eighteenth and nineteenth centuries. Their excellent record keeping means that their business dealings have been well persevered, and with both archives in the process of digitisation, they are readily accessible online. If a study of the Hope and Baring archives has revealed anything, it is that the importance of both archives is yet to be fully appreciated by historians, the author included. It would not be an overstatement to say that any future research on international trade and finance in the eighteenth and nineteenth centuries could benefit from an examination of the Hope and the Baring archives.

References

PRIMARY SOURCES

Archival Sources

The Netherlands, Stadsarchief Amsterdam [NL-SA]:
735 Archief van de Firma Hope & Co. met verwante archiefvormers
London Office:
Outgoing Correspondence:
– 465: 1806–1811.
Organisation of the firm:
– 521: Partners, 1782–1826.
– 524: Powers of Procuration, 1809–1862.
– 525: Circulars on Management, 1811–1938.
– 527: Articles of Agreement, 1813.
Trade Intelligence:
– 1404: 1778–1787.
– 1405: 1791–1803.

– 1406: 1803–1809.
– 1407: 1811–1819.
Business:
International Government Lending:
– 1900: Incoming correspondence on Russian and American loans, 1799–1845.
Personal Archives:
– 2904: John Williams: Testament and Will.
United Kingdom, The Baring Archive [UK-BA]
Northbrook Papers [NP]/1/A:
4. Louisiana Purchase Papers.
Deposits & Gifts [DEP]:
208. Papers of the Labouchere Family, 1621–1822.
House Correspondence [HC]:
1. General.
16. Reports on Business Houses.

SECONDARY SOURCES

Bonney, R., "The Eighteenth Century. II. The Struggle for Great Power Status and the End of the Old Fiscal Regime", in *Economic Systems and State Finance*, ed. R. Bonney (Oxford: Clarendon Press, 1995), 315–390.

Bergeron, L., *France under Napoleon* (Princeton: Princeton University Press, 1981).

Bordo M.D., and E.N. White, "A Tale of Two Currencies. British and French Finance During the Napoleonic Wars", *The Journal of Economic History* 51/2 (June, 1991), 303–316.

Buist, M.G., *At Spes Non Fracta. Hope & Co. 1770–1815. Merchant Bankers and Diplomats at Work* (The Hague: Bank Mees & Hope NV, 1974).

Crouzet, F., *La grande inflation. La monnaie en France de Louis XVI à Napoléon* (Paris: Fayard, 1993).

Davis, J.A., *Naples and Napoleon. Southern Italy and the European Revolutions 1780–1860* (Oxford: Oxford University Press, 2006).

Ellis, G., *The Napoleonic Empire* (London: Macmillan, 1991).

Gabillard, J., "Le Financement des Guerres Napoléonniennes et la Conjoncture du Premier Empire", *Revue économique* 4/4 (July, 1953), 548–572.

Greenfield, J., "Financing a New Order: The Payment of Reparations by Restoration France, 1817-1818", *French History* 30/3 (2016), 376-400.

Haynes, C., *Our Friends, the Enemies. The Occupation of France after Napoleon* (Cambridge, MA: Harvard University Press, 2018).

Herr, R., *Rural Change and Royal Finances in Spain at the End of the Old Regime* (Berkeley: University of California Press, 1989).

Hidy, R.W., *The House of Baring in American Trade and Finance. English Merchant Bankers at Work 1763–1861* (Cambridge, MA: Harvard University Press, 1949).

Kerautret, M., *Documents diplomatiques du Consulat et de l'Empire*, 3 vols (Paris: Nouveau Monde/Fondation Napoléon, 2002–2004).

Lévy, A., *Un grand profiteur de guerre sous la Révolution, l'Empire et la Restauration* (Paris: Calmann-Lévy, 1929).

Marichal, C., *Bankruptcy of Empire. Mexican Silver and the Wars between Spain, Britain and France, 1760–1810* (Cambridge: Cambridge University Press, 2007).

Marion, M., *Histoire financière de la France depuis 1715*, 6 vols (Paris: Rousseau & Co., 1914–1931).

Nicolle, A., *Comment la France a payé après Waterloo* (Paris: E. de Boccard, 1929).

Oosterlinck, K., L. Ureche-Rangau & J.-M. Vaslin, "Waterloo: a Godsend for French Public Finances?" *EHES Working Papers in Economic History* 41 (July, 2013).

Orbell, J., *Baring Brothers & Co., Limited. A History to 1939* (London: Baring Brothers & Co., Limited, 1985).

Riley, J.C., *International Government Finance and the Amsterdam Capital Market 1740-1815* (Cambridge: Cambridge University Press, 1980).

Savant, J., *Tel fut Ouvrard* (Paris: Fasquelle, 1954).

White, E.N., "Making the French Pay. The Costs and Consequences of the Napoleonic Reparations", *European Review of Economic History* 5/3 (Dec., 2001), 337–365.

Wolff, J., *Le financier Ouvrard (1770-1846)* (Paris: Tallandier, 1992).

Wolff, O., *Ouvrard. Speculator of Genius* (London: Barrie and Rockliff, 1960).

Woolf, S., *Napoleon's Integration of Europe* (London: Routledge, 1991).

Xiaolan, Z., "La Crise économique française de 1816 à 1817: La dernière crise d'Ancien régime?", *Revue française d'histoire économique* 2/2 (2014), 86-108.

Ziegler, P., *The Sixth Great Power. A History of One of the Greatest of All Banking Families, the House of Barings, 1762–1929* (New York: Alfred A. Knopf, 1988).

Correction to: Transatlantic Finance in the Age of Revolutions

Correction to:
M. E. Hay, *Transatlantic Finance in the Age of Revolutions*,
https://doi.org/10.1007/978-3-031-65232-5

The original version of the book was inadvertently published before incorporation of final typographical corrections in Chapters 1 and 5 which has now been updated. The book and the chapters have been updated with the changes.

The updated version of this book can be found at
https://doi.org/10.1007/978-3-031-65232-5

M. E. Hay, *Transatlantic Finance in the Age of Revolutions*,
https://doi.org/10.1007/978-3-031-65232-5_6

References

Primary Sources

Archival Sources

The Netherlands, Stadsarchief Amsterdam [NL-SA]:
735 Archief van de Firma Hope & Co. met verwante archiefvormers
Amsterdam Office:
Outgoing Correspondence:
- 5: 1798–1803.
- 6: 1803–1805.

Incoming Correspondence:
- 128: 1801–1811 and undated.
- 131: 1802–1803.
- 134: 1802–1817.
- 152: 1803–1811.

Correspondence with Baring:
- 299: 1803–1805.
- 300: 1803–1805.
- 302: 1803–1810.
- 303: 1803–1811.
- 304: 1804.

London Office:
Outgoing Correspondence:
- 462: 1802–1809.
- 464: 1803–1806.

M. E. Hay, *Transatlantic Finance in the Age of Revolutions*,
https://doi.org/10.1007/978-3-031-65232-5

– 465: 1806–1811.
Incoming Correspondence:
– 477: 1800–1802.
– 480: 1802–1803.
– 484: 1803–1805.
Organisation of the firm:
– 520: Circular 1762.
– 521: Partners, 1782–1826.
– 522: Procuration Cruys, 1795.
– 523: Procuration Taay, 1795.
– 524: Powers of Procuration, 1809–1862.
– 525: Circulars on Management, 1811–1938.
– 527: Articles of Agreement, 1813.
– 538: Contract Nicholas Baudouin, 1765–1772.
Trade Intelligence:
– 1404: 1778–1787.
– 1405: 1791–1803.
– 1406: 1803–1809.
– 1407: 1811–1819.
Business:
Bills of Exchange:
– 1498: Accounts with R.&Th. De Smeth and Tourton Ravel & Co., 1812–1813.
International Government Lending:
– 1892: Receipts, 1792–1818.
– 1893: 1803–1819.
– 1900: Incoming correspondence on Russian and American loans, 1799–1845.
– 1909: America: Notes by Alexander Baring of negotiations in Paris, 1803.
– 1910: America: incoming correspondence on management of American stock, 1803–1811.
– 1911: America: archives relating to the Louisiana operation, 1803.
– 1912: America: American ratification of the Louisiana loan, 1803–1804.
– 1914: Procuration to deal with Office of Treasury, 1804.
Personal Archives:
– 2869: Borski: Archives relating to American stock, 1805–1879.
– 2903: John Williams: Prenuptial Agreement, 1782–1810.
– 2904: John Williams: Testament and Will.
Deposited Archives:
Common Fund of Original Louisiana Stock:
– 3751: Receipts, 1803.

– 3754: Register of correspondence, 1803–1812.
– 3756: Archives regarding to share purchases, 1804–1819.
– 3757: Financial Administration, 1804–1819.

Documentation:

– 4188: Prospectus of the Maine lands by William Bingham, 1793.

The Netherlands, Hoge Raad van Adel:

– III/D/497: De Smeth.

United Kingdom, The Baring Archive [UK-BA]

Northbrook Papers [NP]/1/A:

1. Correspondence between John & Francis Baring & Co., Hope & Co., John Williams and Henry Hope with Francis Baring, 1789–1809.

3. Correspondence between John & Francis Baring & Co., Hope & Co, John Williams and Henry Hope with Francis Baring, 1783–1806.

4. Louisiana Purchase Papers.

9. Northbrook Business Papers A9.

14. Northbrook Business Papers A14.

15. John & Francis Baring & Co., Articles of Partnership, 1788.

17. Northbrook Business Papers A17.

20. Northbrook Business Papers A20.

24. Volume of copies of correspondence. Alexander Baring with Sir Francis Baring, Hope & Co. and William Bingham: 1795–1796.

Northbrook Papers [NP]/1/B:

3. Letters from and papers concerning Henry, William and George Baring, 1802–1836.

13. The will of Jopseph Paice, 1773.

Northbrook Papers [NP]/1/C:

2. Notebooks compiled by Sir Francis Baring.

16. Documents relating to the contract between the East India Co. and Robert Voûte.

Northbrook Papers [NP]/1/D:

1. Papers concerning the affairs of John and Charles Baring in the Exeter House and the Devonshire Bank, Exeter.

11. Papers relating to the Larkbear firm, 1807–1902.

Deposits & Gifts [DEP]:

193/40. Sir Francis Baring's Notebook, 1763–1809.

208. Papers of the Labouchere Family, 1621–1822.

House Correspondence [HC]:

1. General.

16. Reports on Business Houses.

Historical Portraits [PT]

15. Alexander Baring.

31. Pierre César Labouchere.

United States of America, Library of Congress [USA-LoC]:
Louisiana Miscellany:
15 Papers in relation to the purchase of Louisiana, 1803–1804.
James Monroe Papers:
Series 1: General Correspondence, Reel 2: 22 March 1796–8 October 1803.
United States of America, National Archives [USA-NA]:
Record Group 11: *Perfected Treaties.*
Record Group 46: *Records of the US Senate, 1803–1805.*
Record Group 49: *Records of the Bureau of Land Management.*
Record Group 56: *General Records of the Department of the Treasury, Documents relating to the Purchase of Louisiana.*
France, Archives nationales [FR-AN]:
Archives du pouvoir exécutief, 1789–1815 [AF], IV Secrétairerie d'état impériale et cabinet de Napoléon 1er:
1681/A: Relations extérieures: États-Unis, An VIII-1813.

Printed Primary Sources

Barbé-Marbois, F., *Histoire de la Louisiane et de la cession de cette colonie par la France aux États-Unis de l'Amérique Septentrionale; précédée d'un discours sur la constitution et le gouvernement des États-Unis* (Paris: Firmin Didot, 1829).

Jefferson, T., *The Writings of Thomas Jefferson, Being his Autobiography, Correspondence, Reports, Messages, Addresses and Other Writings, Official and Private*, ed. H.A. Washington, 9 vols. (New York: Taylor & Maury, 1853–1854).

Mollien, N.F., *Mémoires d'un Ministre du Trésor public, 1780-1815*, 3 vols (Paris: Guillaumin et Co., 1898).

Monroe, J., *The Writings of James Monroe, including a collection of his public and private correspondence now for the first time printed*, ed. S.M. Hamilton, 7 vols (New York: G.P. Putnam's Sons, 1898–1903).

Nolte, V., *Fifty Years in Both Hemispheres, or Reminiscences of the Life of a Former Merchant* (New York: Redfield, 1854).

[United States Department of State], *State papers and correspondence bearing upon the purchase of the territory of Louisiana* (Washington, DC: Government Printing Office, 1903).

Secondary Sources

Adelman, J., *Sovereignty and Revolution in the Iberian Atlantic* (Princeton: Princeton University Press, 2006).

Aiton, A.S., "The Diplomacy of the Louisiana Cession", in *Louisiana Purchase Bicentennial Series Volume II. The Spanish Presence in Louisiana 1763–1803*, ed. G.C. Din (Lafayette: The Center for Louisiana Studies, 1996), 11–27.

Alberts, R.C., *The Golden Voyage. The Life and Times of William Bingham, 1752–1804* (Boston: Houghton Mifflin Company, 1969).

Alexander, D.S., "Robert R. Livingston. The Author of the Louisiana Purchase", *Proceedings of the New York State Historical Association* 6 (1906), 100–114.

Allis Jr, F.S. (ed.), *William Bingham's Maine Lands, 1790-1820* (Portland: The Anthoensen Press, 1954).

Austin, P.E., *Baring Brothers and the Birth of Modern Finance* (London: Pickering & Chatto, 2007).

Bannon, J.F., "The Spaniards in the Mississippi Valley. An Introduction", in J.F. McDermott (ed.), *The Spanish in the Mississippi Valley 1762–1804* (Urbana: University of Illinois Press, 1974), 3-15.

Bemis, S.F., *Pinkney's Treaty. America's Advantage from Europe's Distress, 1783–1800* (New Haven: Yale University Press, 1960).

Benot, Y., *La démence coloniale sous Napoléon* (Paris: La Découverte, 2006).

Bergeron, L., *France under Napoleon* (Princeton: Princeton University Press, 1981).

Blaufarb, R.,"The French Revolutionary Wars and the Making of American Empire, 1783–1796", in *The French Revolution in Global Perspective*, eds S. Desan, L. Hunt, and W.M. Nelson (Ithaca & London: Cornell University Press, 2013), 148–162.

Boles, J.B., *Jefferson: Architect of American Liberty* (New York: Basic Books, 2017).

Bond, B.G. (ed.), *French Colonial Louisiana and the Atlantic World* (Baton Rouge: Louisiana State University Press, 2005).

Bonney, R. (ed.), *Economic Systems and State Finance* (Oxford: Clarendon Press, 1995).

Bonney, R. (ed.), *The Rise of the Fiscal State in Europe, c. 1200-1815* (Oxford: Oxford University Press, 1999).

Bonney, R., "The Eighteenth Century. II. The Struggle for Great Power Status and the End of the Old Fiscal Regime", in *Economic Systems and State Finance*, ed. R. Bonney (Oxford: Clarendon Press, 1995), 315–390.

Bordo M.D., and E.N. White, "A Tale of Two Currencies. British and French Finance During the Napoleonic Wars", *The Journal of Economic History* 51/2 (June, 1991), 303–316.

Boulle, P.H., "French Reactions to the Louisiana Revolution of 1768", in *The French in the Mississippi Valley*, ed. J.F. McDermott (Urbana: University of Illinois Press, 1965), 143-157.

Branda, P., *Le prix de la gloire. Napoléon et l'argent* (Paris: Fayard, 2007).

Brandt, C., "Robert R. Livingston, Jr. The Reluctant Revolutionary", *The Hudson Valley Regional Review* 4/1 (Mar., 1987), 8–20.
Brasseaux, C.A., "Confusion, Conflict, and Currency: An Introduction to the Rebellion of 1768", *Louisiana History: The Journal of the Louisiana Historical Association* 18/2 (Spring, 1977), 161–169.
Brasseaux, C.A., "The Image of Louisiana and the Failure of Voluntary French Emigration, 1683-1731", *Proceedings of the Meeting of the French Colonial Historical Society* 4 (1979), 47-56.
Brecher, F.W., *Negotiating the Louisiana Purchase: Robert Livingston's Mission to France, 1801–1804* (Jefferson, NC: McFarland & Company, 2006).
Breen, J.C., "De feestelijke stemming na de restauratie van 1787", *Maandblad Amstelodamum* 5 (1918), 89-91.
Broers, M., *Napoleon. Soldier of Destiny* (London: Pegasus Books, 2014).
Broers, M., *Napoleon. The Decline and Fall of an Empire: 1811–1821* (London: Pegasus Books, 2022).
Broers, M., *Napoleon. The Spirit of the Age: 1805–1810* (London: Pegasus Books, 2018).
Brown, E.S., *The Constitutional History of the Louisiana Purchase 1803-1812* (New York: Cosimo, 2005).
Bryant, I., *James Madison. Secretary of State, 1800–1809* (Indianapolis: Bobbs-Merrill, 1953).
Buist, M.G., *At Spes Non Fracta. Hope & Co. 1770–1815. Merchant Bankers and Diplomats at Work* (The Hague: Bank Mees & Hope NV, 1974).
Burnstein, A., and N. Isenberg, *Madison and Jefferson* (New York: Random House, 2010).
Bush, R.D., *The Louisiana Purchase. A Global Context* (New York and London: Routledge, 2014).
Cheney, L., *James Madison. A Life Reconsidered* (New York: Penguin, 2015).
Clapham, J.H., "From the Peace of Versailles to the Second Peace of Paris, 1783–1815", in *The Cambridge History of British Foreign Policy, 1783–1919*, eds A.W. Ward and G.P. Gooch, 3 vols (Cambridge: Cambridge University Press, 1939), I: 1463–215.
Conrad, G.R. (ed.), *The Louisiana Purchase Bicentennial Series in Louisiana History. Volume I: The French Experience in Louisiana* (Lafayette: The Center for Louisiana Studies, 1995).
Cooper, D., *Talleyrand* (London: Bedford Historical Series, 1938).
Cox, I.J., *The West Florida Controversy, 1798–1813. A Study in American Diplomacy* (Baltimore: Johns Hopkins Press, 1918).
Crook, M., *Napoleon Comes to Power: Democracy and Dictatorship in Revolutionary France, 1795-1804* (Cardiff: University of Wales Press, 1998).
Crouzet, F., *La grande inflation. La monnaie en France de Louis XVI à Napoléon* (Paris: Fayard, 1993).

Davis, J.A., *Naples and Napoleon. Southern Italy and the European Revolutions 1780–1860* (Oxford: Oxford University Press, 2006).

DeConde, A., *The Quasi-War. The Politics of the Undeclared War with France, 1797–1801* (New York: Charles Scribner's Sons, 1966).

Desan, S., L. Hunt, and W.M. Nelson (eds), *The French Revolution in Global Perspective* (Ithaca & London: Cornell University Press, 2013).

Din, G.C. (ed.), *Louisiana Purchase Bicentennial Series Volume II. The Spanish Presence in Louisiana 1763–1803* (Lafayette: The Center for Louisiana Studies, 1996).

Din, G.C., "Empires Too Far: The Demographic Limitations of Three Imperial Powers in the Eighteenth-Century Mississippi Valley", *Louisiana History: The Journal of the Louisiana Historical Association* 50/3 (Summer, 2009), 261–268.

Din, G.C., "Protecting the 'Barrera': Spain's Defenses in Louisiana, 1763–1779", *Louisiana History: The Journal of the Louisiana Historical Association* 19/2 (Spring, 1978), 183–211.

Donaldson, T., *The Public Domain. Its History, with Statistics* [...] (Washington DC: Government Printing Office, 1880).

Dwyer, P., *Citizen Emperor. Napoleon in Power* (London: Bloomsbury, 2013).

Dwyer, P., *Napoleon. Passion, Death and Resurrection, 1815–1840* (London: Bloomsbury, 2018).

Dwyer, P., *Napoleon. The Path to Power, 1769–1799* (London: Bloomsbury, 2007).

Egan, C.L., "The United States, France, and West Florida, 1803–1807", *The Florida Historical Quarterly* 47/3 (Jan., 1969), 227–252.

Eeghen, P. van, "Willink", *Nederland's Patriciaat* 36 (The Hague: Centraal Bureau voor Genealogie, 1950), 368-378.

Elias, J.E., *De vroedschap van Amsterdam 1578-1795*, 2 vols (Amsterdam: N. Israel, 1963).

Ellis, G., *The Napoleonic Empire* (London: Macmillan, 1991).

Ellis, J.J., *American Sphinx. The Character of Thomas Jefferson* (New York: Vintage Books, 1998).

Faber, E.L., "The Passion of the Prefect: Pierre Clément De Laussat, 1803 New Orleans, and the Bonapartist Louisiana That Never Was", *Louisiana History: The Journal of the Louisiana Historical Association* 54/3 (Summer 2013), 261–291.

Farrell, D.R., "Reluctant Imperialism: Pontchartrain, Vauban and the Expansion of New France, 1699-1702", *Proceedings of the Meeting of the French Colonial Historical Society* 12 (1988), 35-45.

Fugier, A., *Napoléon et l'Espagne, 1799-1808*, 2 vols (Paris: Félix Alcan, 1930).

Furstenberg, F., "The Significance of the Trans-Appalachian Frontier in Atlantic History", *The American Historical Review* 113/3 (June, 2008), 647–677.

Gabillard, J., "Le Financement des Guerres Napoléonniennes et la Conjoncture du Premier Empire", *Revue économique* 4/4 (July, 1953), 548–572.

Gérard, M., *Messieurs Hottinguer. Banquiers à Paris*, 2 vols (Paris: Banque Hottinguer, 1968–1972).

Gilman, D.C., *James Monroe* (Boston: Houghton Mifflin Company, 1911).

Girard, P.R., "Rêves d'Empire: French Revolutionary Doctrine and Military Interventions in the Southern United States and the Caribbean, 1789–1809", *Louisiana History: The Journal of the Louisiana Historical Association* 48/4 Fall, 2007), 389–412.

Goldwin, R.A., *From Parchment to Power. How James Madison Used the Bill of Rights to Save the Constitution* (Washington, DC: AEI Press, 1997).

Greenfield, J., "Financing a New Order: The Payment of Reparations by Restoration France, 1817-1818", *French History* 30/3 (2016), 376-400.

Greig, J. (ed.), *The Farington Diary*, 8 vols (London, 1922–1928).

Haarmann, A.W., "The Spanish Conquest of British West Florida, 1779–1781", *The Florida Historical Quarterly* 39/2 (Oct., 1960), 107–134.

Hall, C.D., *British Strategy in the Napoleonic War 1803-15* (Manchester: Manchester University Press, 1992).

Haynes, C., *Our Friends, the Enemies. The Occupation of France after Napoleon* (Cambridge, MA: Harvard University Press, 2018).

Hellie, R., "Russia, 1200–1815", in *The Rise of the Fiscal State in Europe, c. 1200–1815*, ed. R. Bonney (Oxford: Oxford University Press, 1999), 481–506.

Hemphill, W.E., "The Jeffersonian Background of the Louisiana Purchase", *The Mississippi Valley Historical Review* 22/2 (Sep., 1935), 177–190.

Herr, R., *Rural Change and Royal Finances in Spain at the End of the Old Regime* (Berkeley: University of California Press, 1989).

Hidy, R.W., *The House of Baring in American Trade and Finance. English Merchant Bankers at Work 1763–1861* (Cambridge, MA: Harvard University Press, 1949).

Hilt, D., *Troubled Trinity: Godoy and the Spanish Monarchs* (Tuscaloosa: University of Alabama Press, 1987).

Hinderaker, E., *Elusive Empires. Constructing Colonialism in the Ohio Valley, 1673–1800* (Cambridge: Cambridge Univertsity Press, 1997).

Josselin de Jong, F. de, "Labouchère", *Nederland's Patriciaat* 49 (The Hague: Centraal Bureau voor Genealogie, 1963), 208–227.

Kakel III, C.P., *A Post-Exceptionalist Perspective on Early American History. American Wests, Global Wests, and Indian Wars* (Cham: Palgrave Pivot, 2019).

Kastor, P.J., *The Nation's Crucible. The Louisiana Purchase and the Creation of America* (New Haven, CT: Yale University Press, 2004).

Kennedy, R.G., *Mr. Jefferson's Lost Cause. Land, Farmers, Slavery, and the Louisiana Purchase* (Oxford: Oxford University Press, 2003).

Kerautret, M., *Documents diplomatiques du Consulat et de l'Empire*, 3 vols (Paris: Nouveau Monde/Fondation Napoléon, 2002–2004).

Kolb, F., "The New Orleans Revolt of 1768", *Louisiana History: The Journal of the Louisiana Historical Association* 59/1 (Winter, 2018), 5–39.

Kuethe, A.J., and K.J. Andrien, *The Spanish Atlantic World in the Eighteenth Century. War, and the Bourbon Reforms, 1713–1796* (Cambridge: Cambridge University Press, 2014).

Kukla, J., *A Wilderness So Immense: The Louisiana Purchase and the Destiny of America* (New York: Anchor Books, 2004).

Labouchere Thorold, A., *The Life of Henry Labouchere* (London: Constable & Company, 1913).

Lee, R., "Accounting for Conquest: The Price of the Louisiana Purchase of Indian Country", *The Journal of American History* 103/4 (March, 2017), 921–942.

Le Pichon (ed.), A., *China Trade and Empire: Jardine, Matheson & Co. and the Origins of British Rule in Hong Kong 1827–1843* (Oxford: British Academy, 2006).

Lemann, S.G., "The Problems of Founding a Viable Colony: The Military in Early French Louisiana", *Proceedings of the Meeting of the French Colonial Historical Society* 6/7 (1982), 27-35.

Lévy, A., *Un grand profiteur de guerre sous la Révolution, l'Empire et la Restauration* (Paris: Calmann-Lévy, 1929).

Lewis Jr., J.E., *The American Union and the Problem of Neighborhood. The United States and the Collapse of the Spanish Empire, 1783–1829* (Chapel Hill: University of North Carolina Press, 1998).

Lyon, E.W., *The Man Who Sold Louisiana. The Career of François Barbé-Marbois* (Norman, OK: Oklahoma University Press, 1942).

Mallet, B., *Thomas George, Earl of Northbrook. A Memoir* (London: Longmans, Green and Company, 1908).

Marichal, C., *Bankruptcy of Empire. Mexican Silver and the Wars between Spain, Britain and France, 1760–1810* (Cambridge: Cambridge University Press, 2007).

Marion, M., *Histoire financière de la France depuis 1715*, 6 vols (Paris: Rousseau & Co., 1914–1931).

McDermott, J.F. (ed.), *The French in the Mississippi Valley* (Urbana: University of Illinois Press, 1965).

McDermott, J.F. (ed.), *The Spanish in the Mississippi Valley 1762-1804* (Urbana: University of Illinois Press, 1974).

McGrath, T., *James Monroe. A Life* (New York: Dutton, 2020).

McGraw, T.K., *The Founders and Finance. How Hamilton, Gallatin, and Other Immigrants Forged a New Economy* (Cambridge, MA: Belknap Press of Harvard University Press, 2012).

Mikaberidze, A., *The Napoleonic Wars. A Global History* (Oxford: Oxford University Press, 2020).

Molhuysen, P.C., P.J. Blok et al. (eds), *Nieuw Nederlandsch Biografisch Woordenboek*, 10 vols (Leiden: K.H. Kossmann, 1911–1937).

Moore, J.P., "Antonio de Ulloa: A Profile of the First Spanish Governor of Louisiana", *Louisiana History: The Journal of the Louisiana Historical Association* 8/3 (Summer, 1967), 189–218.

Nicolle, A., *Comment la France a payé après Waterloo* (Paris: E. de Boccard, 1929).

Onuf, P., and N. Onuf, *Federal Union, Modern World. The Law of Nations in an Age of Revolutions, 1776–1816* (Madison, WI: Madison House, 1993).

Oosterlinck, K., L. Ureche-Rangau & J.-M. Vaslin, "Waterloo: a Godsend for French Public Finances?" *EHES Working Papers in Economic History* 41 (July, 2013).

Orbell, J., *Baring Brothers & Co., Limited. A History to 1939* (London: Baring Brothers & Co., Limited, 1985).

Orieux, J., *Talleyrand ou le sphinx incompris* (Paris: Flammarion, 1970).

Pagé, S., *L'Amérique du Nord et Napoléon* (Paris: Nouveau Monde/Fondation Napoléon, 2003).

Perkins, B., "England and the Louisiana Question", *Huntington Library Quarterly* 81/3 (May, 1955), 279–295.

Peterson, M.D., *Thomas Jefferson and the New Nation: a Biography* (Oxford: Oxford University Press, 1975).

Poniatowski, M., *Talleyrand et l'ancienne France, 1754-1789* (Paris: Librairie Académique Perrin, 1988).

Pritchard, J., "Population in French America, 1670-1730: The Demographic Context of Colonial Louisiana", in *French Colonial Louisiana and the Atlantic World*, ed. B.G. Bond (Baton Rouge: Louisiana State University Press, 2005), 175-203.

Renaut, F.P., *La question de la Louisiane, 1796-1806* (Paris: E. Champion, 1918).

Riley, J.C., *International Government Finance and the Amsterdam Capital Market 1740-1815* (Cambridge: Cambridge University Press, 1980).

Savant, J., *Tel fut Ouvrard* (Paris: Fasquelle, 1954).

Smith, R.D., "Napoleon and Louisiana: Failure of the Proposed Expedition to Occupy and Defend Louisiana, 1801–1803", *Louisiana History: The Journal of the Louisiana Historical Association* 12/1 (Winter, 1971), 21–40.

Smith, W.R., *Brief History of the Louisiana Territory* (St. Louis: The St. Louis News Company, 1904).

Stenberg, R., "The Western Boundary of Louisiana, 1762–1803", *The Southwestern Historical Quarterly* 35/2 (Oct., 1931), 95–108.

Stenberg, R.R., "The Boundaries of the Louisiana Purchase", *The Hispanic American Historical Review* 14/1 (Feb., 1934), 32–64.

Taylor, A., *American Revolutions. A Continental History, 1750–1804* (New York: W.W. Norton & Company, 2016).

Tearle, D., *Barings Bank, William Bingham and the Rise of the American Nation. A Transatlantic Relationship from the Revolutionary War through the Louisiana Purchase* (London and Jefferson, NC: McFarland & Co., 2010).

Tyler, B., "The Mississippi River Trade, 1784–1788", *Louisiana History: The Journal of the Louisiana Historical Association* 12/ 3 (Summer, 1971), 255–267.

Valkenburg, C.C. van, et al., "Voûte", *Nederland's Patriciaat* 63 (The Hague: Centraal Bureau voor Genealogie, 1983), 420-482.

Voort, J. van der, *De Westindische plantages van 1720–1795. Financiën en handel* (Eindhoven: De Witte, 1973).

Ward, A.W., and G.P. Gooch (eds), *The Cambridge History of British Foreign Policy, 1783-1919*, 3 vols (Cambridge: Cambridge University Press, 1939).

Waresquiel, E. de, *Talleyrand. Le prince immobile* (Paris: Fayard, 2003).

Whitaker, A.P., "The Retrocession of Louisiana in Spanish Policy", in *The Louisiana Purchase Bicentennial Series in Louisiana History. Volume II. The Spanish Presence in Louisiana 1763–1803*, ed. G.C. Din (Lafayette: The Center for Louisiana Studies, 1996), 40–58.

Whitaker, A.P., *The Mississippi Question 1795–1803. A Study in Trade, Politics, and Diplomacy* (New York and London: D. Appleton-Century Co., 1934).

Whitaker, A.P., *The Spanish-American Frontier: 1783–1795. The Westward Movement and the Spanish Retreat in the Mississippi Valley* (Gloucester, MA: Peter Smith, 1962).

White, E.N., "Making the French Pay. The Costs and Consequences of the Napoleonic Reparations", *European Review of Economic History* 5/3 (Dec., 2001), 337–365.

Willing Balch (ed.), T., *Willing Letters and Papers, Edited with a Biographical Essay of Thomas Willing of Philadelphia (1731–1821)* (Philadelphia: Allen, Lane and Scott, 1922).

Wills, G., *James Madison* (New York: Henry Hold and Company, 2002).

Winston, J.E., and R.W. Colomb, "How the Louisiana Purchase Was Financed", *The Louisiana Historical Quarterly* 12/2 (Apr., 1929), 189–201.

Winter, P.J. van, "De Verkoop van Louisiana", *Tijdschrift voor Geschiedenis* 47 (1932), 41-61.

Winter, P.J. van, "Louisiana gekocht en betaald", in *Bijdragen en Mededelingen van het Historische Genootschap* 75 (1961), 37*–56*.

Winter, P.J. van, *Het aandeel van den Amsterdamschen handel aan den opbouw van het Amerikaansche Gemeenebest* (The Hague: Martinus Nijhof, 1927–1933).
Wolff, J., *Le financier Ouvrard (1770-1846)* (Paris: Tallandier, 1992).
Wolff, O., *Ouvrard. Speculator of Genius* (London: Barrie and Rockliff, 1960).
Woodward Jr., R.L., "Spanish Commercial Policy in Louisiana, 1763–1803", *Louisiana History: The Journal of the Louisiana Historical Association* 44/2 (Spring, 2003), 133–164.
Woolf, S., *Napoleon's Integration of Europe* (London: Routledge, 1991).
Xiaolan, Z., "La Crise économique française de 1816 à 1817: La dernière crise d'Ancien régime?", *Revue française d'histoire économique* 2/2 (2014), 86-108.
Ziegler, P., *The Sixth Great Power. A History of One of the Greatest of All Banking Families, the House of Barings, 1762–1929* (New York: Alfred A. Knopf, 1988).
Zylberberg, M., *Capitalisme et catholicisme dans la France moderne. La dynastie Le Couteulx* (Paris: Éditions de la Sorbonne, 2001).

Newspapers

Un radical d'outre mer', *Le Temps*, 23 January 1912.

Unpublished sources

Klein, M., "Louisiana: European Explorations and the Louisiana Purchase. A Special Presentation from the Geography and Map Division of the Library of Congress", unpublished essay (Library of Congress, Geography and Map Division, undated0, accessed via: https://www.loc.gov/collections/louisiana-european-explorations-and-the-louisiana-purchase/about-this-collection/

Index

M. E. Hay, *Transatlantic Finance in the Age of Revolutions*,
https://doi.org/10.1007/978-3-031-65232-5

The manufacturer's authorised representative in the EU is Springer Nature Customer Service Centre GmbH, Europaplatz 3, 69115 Heidelberg, Germany. If you have any concerns regarding our products, please contact ProductSafety@springernature.com

Printed and bound by CPI Group (UK) Ltd, Croydon, CR0 4YY
21/09/2026
02220011-0012